Hustle and Gig

Hustle and Gig

STRUGGLING AND SURVIVING IN
THE SHARING ECONOMY

Alexandrea J. Ravenelle

UNIVERSITY OF CALIFORNIA PRESS

University of California Press, one of the most distinguished university presses in the United States, enriches lives around the world by advancing scholarship in the humanities, social sciences, and natural sciences. Its activities are supported by the UC Press Foundation and by philanthropic contributions from individuals and institutions. For more information, visit www.ucpress.edu.

University of California Press
Oakland, California

© 2019 by Alexandrea J. Ravenelle

Library of Congress Cataloging-in-Publication Data

Names: Ravenelle, Alexandrea J., 1980– author.
Title: Hustle and gig : struggling and surviving in the sharing economy / Alexandrea J. Ravenelle.
Description: Oakland, California : University of California Press, [2019] | Includes bibliographical references and index. | Description based on print version record and CIP data provided by publisher; resource not viewed.
Identifiers: LCCN 2018033918 (print) | LCCN 2018038179 (ebook) | ISBN 9780520971899 (ebook) | ISBN 9780520300552 (cloth : alk. paper) | ISBN 9780520300569 (pbk. : alk. paper)
Subjects: LCSH: Precarious employment. | Independent contractors. | Employee rights. | Flexible work arrangements—United States. | Labor—United States. | Labor market—United States.
Classification: LCC HD5857 (ebook) | LCC HD5857 .R38 2019 (print) | DDC 331.25/96—dc23
LC record available at https://lccn.loc.gov/2018033918

Manufactured in the United States of America

27 26 25 24 23 22 21 20 19 18
10 9 8 7 6 5 4 3 2 1

For Anna

Contents

Illustrations

MAP

TABLES

BOX

Acknowledgments

First and foremost, I owe a debt of gratitude to the workers who took time out of their days—in lives where time truly is money—to talk to me about the experience of working in the gig economy. Without their honesty and openness, this would have been a very different project.

I started my career in journalism and nonprofits, and my journey to researching the sharing economy was a multistep process with numerous mentors, colleagues, and loved ones providing support and advice along the way.

I finished this manuscript while working as a visiting instructor at Mercy College in New York, where Karol Dean, Diana Juettner, and Dorothy Balancio offered their tireless encouragement and support. My students and colleagues at Mercy have been especially gracious and eager to help, regularly forwarding me articles about the gig economy and inquiring about the status of my research.

My editor, Naomi Schneider, showed early interest in this project, when it was just a one-page proposal, and has provided valuable feedback and advocacy. Her editorial assistant, Benjy Malings, has been exceptionally patient with the numerous questions associated with a first-time author.

The production team—Jessica Moll and Bonita Hurd—have been the epitome of patience. Thank you to P. J. Heim for building the index.

As a graduate student at the University of Missouri, I was assigned Barbara Katz Rothman's essay "Now You Can Choose! Issues in Parenting and Procreation" in one of my classes. Amid my orange highlights, I scrawled "good writer" in the margins, with a notation to revisit how she brought stories into her argument. A decade later, I found myself in Barbara's food studies course at the City University of New York Graduate Center and eventually became her advisee in matters both academic and personal. I consider myself exceptionally lucky to have connected with such a talented and thoughtful writer and mentor.

Philip Kasinitz, the executive officer of the Graduate Center sociology program during most of my tenure, was also generous with his time, humoring my occasional office drop-ins with hour-long conversations on everything from article topics to job applications—even making time to meet with me while traveling internationally. Paul Attewell provided additional advice on theory and writing, and Vilna Bashi Treitler provided me with a crash course in matrix interviewing, courtesy of *Learning from Strangers*, that made it possible for me to collect these stories.

John Torpey and Samson Frankel took a chance on my academic aspirations when these aspirations amounted to little more than optimism. John was especially gracious with his time, reading funding proposals and providing the feedback and reassurance that I so desperately needed at times, while Samson's encouragement was a decisive step in my return to graduate school.

Juliet Schor shared her transcription resources and offered professional guidance early in my academic career, serving as a crucial resource and a welcome addition as a mentor. Wayne Brekhus, in his first semesters as an assistant professor, showed me how to bring research into the classroom and inspired my own categorization of workers. I owe a debt of gratitude to Jennifer Silva and Tamara Mose for their valuable suggestions for strengthening the manuscript, and to David Brady for skilled mentoring.

I have also benefited greatly from mentoring by former Graduate Center colleagues. Jonathan Davis and Alexandre Frenette provided feedback and advice on proposal and article writing and generously shared their own work, while fellow cohort members Sarah D'Andrea and Rachel Bogan were a source of equally important commiseration.

While at the CUNY Graduate Center, my work was supported by an Ewing Marion Kauffman Foundation Dissertation Fellowship in Entrepreneurship, an Early Research Initiative Award in Interdisciplinary Research in the Service of Public Knowledge, a Dissertation Year Award, and a Doctoral Student Research Grant. I remain grateful to the Kauffman Foundation for providing ongoing support and networking opportunities, and to the Graduate Center's sociology department, including Rati Kashyap and Lynn Chancer, for their backing.

Research can be myopia inducing, and I thank the family and friends who have provided support, reassurance, and encouragement. Dena Kessler, Joel Rosner, Digs Majumder, Isaiah Akin, Chani Kavka, Jonathan Weinberg, and Jamie Moore served as sounding boards and offered invaluable friendship. Brian Kennedy and Alex Palmer, members of my writing group, were a source of competitive encouragement.

My mother was an early advocate of my writing career, battling rush-hour traffic to bring me to newspaper meetings and supporting my entrepreneurial efforts. My aunt Diane Lefebvre challenged me to publish my work and has never stopped believing in me. Both Diane and my mother-in-law, Eva Duncan, gave the ultimate gift of their time, generously cooking meals, helping with childcare, and offering their support and understanding when I was overwhelmed with deadlines. My brother Chuck shared his own experiences in the gig economy world and was an upbeat cheerleader.

My husband, Sam Duncan, kept me fed, the dog walked, and the baby sleeping, and prevented the ever-present dishes on my desk from turning into a moldy avalanche. I love you and appreciate all that you do. Thank you.

This book is dedicated to Anna Addison, who inspired me to write multiple chapters in a summer and was the perfect "dissertation baby," happy to watch me write and even happier to play with my discarded drafts. May you always achieve your dreams.

1 Strugglers, Strivers, and Success Stories

Sarah was unemployed.[1] After leaving a position in casting for a critically acclaimed Netflix show, the twenty-nine-year-old waited for a series of promised jobs that never panned out. A friend recommended TaskRabbit.

At first, Sarah thought the site was a waste of time, but the traditional nine-to-five jobs she was finding elsewhere were unappealing. "Everything I wanted to do pretty much didn't pay, like film work," she said. "So I just kind of stayed with TaskRabbit. I could build a schedule, and it was just really reliable. I couldn't believe that I could make a living off of it."

Before long, more than 90 percent of her income was coming from TaskRabbit, and Sarah made plans for her first "actual vacation," a trip to Puerto Rico. A week before her trip, TaskRabbit announced its first pivot, changing from a bidding marketplace to more of a temporary-agency model, with Tasker availability posted in four-hour increments. Workers were required to respond to client emails within thirty minutes and accept 85 percent of their offered gigs.

"I was just freaking out the entire time, and I didn't know if I should spend any money on fun things on my vacation. I didn't know what was going to happen, and [TaskRabbit] kept saying it was a really good thing," she said. "But [the Taskers] kept saying, 'It's not a good thing,' and everyone was really worried."

Concerned that she would slip below the 85 percent acceptance rate, Sarah felt a lot of pressure to accept any work she was offered. "I had no control over what I would be getting and when. So I just took pretty much everything that I could," she said, including cleaning an apartment that she described as "a crack den." She told me, "I was actually nervous in there. . . . You would think that a lot of drugs happened there—basically everything just looked like it was covered in dirt and mud. It almost looked like there was mud even on the pillows. And I was like, 'I can vacuum and clean your bathroom.'"

But being picky about tasks has its own risks. In Sarah's experience, TaskRabbit's algorithm highlights people with high acceptance rates or high availability. "They want you on call for free," she said, before describing her schedule instability as "frustrating. . . . [Y]ou are always thinking, 'Oh, in five months I am going to be [sleeping] on a bench somewhere.'"

Baran, twenty-eight, is a college student at a local university who drives for Uber and Lyft. In New York, app-based drivers have the same insurance and licensing requirements as taxi drivers, a cost that usually runs several thousand dollars. To sidestep this considerable start-up expense and the associated annual costs, some drivers rent a licensed, insured, and Uber-approved car through local services or utilize Uber's fleet-owner and driver matching service. Baran rents such a car for four hundred dollars a week. "You have to work at least three days to just cover your [car] expenses," he says. "Two days for the rent, and one more day sometimes for the gas and other things. After the three days, whatever you make, it just belongs to you."

Baran works twelve-hour shifts, from eight a.m. to eight p.m., on his workdays and tries to make $250 per day after accounting for the Uber fees, but before paying for tolls. He showed me his weekly earnings: most were under $800. His earnings showed a single week of making over $1,000. "That week I was really lucky," he said. "I kept going back and forth to the airport. It was like finding a unicorn."

In the tech world, a "unicorn" is a statistical rarity, a privately held start-up worth over a billion dollars.[2] In Baran's experience of driving for

Uber, making a thousand dollars—before paying for weekly car rental expenses—is equally mythical.

Baran describes his costs as "spending money to make money," but each week he incurs a considerable debt that he must work off before he can earn the money he needs for rent and food. He's thankful he isn't using one of the Uber or Santander financing programs (discussed in chapter 3), either of which, he says, amounts to "a deep hole" and "modern slavery." But his current pay-to-work situation also sounds suspiciously like indentured servitude, a practice outlawed more than a hundred years ago.

"The *sharing economy* is the term which they use for getting around rules so they don't have to pay taxes. . . . I'm not a partner. I'm an independent contractor. *Partner* means that you are sharing somewhat, because you are partners. All of the costs have been covered by me. . . . I'm not a partner. I'm an independent contractor. They can kick me out anytime they want. If I was a partner, they couldn't do that," he said. "They can do whatever they want. [Uber] became a forty-billion-dollar company. What can you do?"

Baran tries to not think about his gig work too much. "Uber is for me—it's like I go to an isolated place. I don't want to, you know, bring anything home from that place to my normal life," he said. "I don't want anybody to think I have something to do with it."

Shaun, thirty-seven, an African American male, is another New York City transplant. Previously living in Westchester, a suburb north of New York City, he turned to TaskRabbit when the cleaning service he was affiliated with couldn't provide any work. "I came to New York City basically out of desperation to find some type of work," he said.

When I met Shaun, he was splitting his time between two part-time gigs: four days a week as a part-time personal assistant and two to three days a week on TaskRabbit. "Normally I try and set goals, saying, 'If I make at least two hundred dollars in two days, then I could just rest on a Sunday,'" he said. "The only thing that I kind of regret is that I lack a social life."

Working seven days a week doesn't leave much time for friends, but Shaun has credit card debt and firsthand experience with the challenges of finding housing on a low income. "I was homeless a couple of times before. I was literally living on the streets," he said. "Since it was September and it was still warm, I decided to just stay on the streets versus going to the shelter. Every once in a while I'd actually go to Airbnb and get some place to sleep. But I mostly remained on the streets until I was able to afford a place where I could go weekly. The first place I went to was Long Island City [a neighborhood in Queens]; but the roommate was an asshole, so I moved into an illegally run hostel. When I got tired of that, I moved to a room. And I've been there ever since."

"The personal assistant job is enough by itself to rent the room and take care of myself, but it is not enough to help me unload the credit card debt and to save up money," he explained. "So this basically helps me save money and to help get rid of debt. . . . I'm not planning on doing this for long; I'm just trying until I can work at a stable job. . . . [A]nd then afterwards I'll do TaskRabbit once in a while just for extra money, instead of depending on it like a second job."

Shaun doesn't think of himself as a entrepreneur. "I think of myself as a hustler," he said. "Basically, right now I'm just money-motivated. I have the attitude where I am basically doing things that I don't think I can do to get by. So there are times when I would look at a job, and someone might say, 'You're sure you can handle it?' And I'm like, 'I don't know what I'm doing.'"

Unlike driving for Uber or working as a Kitchensurfing chef, Taskers can be hired for a variety of tasks. In some cases, Shaun has proven to be a quick study, such as when it came to building Ikea furniture. "The one thing that I've done that I kind of regret doing was [when] someone hired me to tune a door handle, one of those automatic door handles. And I went there thinking I know what's going on—until I looked at the door handle," he said. "It took me like a good thirty minutes to figure it out, but not before the [door swung out and the] glass hit the desk. They gave me a negative review, saying, 'I don't think he knows what he's doing.'"

Shaun has since sworn off fixing automatic doors. And after getting injured on a TaskRabbit gig, he's also stopped accepting moving tasks. "I helped lift a dresser. Had to pull [it] up a flight of stairs. It was two dressers, and even though I had assistance, I'm carrying stuff that weighs about 125, and my current abilities can only allow me to carry 50 pounds. So yeah, I stretched my back, and I just walked out of there saying, 'I'm okay.'

But when I'm out, I'm like, 'Ouch.' My mind thinks I'm twenty-five, but my body is way older," he said with a chuckle. "And I keep telling myself, 'Yeah, let me just lose a couple of pounds, let me just lose the stomach or at least get my flexibility back before doing things like that again.'"

The stories from these twentysomething and thirtysomething workers underline the volatility of working in the twenty-first-century gig economy. Taking jobs in what has been heralded as a futuristic utopia of choose-your-own-adventure employment with flexible schedules and unlimited earnings, these young workers have instead found themselves working long hours for little pay and less stability. The autonomy they expected—work when you want, doing what you want—has been usurped by the need to maintain algorithm-approved acceptance and response rates. Sarah and Shaun find themselves pressured to accept unpleasant tasks, constantly hustling, while every week Baran must earn more than four hundred dollars just to break even on his Uber rental. Rather than finding financial freedom, these workers find themselves on the losing side of an outsourcing equation where they are responsible for platform "service fees" and encounter workplace expenses usually financed by employers. The promise of modern-day, app-driven entrepreneurship has yielded the bleak employment and living conditions of the early industrial age.

THE SHARING ECONOMY IS A MOVEMENT FORWARD TO THE PAST

Welcome to the sharing economy, a nebulous collection of online platforms and apps that promise to transcend capitalism in favor of community. Supporters argue that this new economic movement, alternatively described as the on-demand, platform, or gig economy, will build community, reverse economic inequality, stop ecological destruction, counter materialistic tendencies, enhance worker rights, empower the poor, and bring entrepreneurship to the masses.[3] The sharing economy promises both an idyllic, boss-free future, where workers control their incomes and hours, and to be a cure-all for the woes of modern society.

Yet for all of its app-enabled modernity, the gig economy resembles the early industrial age, where workers worked long hours in a piecemeal system, workplace safety was nonexistent, and there were few options for redress. Despite its focus on emerging technology—apps, smartphones, contactless payment systems and review systems—the sharing economy is truly a movement forward to the past. Workers find themselves outside even the most basic workplace protections regarding discrimination and sexual harassment, the right to unionize, and even the right to redress for workplace injuries. The sharing economy is upending generations of workplace protections in the name of disruption and returning to a time when worker exploitation was the norm.

This book explores contradictions between the lofty promises of the gig economy and the lived experience of the workers, between app-enabled modernity and the reality of rolling back generations of workplace protections.

The sharing economy promises flexibility and work-life balance, but while Baran works only four days a week, those days are twelve-hour shifts. Sarah and Shaun are free from reporting to a single employer, but the gig economy increasingly tethers them to work: they're constantly on call, hustling to make money. Thanks to service algorithms, the decision to work isn't always in their hands. The gig economy offers "flexibility," but if they spend too much time away from the platform, they may discover they've been "removed from the community," or "deactivated."

When it comes to the sharing economy's promise to bring entrepreneurship to the masses, their careers diverge even more. Sarah doesn't think of herself as an entrepreneur, but TaskRabbit tells her she is, and that the service is "incentivizing" her entrepreneurship through its commission structure. Yet successful Airbnb entrepreneurs (discussed further in chapter 7) are described by the platform as "bad actors" who are using the service to run de facto hotels, instead of just making extra money on the side.[4] And Shaun? He's just hustling.

Much like fledgling entrepreneurs, gig economy workers find that getting work often requires doing unpaid work. Workers must maintain profiles and respond to emails from prospective clients or even just keep clicking "refresh" on their app—all of which is unpaid work. Sarah and Shaun are not always being paid to work, but they are always working. And Baran is "spending money to make money," but his ability to make money is dictated by Uber's policies and algorithms. Such contradictions lie at the center of the sharing economy. And yet, questioning these contradictions is not merely an academic exercise but one that has real implications for millions of people.

In 2016, the Pew Research Center found that nearly a quarter of American adults had earned money in the "platform economy" over the last year.[5] Economists Lawrence F. Katz and Alan B. Krueger found that online services such as Uber and TaskRabbit accounted for .5 percent of all workers in 2015— an impressive level of growth for a five-year-old industry.[6]

Yet for all its growth, little is known about the actual, lived experience of working in the gig economy. Who are these workers? Why are they willing to work without hard-earned workplace protections? Are they entrepreneurs or idealistic "sharers," or is this simply "unemployment lite"? Why are they investing their time and personal financial resources in work that is entirely out of their hands? What types of challenges and dangers— emotional, physical, or financial—do they experience? What does this mean for the future of work? And what does this mean for our society?

My book is the first—and perhaps still the only one—to build on firsthand accounts from nearly eighty workers and to place their stories in the context of larger social structures and trends in American society. It's also the only one to focus on four very different services—Airbnb, Uber, TaskRabbit, and Kitchensurfing—that illustrate the larger issues of skill and capital in the gig economy. (It's highly illustrative that two of those services are doing better than ever, one is trying to establish a clear identity, and one is already defunct.)

Many of the sharing economy books written to date have been by journalists or business school professors. Most serve as cheerleaders—the trend is great, the problems are minor, and so on. But as a sociologist, I take a more critical perspective. My book acknowledges the potential of the sharing economy and examines the challenges for workers. Instead of just telling readers about the sharing economy, I raise important questions about this new economic movement. My goal is to leave you reexamining some of what you've read previously. For instance, if this is a great opportunity for people to own their own businesses, why are workers embarrassed to work in the gig economy? What does it say about this type of work that workers lie to family and friends rather than admit that they drive for Uber or clean homes via TaskRabbit? If this is the so-called sharing economy, why does everything have a price?

As a sociologist, I examine the larger social forces that lead workers to take on gig work or turn to multiple jobs to make ends meet. I link trends in outsourcing, wage stagnation, income volatility, and mass layoffs to the rise of this "alternative" work. I focus on the stories of the workers in order to put the sharing economy in the context of larger trends related to income inequality and American labor struggles over the past two hundred years. This historical connection demonstrates that while the underlying notion of a "gig economy" is fundamentally forward-facing—new tools, new capabilities, and new ventures—most of its basic practices are distressingly familiar. It's an exercise in regression, returning workers to an era of rampant exploitation. It may be app-enabled, but this so-called disruption is definitely not leading to anything new.

FROM SHARING TO EARNING

From the beginning of the Great Depression and until the early 1970s, the trend in income distribution in the United States was toward greater equality, with the percentage of national income held by the wealthiest 1 percent of families dropping by more than half. But by the mid-1970s, that trend began to reverse. From 1993 to 2010, for the bottom 99 percent of the income distribution, the real growth rate in income was 6.4 percent, while the top 1 percent experienced a real growth rate of 58 percent. More than half of all real income growth in the economy went to families at the very top of the income distribution, a reversal described by Paul Krugman as the "Great Divergence." But while worker wages stagnated, the pay received by top business executives has soared in the last twenty-five years. "In 1979 the ratio of the pay received by the average CEO in total direct compensation to that of the average production worker was 37.2:1. By 2007 (the year before the recession) it had grown to 277:1."[7]

The high levels of income inequality immediately before the Great Depression and Great Recession have led some to suggest that high levels of income inequality may precipitate economic crises by destabilizing the economy as a whole. Although the incomes of the wealthiest also declined during the Great Recession, the Federal Reserve's triennial report, the 2014 *Survey of Consumer Finances,* shows that in the three years following the Great Recession, the typical American family's income declined 5 percent. In addition to seeing their overall wealth fall by 2 percent, cash-strapped families did not save any additional money for retirement, and student loan debt continued to increase. Only the highest-earning households experienced income gains, causing the gap between the wealthiest and the poorest families to widen.[8]

Early in the first decade of the twenty-first century, the gap between earnings and expenses was met with an increased use of credit cards and revolving lines of credit. By 2001, 75 percent of households utilized credit cards—a 50 percent increase since 1970.[9] Credit card debt became increasingly common as the millennium continued: by 2007, 72 percent of households were carrying a balance.[10]

In 2008, the Federal Reserve Board reported that Americans carried $2.56 trillion in consumer debt, up 22 percent since 2000. Household debt, which included mortgages and credit cards, represented 19 percent of household assets, according to the Federal Reserve, compared with 13 percent in 1980. The nation's savings rate—which exceeded 8 percent of disposable income in 1968—was just 0.4 percent by 2008, according to the Bureau of Economic Analysis.[11]

There are two general solutions when one's income doesn't match expenses: either cut expenses or increase income. The early days of the sharing economy—often described as collaborative consumption—included such free services as Couchsurfing.com and Craigslist, which were viewed as a way to decrease the expenses of consumption. Makerspaces and swaps allowed users access to low-cost or free products. As the sharing economy grew, free services were replaced with fee-based services. Couchsurfing.com was largely usurped by Airbnb.com; clothing swaps were replaced with Tradesy.com, an online designer-clothing reseller marketplace. Instead of cutting expenses through sharing, the focus moved to growing income by renting out one's "surplus," such as an unused room or one's free time on evenings or weekends. In this way, the sharing economy became a way for workers to supplement their incomes.

And the sharing economy appears to be fulfilling a real need. According to the Economic Policy Institute, the hourly wages of middle-wage workers were stagnant from 1979 to 2013, rising just 6 percent—less than 0.2 percent per year.[12] The Pew Research Center notes that after adjusting for inflation, today's average hourly wage has stagnated: "The $4.03-an-hour rate recorded in January 1973 has the same purchasing power as $22.41 would today."[13] Although the US unemployment rate has reached record lows, there's a real perception that workers are not making enough and are taking a step backward, or at least remaining static.

Millennials (born between 1980 and 2000) are known for early adoption of technology, but also for being disproportionately affected by the Great Recession.[14] According to Bureau of Labor Statistics data, young people ages sixteen to twenty-four had an unemployment rate of 15.5 percent in 2013 and 14.2 in early 2014, leaving many of them unable to rent apartments and purchase or furnish homes. In contrast, the unemployment rate for people ages twenty-five and over was 5.4 percent in early 2014. Unfortunately, graduating college in the middle of an economic recession appears to have long-term effects on one's earnings potential; such graduates experience a statistically significant wage loss even fifteen years after college graduation.[15] Given this wage loss and high levels of student loan debt, it's not surprising that almost half of twentysomethings in major cities are relying on rent subsidies from their parents.[16] For millennials contending with the possibility of downward mobility, earning additional income through the sharing economy can be a popular stopgap measure—the majority of gig economy workers are between the ages of eighteen and thirty-four.[17]

STRUGGLERS, STRIVERS, AND SUCCESS STORIES

As I met and interviewed workers, the same themes arose again and again: some workers were struggling, others were excelling, and a large portion fell somewhere in between. I characterize the workers as falling into three main types: Strugglers, Strivers, and Success Stories.[18]

The Success Stories have used the gig economy to create the life they—and many of us—want. They are their own bosses, they control their day-to-day schedule, and the sky seems to be the limit in terms of how much money they can make. The flexibility of the sharing economy means that they aren't tied to a desk or even a city; they can run their companies via app while lounging on a beach or passing time in a bar.

At the other end of the spectrum are the Strugglers. These are the workers who have turned to the sharing economy in a fit of desperation. They include the long-term unemployed and undocumented workers, who—thanks to the growing prevalence of E-Verify, a federal program that confirms employment eligibility—struggle to find work. In some cases, they are simply temporarily down on their luck: a job loss or personal crisis caused a major setback and their already-strained savings couldn't handle the increased pressure. These college-educated workers found themselves struggling to pay rent, to afford food, even to collect enough quarters to do laundry. Finally, some of the Strugglers were reasonably successful—even believing themselves to be Success Stories—until the platform they were on performed a "pivot," techspeak for a mission change and policy overhaul. Much like automation led to the wholesale layoffs of automotive workers, pivots lead to Strugglers trying to reinvent themselves. But unlike automotive workers, sharing economy workers generally receive little to no advance notice of major workplace changes, and they have no unemployment safety net to fall back on.

The appeal of the Success Story is unmistakable. The fear of the Struggler situation is overpowering.

And yet, these two extremes don't tell the whole story. There's also a third possibility for sharing economy workers. The Strivers are those who have good jobs and stable lives and who turn to the sharing economy for a bit of added excitement or extra cash. Unlike the Success Stories, they aren't looking to make thousands of dollars from their sharing economy work; they don't talk about scaling up or incorporating. Although some Strivers discuss making this a full-time job, they remain hesitant to leave their mainstream stability and workplace benefits or are using the gig economy while they transition to a new career or start a business. Unlike the Strugglers, these workers don't necessarily need this money to survive, although it can provide a more comfortable lifestyle: the occasional vacation, additional funds in the bank, a bit more financial security.

I use the term *worker* here as a matter of convenience but also of accuracy. These individuals are not employees, a specific workplace classification that I discuss further in chapters 3 and 4. But even though they are not employees, they are definitely working. While hosting an Airbnb guest or cooking as a Kitchensurfing chef may be fun, there is work involved. Few people would participate in this activity without the cash reward that follows, a fact that many workers freely admit.[19]

I caution, however, that the categories I provide here are ideal types.[20] Although I describe these distinctions as clear-cut, it's not uncommon for a Striver to have qualities in common with the Strugglers or the Success Stories. In some cases Strivers would be considered Success Stories in the mainstream, nonsharing economy, even as they struggle to provide a middle-class lifestyle for their families.

Amy, a thirty-six-year-old white woman, is a perfect example of this contradiction. A former nonprofit executive married to a lawyer, Amy had several children and was expecting another. I met Amy in a coffee shop near her East Village brownstone on a muggy summer day in New York City. I was excited that she had accepted my interview request. Many Airbnb hosts talked about hosting until they had kids, but Amy's children were the impetus for her Airbnb hosting.

She and her husband rented a brownstone in district 1, one of the few "choice" districts with no zoned schools. Part of the Lower East Side/East Village, district 1 has a number of alternative and experimental schools, but it's also just blocks away from district 2, which has some of the best public elementary schools in the city.

Unwilling to give up their apartment, but also wanting their oldest child to attend a strong school, Amy and her husband moved to a local rental complex that was comfortably ensconced in district 2. They turned their brownstone into an Airbnb rental. "We were essentially trying to figure out how we could recoup some of the rent," she said. "If we can't afford private school, I at least wanted to get into a good public school—you know, not right at the bottom of the barrel." New York gives siblings preferential access to neighborhood schools, so Amy's family can return to their apartment later, confident that their younger children will get into their preferred school.[21]

Renting out their primary home hasn't been easy. Their apartment tends to attract fellow families, something Amy and her children have struggled with. "Renting it to families creates a lot more work in turning it over," Amy said, detailing her efforts to clean and reorganize toys after each stay. "I went once with my son because my nanny was sick. I just had to go. [I brought] both kids, and they had a really hard time walking in and realizing someone had slept in their beds, someone had played with their toys. They were really upset about it."

As in the cases of many other Airbnb hosts, Amy hasn't told her landlord about her rental activities. The need to be discreet further adds to the stress. Unable to afford the carrying costs of both homes, Amy maintains a balancing act, being attentive to the needs of her guests to ensure that they give her positive reviews and making certain that her landlord doesn't find out about the rental.

A recent situation with a maintenance worker highlighted the difficulties of that discretion. Amy's landlord notified her that a worker needed access to her apartment, and she let her guests know. Unfortunately, the worker was there for several hours and repeatedly needed to be buzzed in, effectively transforming the Airbnb guests into de facto doormen for most of a workday. The guests were understandably frustrated and requested a rent reduction.

"We were really nervous. . . . [W]e were just paranoid that they were going to write a review that was awful and give us two stars," Amy said. "I was like, 'Let me treat you to dinner. . . . [T]ell me where you want to go; I will call ahead.'" The guests declined her offer, noting that they would be around for only a few more nights and didn't plan to go out. "I bought wine and chocolates and a little thing for the kid, and I'm like, 'Well, at least enjoy your few nights home,'" she said. "We felt really responsible, but this was out of our control and we were so worried about making amends with them. [If you get] one bad review or one low star rating, it just affects everything, and then you don't come up [in the search algorithm] and it looks like it's not a place that's worthwhile to stay in."

Maintenance worker snafus aren't the only challenge. Needing to charge a premium for the apartment, Amy has become an on-call concierge, putting her guests in touch with local babysitters, suggesting activities for kids, and making restaurant recommendations. Like many hosts, she provides an extensive booklet of suggestions, but people often have questions or special requests that she feels obligated to fulfill. Indeed, when we met, she was just finishing an hour-plus meeting with a guest who needed additional hand-holding. Amy and her family may be mainstream Success Stories, but they're sharing economy Strivers.

Likewise, Ashley, a twenty-six-year-old white female, highlights how some Strivers are precariously close to Strugglers. Ashley has a full-time job, with benefits, managing local drugstores, but she still describes herself as "trying to make ends meet." When an unemployed friend turned to TaskRabbit, the personal assistant site, and was able to set her own hourly rates, Ashley decided to do the same. "I can actually use my main job for serious expenses, and then the side jobs that I do are for my little minuscule expenses," she said. "Major expenses would be paying rent or going on vacations or having to go to a doctor appointment or if something medically went wrong and I had to go to a hospital—anything of that kind of nature, where my main job would have to cover those finances. . . . I can use the side job for the little things, because they always add up to the big things."

Working two jobs is a good way to make extra money, but it's time-consuming—and exhausting. Ashley tries to balance jobs that require extensive manual labor, such as a deep cleaning, with easier jobs like errand running. Accepting a deep-cleaning job requires an expected-energy-level calculation. "I have to think to myself: 'Am I willing to sacrifice my exhaustion level for the pay?' Or am I going to just say, 'You know what? I need a day off.' But the problem is, if I already put that availability, it wouldn't matter how tired I am. I would have to go," she said. "Every day, you don't know what can happen but you have to plan—like, could you see yourself being exhausted that day regardless of what you worked? So that's always the Catch-22. But even when there are days that I would be extremely tired, I would still make sure that I would get there. Because that person needs the help, and I'm not usually the kind of person to say, 'Sorry, I'm too tired to come.' I would never say that to someone. . . . So there's a sense of professionalism involved."

As a result, Ashley must weigh the obligations of her full-time job with the requirements of her part-time work. "If I know that I'm staying God-knows-how-many hours in the store, I'll make sure I take off that day so I can relax. But if it doesn't happen that way, I would come home, sleep for two or three hours, wake up, and get myself ready to go to the client's house," she said. "There have been a lot of instances where I would get three clients within a day, and each one booked, from eight o'clock to twelve o'clock, twelve o'clock to four o'clock, and four o'clock to eight o'clock. Some of them do take the entire three, four, hours. Some of them only take an hour. It creates a lot of gaps in between, but it helps also for traveling, too, if I have to travel from place to place." The time spent traveling is unpaid however, so although she may be working up to a dozen hours, Ashley is paid for only a fraction of her time.

"At first, it was fun getting job after job after job after job. And it's like, 'Oh, I'm on a roll!' But now I'm burning out, balancing that tightrope, that juggling act of trying to benefit myself in some way. But then I realized the exhaustion level started taking a toll on me. So now I have to start creating a balance. 'Okay, if I start getting tired, I need to take a week off from TaskRabbit,'" she said. "There are just some days when I'm like, 'I need to be away from everybody and everything and lie down, because I'm not going to be helping my main job or my side job if I'm not focused. And I won't be helping either of them if I, God forbid, do something to myself because I'm not fully awake.'"

Ashley and Amy illustrate the precarious nature of work in the gig economy, even for the college-educated middle class. The gig economy promises flexibility and more free time, yet workers are increasingly tethered to work because of the on-demand nature of the work. The work is seemingly flexible, but it doesn't end. And while the workers are "self-employed" contractors and don't answer to bosses, they remain under constant observation through a technological panopticon. But unlike Bentham's original prison model, where prisoners cannot see the watchers and never know when they are being watched, in the gig economy everything can be collected and viewed at any point. Chat logs in TaskRabbit, emails in Airbnb, travel locations for Uber—all of this is collected and can be viewed by the platform administrators.

There's also a bigger social and economic issue at play here. In February 2005, President George W. Bush, after meeting with a divorced mother of three who worked three jobs, was ridiculed for describing her workload as "fantastic" and "uniquely American." The general consensus, at the time, was that having to work multiple jobs in order to support oneself might be uniquely American, given our lack of a social safety net, but it was hardly to be applauded.

Why have we gone from questioning why anyone should have to work multiple jobs to accepting and embracing this as our new reality? Why do workers feel the need to forgo their leisure time? Why are PhDs running errands for twenty dollars an hour, and why are former finance professionals cleaning houses?[22] Why is driving part-time for Uber or renting a spare room on Airbnb seen as a postrecession solution to stagnating wages and the lack of job security? Why are workers who spend their "free" time on a technologically enabled second or third job, on a platform controlled by other people, hailed as entrepreneurs?

Americans already work a lot. Although direct comparisons can be difficult to make owing to data gaps and different data collection methods, American work weeks are longer than in most industrialized countries.[23] Even though the United States doesn't require paid time off, and many workers don't receive paid vacation time, research suggests that Americans neglect to take what time they do receive: on average in 2013, employees with paid time off neglected to use 3.2 days of paid time off.[24] The problem seems to be growing. In *The Overworked American,* Juliet Schor concluded that in 1990, Americans worked an average of nearly one month more per year than in 1970.[25] American women who work outside the home already contend with the "second shift," the additional hours of housekeeping and childcare that occur on weekends and in the evenings after daytime employment.[26] Men have also been increasing their levels of household work and childcare involvement, although their baseline is much lower.[27]

People are not robots. Every additional hour of work must come from somewhere, leading to either reduced sleep, limited leisure, or split-attention parenting. In 2003, Robert Putnam raised an alarm, telling us that Americans were no longer "bowling together" in leagues or participating in high numbers in the types of voluntary organizations that Alexis de Tocqueville first identified as a uniquely American phenomenon. Instead, they were spending more and more time camped out in front of the television, decompressing from an ever-increasing workday.

The sharing economy promises to bring people together, but instead it may further decrease American leisure time by providing workers with the opportunity to work more. Instead of simply reporting for a several-hour shift, workers may find themselves picking up tasks or gigs here and there, the flexibility of scheduling inadvertently increasing their workload by more than they intended. Or the proliferation of outsourcing—of hiring others to do everything from walking dogs to cleaning homes to grocery shopping and chauffeuring—may further increase the "commodification of intimate life" and lead to additional pressure to make enough to pay for market services.[28]

Hiring workers off of platforms risks creating platform monopolies. As noted by Andrew McAfee and Erik Brynjolfsson, when more and more people use a platform or tool, a "network effect" arises, which is economist speak for the idea that certain goods become more valuable as more and more people use them. The most frequently given example is that of a fax machine. If only one person has a fax machine, it's not very useful. But as more and more people get fax machines, the tools become increasingly useful. One tool gives you access to many people. Eventually the tools are so prevalent than even spammers use them for sending scam offers. The fax machine is also an apropos example because most people no longer have, or use, fax machines. That doesn't seem like an issue unless you're invested in a fax machine company or are wedded to your fax, for whatever reason. When other people stop using faxes, your fax machine stops being useful.

McAfee and Brynjolfsson note that "economics of network effects are central to understanding business success in the digital world," and they use the example of WhatsApp to illustrate network effects. They explain that as WhatsApp became more popular, users of regular text messages (SMS) felt left out and increasingly turned to the app: "As more and more of them did this, the network effects grew stronger. Computer pioneer Mitch Kapor observed that 'architecture is politics.' With platforms, it's also economics."[29]

But the idea that, for platforms, architecture can be economics might not be a good thing. As these platforms grow in size and become the "go-to spot" for everything from furniture assembly to taxis to hotel rooms, we run the risk of creating monopolies. When TaskRabbit, as part of its first pivot, transitioned into an app-based service (as opposed to remaining accessible via the website), workers who didn't have smartphones with generous data plans found themselves at a serious disadvantage. Continuing the fax machine analogy, these workers had fax machines but everyone else was using email.

For Strugglers, the sharing economy is an occupation of last resort. What happens to those workers if their work of last resort requires a thirty-dollar phone activation first? Do we want to live in a world where

Figure 1. Union Square Park in New York City, October 2017. The young man's sign reads, "Hired with courier co, UberEats. Can show proof. Unable to start my job without an operating phone cause I have to work off an app. Trying to raise $30 to pay 4 activating my phone. Willing to work 4 it." Photo by author.

work becomes a luxury good, available only to those who can pay a marketplace entry fee or meet platform requirements? As fig. 1 shows, such a possibility has already become a reality for some workers.

SUCCESS STORIES STILL FACE INCREASED RISK

Workers who make a comfortable living in the sharing economy—the Success Stories—are a far cry from the unemployed young man panhandling for phone activation funds. But even Success Stories face the implications of platform monopolies and an outsourcing of risk.

Ryan, a twenty-seven-year-old white man, is a successful entrepreneur by any account. The owner of several laundromats in New York City—where most residents don't own washer-dryers—Ryan has a high-demand business. Having previously lived in the suburbs, Ryan had one requirement when he wanted to move to New York City after college: his apartment had to be nice. So he and his business partner became roommates and rented a three-bedroom apartment for six thousand dollars a month. "We rented out one of the bedrooms, and that's how it all started, actually," he said, describing his entrée to Airbnb. "We ended up making about four thousand dollars a month from it, from one bedroom."

Impressed by the income possibilities, Ryan and his partner soon expanded their Airbnb offerings and now rent six apartments throughout New York City that they use exclusively for Airbnb hosting. Ryan's schedule is generally open except when he gets a new apartment, then it's "crunch time." His goal is to have that apartment up and functioning as an Airbnb rental within a week. "It's my whole day. Once I get into the apartment, I become very busy. We're in New York City, with a lot of contractors that can come and mount TVs, mount shelves, and make it the best. And they put together couches and furniture if you need it. So we get it going pretty quick. What we usually do is to get the apartment, and about five days later we'll schedule a photographer; so we know that we have five days to get everything in there. Every day it's not on Airbnb, you are losing money."

And the money that can be made is significant. Ryan tries to charge at least $300 a night per property, with two-bedroom apartments renting for $300 to $400 a night, and three bedrooms billed at $450 to $650 a night. According to the website RentCafe, in 2018 a Manhattan one-bedroom apartment rents, on average, for $3,757 a month; the average rent for a two-bedroom apartment is $5,474.[30]

Ryan is a successful Airbnb entrepreneur. And yet, he questions the promise that such entrepreneurship is readily available. First there's the barrier to entry. Ryan knows that it takes a certain level of financial capital to take advantage of the arbitrage between the annual cost of an apartment and the price he can charge nightly on a short-term rental. "I mean, I guess not everyone can do it," he said. "I spent the money to start these apartments up, and every apartment is twenty to thirty thousand dollars. . . . First month [rent], last month, security deposit, and some-times a broker's fee, furnishing the whole thing."

It's a big investment and one that could easily disappear. To start with, there's the question of legality. Using an apartment for short-term rentals of less than thirty days has been illegal since 2010, and fines from the city start at twenty-five hundred dollars per day. And Airbnb has cracked down on commercial users in the past, removing them from the platform. If Ryan were prevented from hosting, he would still be responsible for paying more than twenty thousand dollars in monthly rent for the six apartments. There are other short-term rental sites, like HomeAway, but guest reviews don't transfer between sites, and Airbnb tends to dominate the New York market. Ryan has a fairly precarious business model.

As a result, Ryan and his partner utilize strategies designed to skirt detection by their landlord and the city. They've divided their listings between their two profiles. And they are particular about the properties they rent, preferring apartments that don't have on-site superintendents or doormen, and that feature easily replicable front-door keys as opposed to magnetic fobs. "I actually have one building on the Lower East Side where the whole building is mine," he said. "There is a restaurant on the first floor. Another restaurant on the next floor, then an apartment and another apartment. I have both apartments, so that one is a completely secure building. That's kind of what I look for."

Keeping his investment "secure" also means allaying his landlord's sus-picions. Instead of calling building staff, Ryan tries to do his own repair work. "My apartments are pretty much booked, so I don't want to ever involve my building [staff]. Unless it's a problem where I need—like if it's five-thousand-dollar problem, I will have [them] take care of that," he said. "If it's a pipe, and it costs me a few hundred bucks, I'll take care of it just because I don't want building [staff] to come in and, you know, what-ever. I'm very cautious, basically."

But even beyond the legal and business concerns, Ryan remains ambiv-alent about his business. He'd like to see the city tax or regulate Airbnb and thereby reduce some of the uncertainty. But this would also reduce his profits.

Perhaps most surprisingly, Ryan—a thriving entrepreneur in the shar-ing economy—doesn't feel entirely comfortable telling people about what he does for a living. He prefers instead to "keep to myself." He's a success story who has a hard time telling the story of his success.

RESEARCHING THE SHARING ECONOMY

My research is based on nearly eighty ethnographic interviews with workers for Airbnb, Uber, TaskRabbit, and Kitchensurfing. When I discuss my gig economy research, I often hear a response that sounds like this: "I love Uber/Airbnb/TaskRabbit! I spoke to my driver/host on the way here/ when I was staying in exotic city, and they told me that the platform changed their life! Now they get to be their own boss and aren't stuck in an office and life is fantastic!" These days, my response is equally canned: "That's great! You may have found a really happy worker. But when your boss asks if you like your job, what do you say?"

The sharing economy markets itself as offering a peer-to-peer connection, but that message ignores a larger reality: when you get in an Uber or hire a TaskRabbit, you become the boss, at least temporarily. You are paying them, albeit through an app that will first take a cut. You are ranking and rating their performance. Your perception and rating of their demeanor or skills may affect their ranking in the app's algorithms and their ability to find and be hired for work. With that type of power, it's unlikely that workers will be entirely honest about what their experience is like. Most of us have also been cautioned not to complain about our last boss to a current or prospective employer—another strong deterrent to an honest conversation.

In many apps, such as Airbnb and Uber, the worker can also provide a rating for the employer. But as I discuss in later chapters, workers—who are intimately familiar with the often-damaging implications of a four-out-of-five rating as opposed to a five-out-of-five—rarely give low scores. Additionally, as service providers, although they may prefer to not work with an employer with a low score, there will always be someone who needs the income enough to risk it. A low rating has a much bigger effect on a worker than an employer.

Although I approached interviews with some general questions (available in the appendix), the interviews were participant driven and averaged two hours, with some exceeding three hours. For most workers, the interview was the second, third, or even fifth time that I had seen them. Instead of creating the power imbalance usually found in the worker-employer interaction, I made it clear that I was relying on them as experts; interviews were often done over lunch or at cafes where I provided snacks. Even with my attempts to build rapport, many of the stories presented in these pages didn't come up until well into the interview. These are not the stories that workers bring up in a fifteen- or twenty-minute interaction.

While I used a survey to obtain basic demographic information, qualitative interviews allow for more detail. Interviews allow for follow-up questions and clarifications, such asking why something happened or how it made someone feel. And the participant-driven model enabled respondents to branch off into tangential stories that often became theoretically rich data. It was these tangents that first brought the issues of sexual harassment (chapter 5) and crime (chapter 6) to my attention.

PLAN FOR THE BOOK

In chapter 2, I provide a background on the sharing economy and an overview of the four platforms I studied: Airbnb, Uber, TaskRabbit, and Kitchensurfing. I discuss participant recruitment and worker demographics in more detail and frame my research within the larger literature available to date on the sharing economy.

In chapters 3 and 4, I address the lived experience of the workers and the dangers that result from the gig economy's shifting of risk and liability as part of a larger casualization of labor.[31] I focus on the past by describing how the gig economy resembles the industrial age, in which workers worked long hours in a piecemeal system, workplace safety was nonexistent, and there were few options for redress for injustices. I outline how the gig economy's lack of responsibility for workers results in an effective destruction of Occupational Safety and Health Administration protections and worker's compensation as workers clean ponds and remove construction dust with their bare hands, get bitten by dogs, and experience on-the-job injuries for which they have no financial recourse.

Although the workplace protections dealing with safety and the right to unionize date back to the early industrial age and the beginning of the 1900s, American protections against sexual harassment are a direct outcropping of second-wave feminism and the current #MeToo movement. Yet even the latest workplace policies are no match for the sharing economy's bulldozing of workplace protections. Chapter 5 examines sexual harassment in the sharing economy and how the egalitarianism of peer-to-peer employment results in the loss of political language as workers "explain away" sexual harassment.

In chapter 6, I explore the shady underbelly of the sharing economy through stories of workers who find themselves engaging in illegal or at least legally questionable activities as part of their sharing economy work. I argue that the anonymity of the sharing economy can make it easier to source otherwise law-abiding workers for drug deliveries and can lead to unsuspecting workers involved in various scams. In many ways, the gig economy creates a new future for criminal activity even as it rolls back worker protections.

Finally, in chapter 7, I discuss gig economy workers whose higher skills and capital give them many more choices in the sharing economy: successful Airbnb hosts and Kitchensurfing chefs. I found that workers on these two platforms were much more likely to view themselves as entrepreneurs and to take advantage of the outsourcing opportunities of the gig economy to hire others. By juxtaposing the stories of those who are thriving with those who are barely surviving, I highlight the role of capital and skills in the gig economy.

My concluding chapter provides interviews with the leaders of services who are working to change the sharing economy status quo by paying their workers a living wage and providing benefits and workplace protections. I also provide policy recommendations on how to best address the differing challenges experienced by Strugglers, Strivers, and Success Stories.

In the debate between capitalism and community, the experience of gig workers often gets lost along the way. Workers' stories suggest that while the sharing economy offers a select few an opportunity to manage a small business, the experiences of many others are decidedly less pleasant. In many ways, the sharing economy is the millennial's version of the minimum-wage, precarious work that Barbara Ehrenreich detailed in *Nickel and Dimed: On (Not) Getting By in America.*[32] Workers are underpaid, they're subject to capricious policies, and ultimately, they are expendable. Studying the experiences of workers in the sharing economy—and the different challenges encountered by Strugglers, Strivers, and Success Stories—can provide a better understanding of the costs, benefits, and societal impact of this new economic movement and help us create a new narrative rather than an equally exploitative sequel.

2 What Is the Sharing Economy?

Be Your Own Boss. Make $7,000 in December, Guaranteed.

—Uber

Find jobs you love. At rates you choose. Make a schedule that fits your life.

—TaskRabbit

Airbnb provides supplemental income for tens of thousands of New Yorkers.

—Airbnb

Mimic a restaurant experience . . . without all of the chaos and uncertainty that inevitably comes with running a NYC kitchen.

—Kitchensurfing

We've probably all daydreamed about quitting our jobs to pursue our passion: to open a cupcake shop, pursue novel-writing full time, or simply lead guided tours through exotic locales. For many of us, that daydream is a refuge from daily stresses and pressures.

But there's a new economic game in town that promises to place the dream of setting one's own hours, being one's own boss, and deciding one's own paycheck in the hands of ordinary Americans. These companies comprise the sharing economy and include such services as Airbnb, Uber, TaskRabbit, Etsy, and Kitchensurfing.

Sharing economy is a catchall term for "'peer-to-peer' firms that connect people for the purposes of distributing, sharing, and reusing goods and services."[1] The concept encompasses everything from multibillion-dollar companies such as Airbnb (room rental) and Uber (on-call taxi service) to free durable-goods-sharing sites such as Neighborgoods. Definitions of the field vary and often seem arbitrary: Airbnb is seen as the epitome of the sharing economy, but traditional bed-and-breakfasts are not. eBay, the online marketplace of essentially everything, is hailed as an early founder, but free local libraries and parks are not—even though libraries involve sharing and eBay requires payment. Juliet Schor, a preeminent researcher in the field, notes that definitions of the sharing economy tend to be "pragmatic, rather than analytical: self-definition by the platforms and the press defines who is in and who is out."[2]

After the Great Recession in 2009, there was increased attention on utilizing unused assets for economic gain, with particular focus on "durable goods, such as lawn mowers, tools, or expensive equipment for specialized uses."[3] These efforts, although often compared to Zipcar (the hourly car rental service, which was an early entrant in the sharing economy),[4] are perhaps most similar to the tool libraries that had developed decades earlier in low-income communities. Much like the tool libraries, most of the free websites that originally comprised the sharing economy are now defunct: Snapgoods, Neighborrow, Crowd Rent, and Share Some Sugar.[5] The somewhat better-known Neighborgoods lingers, but only as the pet project of an investor; among its forty-two thousand members, only ten thousand users are active.[6]

The technological version of the sharing economy, also described interchangeably as connected consumption, collaborative consumption, or the gig economy, is often dated back to the 1995 inventions of Craigslist by Craig Newmark and PayPal by Pierre Omidyar.[7] Later contributory organizations included the free hospitality-exchange website couchsurfing.com, founded in 2003. The increased interest in the sharing economy is thought to be fueled by the convergence of three technological advancements: smartphone ubiquity; secure, cashless payment systems; and customer review sites. But not all of the impetus is technological. The recession and postrecession fallout led to the rampant underemployment of college graduates—with almost half working in jobs that didn't require a college degree—and to a need to monetize possessions and make do with less.

As noted in the journal *Contexts*, "The sharing economy is a floating signifier for a diverse range of activities. Some are genuinely collaborative and communal, while others are hotly competitive and profit-driven."[8] Juliet Schor groups sharing economy activities into four broad categories:

- *Recirculation of goods.* These services reduce transaction costs (such as consignment shop fees and the risk of financial loss) and provide reputational information on sellers to reduce the risks of financial transactions with strangers.

- *Increased utilization of durable assets.* These services, such as Airbnb and its earlier, free predecessor, Couchsurfing.com, allow some people to earn additional money to supplement traditional incomes, while providing others with low-cost access to goods and space.

- *Exchange of services.* These services, such as TaskRabbit, Handy, and Zaarly,[9] pair users who need tasks done with individuals who need or want work.

- *Sharing of productive assets.* These services enable production rather than consumption and include hackerspaces (for programmers) and makerspaces, which bring together shared tools and coworking spaces.[10]

While Schor's definition seems clear, others argue that there are distinct differences between the sharing and the on-demand economies. For instance, a team of Dutch researchers defines the sharing economy as limited to "consumers (or firms) granting each other temporary access to their under-utilized physical assets ('idle capacity'), possibly for money" (see fig. 2). Under this definition, UberBLACK, the luxury car service, while innovative, is just an app-based black car service. UberPOOL is part of the sharing economy because, when someone requests a car, a ride is already under way and excess space is then used, while "UberX is only a form of the sharing economy if the driver would have made the trip anyway." Under this definition, TaskRabbit and Kitchensurfing are part of the on-demand economy, while eBay, with its focus on consumer-to-consumer sales (C2C), is part of the secondhand economy. Airbnb is further differentiated by the method behind the rental: if a person is hosting while

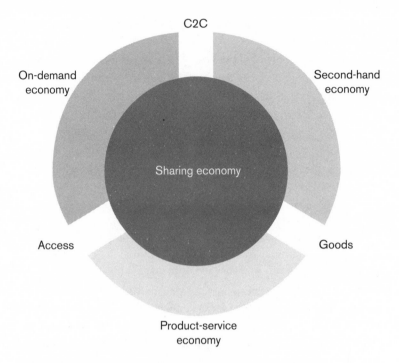

Figure 2. The sharing economy and related forms of the platform economy. Source: Frenken, Meelen, Arets, and van de Glind (2015). Used by permission.

on-site or while on vacation, it is part of the sharing economy; but "if people live permanently in another house, and continuously rent out their own house, they are actually just running a (often illegal) hotel."[11]

"A WORD . . . MEANS JUST WHAT I CHOOSE IT TO MEAN—NEITHER MORE NOR LESS"

Adding to the confusion, the sharing economy regularly feels like a trip through Alice's looking glass or into Bizarro World, where the meaning of standard words is twisted and changed. The first of these is, of course, *sharing*. Although early sites such as couchsurfing.com and ShareSomeSugar. com didn't charge fees, most current "sharing economy" sites do charge them. An Airbnb host isn't so much "sharing" her home or "hosting guests" as she is renting her home out. TaskRabbit assistants and Kitchensurfing chefs aren't "sharing" their services but being paid. Likewise, even though Uber and Lyft describe themselves as "ride-sharing," charging for private vehicle transportation is simply a taxi or chauffer service by any other name. While Lyft (slogan: "Your friend with a car") originally encouraged riders to "sit in the front seat like a friend, rather than in the backseat like a fare," such "friendship" didn't eliminate the need to pay the fare.[12]

The reinvention of terms isn't limited to the companies themselves but can also carry over into descriptions of the services by researchers. For instance, TaskRabbit and Handy are often grouped in the category "exchange of services."[13] Yet these two services aren't time banks, and they don't allow for bartering. They are not an "exchange" of services but instead operate according to the usual practice of offering services for cash. Likewise, used-goods-sale sites are also often included in the sharing economy. While these services may have helped create the sharing economy, once an item is sold on eBay it is no longer available for "sharing."

Also integral to the sharing economy is the idea of trust. Although trust would seem to be at odds with the idea of background checking, many sites promote their background checks and identity verification as part of the trustworthiness of their service. In an unintentional irony, the section of Airbnb's website dealing with trust and safety is unreachable unless one agrees to the site's terms of service, which leads with an arbitration clause. One is reminded of the motto "In God we trust, all others pay cash." While Airbnb markets trust, the company prefers to rely on lawyers.

The sharing economy claims to make trust easier because electronic trails are supposed to make it easier to know everyone. In the small community of old, reputations could follow a family for forever; today one's Facebook trail is everlasting. Sharing economy services often link through Facebook accounts for identity verification, making a "digital re-creation of the neighborly interactions that defined pre-industrial society."[14] In addition to linking to Facebook, these services often ask users to post pictures of themselves and, in the case of Airbnb and TaskRabbit, to communicate before each stay or task. Although almost every sharing platform requires users to create a profile, and many utilize community ratings, organizations such as Traity, and the now-defunct TrustCloud, work to collect information on people's online reputations based on their social media footprint and information data exhaust, the trail that users leave as they engage with others on Facebook, LinkedIn, Twitter, and TripAdvisor.[15] This information could possibly be used to calculate "reliability, consistency, and responsiveness[,] . . . a contextual badge you'd carry to any website, a trust rating similar to the credit rating" of the offline world.[16] Relying on a credit rating is the antithesis of trust.

Trust is generally defined as a firm belief in the reliability, truth, and ability of something; but in the sharing economy, trust is easily conjured—Airbnb's website even features a TED Talk by cofounder Joe Gebbia on how the service "designs for trust." TaskRabbit also markets its "trust and safety" efforts, which include an identity check, criminal-offense screening, and a two-hour orientation that discusses the best practices for success on the TaskRabbit platform. As the TaskRabbit website explains, "We share knowledge of what creates a great task so that [Taskers] can deliver safe and superior experiences." Again, trust is something the user demonstrates to TaskRabbit and its workers—not something TaskRabbit is willing to rely on. This expropriation of positive terms such as *trust* and *sharing* is often crucial to the marketing of the sharing economy and serves to mislead and redirect, painting an image of trustworthy friends as opposed to workers and de facto temporary employers.

Likewise, in regard to the use of *disrupting,* many sharing economy companies use this term to describe their services, even though their use of the term is often at odds with commonly accepted definitions of disruption as "groundbreaking" or "wreaking havoc." Instead of truly changing the world, the services are just taking standard services and putting them on an app. They're not inventing hoverboards to replace taxis; they're simply making it easier to get a for-hire vehicle.

The popularity of the sharing economy as a concept means that companies regularly declare themselves to be part of the sharing economy. For instance, a recent white paper by PricewaterhouseCoopers grouped Spotify and Amazon Family with Airbnb and Uber as part of the sharing economy.[17] Amazon Family allows adult members of the same household to access books and videos purchased from different Amazon accounts. Although these are definitely sharing activities—and involve more sharing than is entailed in renting out an apartment on Airbnb—this is simply the technological equivalent of family members accessing the same communal DVD collection or family-room bookcase. If family members' acts of sharing the same TV or tube of toothpaste are part of the sharing economy, the term is essentially meaningless.

In my research, I define the sharing economy as a collection of app-based technologies that focus on the lending/renting of assets or services either for profit or for a higher good. While food swaps and makerspaces are useful and raise a number of theoretically interesting issues regarding race, class, and the creation of "belonging," I am especially interested in sharing economy platforms that provide a source of work and income and that claim to be bringing entrepreneurship or financial sustainability to the masses.[18] I categorize these platforms as part of the gig economy, owing to their focus on short-term income opportunities. While not all aspects of the sharing economy are part of the gig economy, platform-based gig-economy services fall under the sharing economy heading, and I use these two concepts interchangeably.

The guiding questions of my research are: What is life in the sharing economy like for workers? To what extent do the workers consider or experience themselves as entrepreneurs, workers, or sharers who are creating a new type of economy? What types of skills and capital do workers bring to the gig economy?

My research draws on three main theoretical themes: the *Gemeinschaft/Gesellschaft* trust divide; the increasing casualization of labor with a related shift in risk; and the resulting increase in social inequalities.

Gemeinschaft/Gesellschaft, *or Technology Leading to the Revival of Trust and Community*

Originally seen as centers of trade, government, culture, and religion, cities took on new importance in the Industrial Revolution, making citizens out of people who had been peasants the day before. The increasing size and importance of cities made early political leaders suspicious. Thomas Jefferson believed that "urban culture would ruin the American desire for freedom," while Alexis de Tocqueville complained about Cincinnati, describing it as "a picture of industry and work that strikes one at every step."[19] Even worse than being disorganized, cities were seen as destroying humanity. As Bonnie Menes Kahn points out, one of the most disturbing consequences of city life seemed to be the change in human relationships, creating "a breed of savage, self-interested machines[,] . . . strangers, tearing human beings away from one another, rendering men and women less human."[20] Theorist Georg Simmel believed that the overstimulated world of strangers created a city dweller who was callous and blasé, forced to shut down in the face of so much mental stimulation.[21] Cities contributed to a "lonely crowd" of people who were looking for clues to how they should act, a people who felt "no moral responsibility because they have no history— no past to honor, no land to defend, no traditions to follow."[22] In this view, cities were at odds with community and human connections.

This fear of cities as destroyers of community can also be seen in Ferdinand Tonnies's concept of *Gemeinschaft* and *Gesellschaft*. For Tonnies, *Gemeinschaft* was a community focused on primary relations organized by natural will, house, village, and town, with a focus on collective consciousness and effervescence. *Gemeinschaft* required that people interact with each other face to face; lacking a division of labor, people knew each other in many contexts. Social conformity was maintained through stigma, informal sanctions, and social traditions—there might be blood feuds, but no lawsuits. By comparison, "the city is typical of *Gesellschaft* in general." In a *Gesellschaft*, connections are abstract and more tenuous, bonds have to be imagined. Connections have to be organized through contracts because members can no longer trust that someone's word and firm handshake are trustworthy—courts, cops, and lawyers serve as an enforcement mechanism. By definition, when one moves to a "modern"-day society—or at least a city—one loses the community connections of *Gemeinschaft;* it is also in *Gesellschaft* that "the family is decaying."[23]

The sharing economy paints itself as a solution, as a return to small-town or even village life. New York University Stern School of Business professor Arun Sundararajan argues that "the extent to which people are connected to each other is lower than what humans need. . . . Part of the appeal of the sharing economy is helping to bridge that gap."[24] John Zimmer, a cofounder of the taxi app Lyft, compares the sharing economy to his time spent on the Oglala Sioux reservation in Pine Ridge, South Dakota: "Their sense of community, of connection to each other and to their land, made me feel more happy and alive than I've ever felt before," he says. "I think people are craving real human interaction—it's like an instinct. We now have the opportunity to use technology to help us get there."[25] Although Uber and Airbnb can be found all over the world, true economies of scale are most often found in cities. It's easier to be a Sprig messenger, responsible for delivering healthy meals in twenty minutes or less, if you live in a concentrated city like San Francisco—the same model doesn't work in rural Idaho or in Atlanta's suburban sprawl.

But our trust in humanity doesn't seem to be increasing. Data from the 2012 *General Social Survey,* the National Opinion Research Center's poll of American attitudes, found that only 32 percent of respondents agreed that people could generally be trusted, down from 46 percent in 1972.[26] An October 2013 report by the Associated Press and the market research firm GfK found that only 41 percent of respondents (n = 1,227) express "a great deal" or "quite a bit" of trust in the people they hire to work in their homes, 21 percent trust others when they are driving cars, and only 19 percent trust "people you meet when you are traveling away from home."[27]

As for the promise of community offered by these services, academic research to date suggests that it, too, may be a bust. Anny Fenton, a Harvard graduate student who studied social interactions among RelayRides users, found that car owners using the site said their relationships with users were "sterile," "anonymous," and "nothing"; however, they felt that they had something more personal to offer and assumed that users would treat their cars better than a typical rental car.[28] Research on Zipcar, a service often described as part of the sharing economy, found that users experienced the service in the same anonymous way that one experiences a hotel: "They know others have used the cars, but have no desire to interact with them." Rather than viewing fellow Zipsters as cosharers of the cars, users were mistrustful of them and relied on the company to police the system. Researchers have suggested that Lyft's lack of success in relation to Uber may be a result of Lyft "putting too much emphasis on consumers' desire to 'share' with each other," and that "consumers are more interested in lower costs and convenience than they are in fostering social relationships with the company or other consumers."[29]

My own research echoes this lack of interest in interaction. Rather than create long-lasting relationship with their guests, many Airbnb hosts never meet the person who will be sleeping in their bed or using their bathroom.

Figure 3 (above) and *figure 4 (opposite)*. Lockboxes, like these, are a common sight in the East Village. Airbnb hosts provide guests with the location of the box (usually a tree guard or nearby fence) and the combination when sending confirmation messages. The lockboxes allow for an interaction-free key transfer between host and guest. Photos by author.

As a matter of both convenience and personal preference, hosts often make use of strategically located street-side lockboxes (see figs. 3 and 4), KeyCafes (lockboxes in local stores and restaurants), and TaskRabbit workers to allow for interaction-free key transfer between host and guest. This avoidance of contact is so prevalent that in an undergraduate observational study I conducted in the East Village, a popular Airbnb neighborhood, I found numerous lockboxes allowing hosts to exchange keys without any human interaction whatsoever. While the sharing economy may market itself as bringing people together, it results in the ultimate *Gesellschaft* as fleeting interactions and urban anonymity rule the day.

Although the sharing economy—a term that increasingly feels inappropriate—may have been intended to democratize entrepreneurism, evi-

dence suggests that it may simply be furthering the discriminatory status quo. Discrimination in the marketplace has been well documented by researchers. We know that those with "black-sounding" names are 50 percent less likely to be called in for an interview, and female job candidates are given lower salary offers than men.[30] Users hope that the sharing economy makes discrimination harder or less likely, and anecdotal reports about Uber suggest that it may make hiring a cab easier for African Americans by increasing the salience of social class—using Uber entails a credit card, a smartphone, and at least originally, higher rates, and so Uber users are considered wealthier.

Yet the sharing economy's emphasis on user names and profile pictures may make discrimination easier. Black Airbnb hosts charge 12 percent less than comparable properties hosted by white hosts, possibly owing to discrimination.[31] Meanwhile, iPods for sale on eBay that are photographed while held in a black hand get bids that are 20 percent lower than those held in a white hand.[32]

In my qualitative interviews with Airbnb hosts, I've found that although some hosts admit to discriminating on the basis of race, hosts actually consider a slew of factors, including profile photos, email communication, reviews, and even outside information gathered through "Internet stalking." As a result, host discrimination against potential guests may be broader and more extensive than previous studies may suggest. The increase in discrimination, partnered with a reliance on reviews and profiles and a declining level of trust, suggests that the sharing economy—while many things—is hardly a positive return to the ideal of small town life.

The Increasing Casualization of Labor and the Related Risk Shift

The sharing economy also brings to the forefront issues regarding the changing relationship between worker and firm and the resulting workplace risks encountered by sharing economy workers. The majority of sharing economy workers—including Uber/Lyft drivers, TaskRabbit runners, Airbnb hosts, and Handy cleaners—are independent contractors. In recent years, the number of workers classified as independent contractors has grown steadily as employers seek to avoid social responsibilities, including workers' compensation, overtime, and disability accommodations.[33] A 2015 Occupational Safety and Health Administration report suggests that temporary workers and independent contractors also receive less training and are more likely to be injured on the job as a result.

Although researchers have addressed how classification as an independent contractor, as opposed to employee, can affect workers, the concept of risk is more commonly used when discussing entrepreneurs.[34] Since the late 1700s, entrepreneurs have been linked with risk-taking based on Ricard Cantillon's observations that the entrepreneur "buys at certain prices and sells at uncertain prices," thereby bearing the risk of the transaction.[35] Harvard Business School's Howard Stevenson describes entrepreneurship as "the pursuit of opportunity beyond resources controlled."[36] Although an entrepreneur is often thought of as creating something new, the Oxford dictionary emphasizes control and risk in its definition of an entrepreneur, describing one as someone who "undertakes or controls a business or enterprise and bears the risk of profit or loss."[37] The concept of risk is particularly salient for entrepreneurs, especially in the United States; statistics from the Bureau of Labor Statistics demonstrate that roughly a third of new businesses will fail in the first two years, and that more than half won't last five years.[38]

Yet Jacob Hacker has noted that risk in the workplace is no longer assumed entirely by entrepreneurs or capitalists.[39] Workers have seen their health insurance coverage transformed into high-deductible plans and their company pensions converted from defined benefit to defined contribution plans (401ks), pushing the financial risk of health problems and bad investments onto the workers. The rise of outsourcing and focus on short-term profits further means that workers are constantly competing for jobs in a "spot market" that resembles a trading floor. Thanks to stagnating wages, many families rely on two incomes, and the loss of either can be devastating.

In 1994, sociologists Stanley Aronowitz and William DiFazio published *The Jobless Future*, arguing that companies were "scratching every itch of everyday life with sci-tech," leading toward "more low-paid, temporary, benefit-free blue- and white-collar jobs and fewer decent permanent factory and office jobs." The secondary labor market is defined as providing workers with low pay, few benefits, and a level of economic insecurity in which work today doesn't necessarily mean work tomorrow—the very definition of gig employment. While this casualization of the workplace and increasing transfer of risk to workers was once a defining characteristic of the secondary labor market, it has become much more pervasive and generalized, increasingly affecting managerial and professional workers.[40] British economist Guy Standing warns that this instability has led to the "precariat," a growing number of people "living and working precariously, usually in a series of short-term jobs, without recourse to stable occupational identities or careers, stable social protection or protective regulations." This precariousness often leads to a sense of anxiety, anomie, alienation, and anger.[41]

The *Wall Street Journal*, a bastion of big business, suggests that the rumblings of worker discontent "highlight the ambivalence that many workers feel towards the platforms that supply or supplement their income." Workers argue that the on-demand platforms give them little control over their labor, and that they are forced to shoulder personal and financial risks. Numerous lawsuits brought by workers of Uber, Lyft, and Handy argue that the restrictions on, and requirements for, workers mean they should be considered employees—not independent contractors. Other suits, such as one against CrowdFlower.com (renamed Figure Eight in 2018), a start-up that breaks digital jobs into tiny tasks performed by millions of workers, argues that workers were paid less than minimum wage. In a video interview, one of CrowdFlower's cofounders noted that "the firm sometimes paid workers $2 to $3 an hour, rather than the federal minimum wage of $7.25, or paid workers in points for various online reward programs and videogame credits."[42]

Sociologist Allison Pugh suggests that how this instability is experienced depends on the social class and desirability of the worker. In *The Tumbleweed Society,* she argues that for upper-class people with in-demand job skills, "insecurity looks more like 'flexibility.'"[43] These workers can pursue jobs that are meaningful and that provide the best fit between job and self. For lower-class workers, reduced security in the workplace has also led to an inability to commit in personal relationships. Upper-class workers avoid the same fate in part by creating a moral wall between work and family. Could the sharing economy—by reducing barriers to entrepreneurship—transform insecurity into flexibility for lower-class workers?

The central role of entrepreneurship in economic growth and development is well researched in economic literature. Entrepreneurs can play a transformative role by increasing competition, shaping markets, and driving innovation and technological improvements.[44] But not all entrepreneurism is created equal. As MIT economist Antoinette Schoar notes, "Much less effort has been devoted to studying the actual entrepreneurs who are the agents of this change and the heterogeneity among these individuals." Schoar argues that there's a difference between subsistence entrepreneurism, which provides a subsistence income, and transformational entrepreneurs, "who aim to create large, vibrant businesses that . . . provide jobs and income for others."[45]

Where do sharing economy workers fall on this spectrum? Uber-financed research by Jonathan Hall and Princeton economist Alan

Krueger notes that more than 90 percent of Uber drivers say they drive with Uber to "earn more income to better support myself and my family," though only 71 percent of respondents agree that working for Uber actually makes them better off financially.[46] In New York City, Airbnb launched a public relations campaign "highlighting its positive economic impact on the city's predominantly-black neighborhoods, from Crown Heights and Bedford-Stuyvesant in Brooklyn, to West Harlem."[47] Airbnb's *Economic Impact Report* utilizes internal research (based on guest stays from 2012 to 2013) to argue that the typical host earns $7,530 per year, and that the funds are used to help people stay in their homes. Etsy, the online craft space, notes that sellers report higher levels of education and lower household income than the general population in the United States: 52 percent of sellers have a college education, but the median income is just $44,900, 10 percent lower than the national average. More than a quarter (26 percent) of Etsy sellers earn less than $25,000 in annual household income. The same report further notes that "68% [of sellers] said that Etsy provides supplemental income for themselves or their family . . . contributing 7.6% to household income[,] . . . enough to cover the cost of annual car payments or several months' rent."[48] Based on these reports—issued by the companies themselves—it appears that while the gig economy may offer workers a way to fight stagnating wages and workplace instability, at best, this work is subsistence entrepreneurism.

Increasing Social Inequalities

As the Success Stories show, some workers are able to create a middle-class, or higher, living from the sharing economy. Even individuals who are renting out a spare bedroom on Airbnb, ostensibly to make rent, like Ryan in the first chapter, soon discover that if they have the available capital, they can quickly realize considerable profits on their investment. A *New York Times* article on the business tycoons of Airbnb discusses a real estate agent who started off renting his spare bedroom when the monthly rent on his apartment increased suddenly from twenty-eight hundred dollars to five thousand dollars.[49] When the agent realized the potential to exploit the difference between long- and short-term rental prices, he signed a lease for a second apartment. In October 2014, already making up to six thousand dollars a month in profit from his second apartment, "he added a third rental—this one under his wife's account. He plans to add more he said, possibly even under phony accounts to avoid legal scrutiny."[50] Other documented Airbnb empires include a San Francisco stockbroker who rented six different apartments in order to "create a makeshift hotel that could net him almost $100,000."[51]

In some cases, sharing economy services are used to pad the incomes of the already wealthy. In 2014, the New York State attorney general released a report highlighting Airbnb's illegal listings, finding that as many as 72 percent of Airbnb listings in New York were illegal. This report, *Airbnb in the City*, found that although more than 90 percent of hosts in New York City rented two or fewer units on Airbnb, 1,406 hosts (6 percent) during a four-year period acted as "commercial users," running larger operations that administered as many as 272 unique units each. The sheer number of commercial users meant that they "controlled more than 20% of unique units in New York City booked on Airbnb as private short-term rentals, accepted more than 33% of private reservations, and received more than one of every three dollars in revenue from private short-term rentals on Airbnb for a total of $168 million."

These multilocation hosts are not as rare as one might expect. More than a fifth of my Airbnb hosts respondents have multiple units; one respondent in particular maintains space for twenty-five guests a night. In his words: "I own a hotel. I'm a hotelier. I just have a room here and apartment there. . . . Until I have that chain of hotels, I just have a chain of different apartments all over this island."

In *Capital in the Twenty-First Century*, Thomas Piketty notes that in a slow-growth economy, wealth provides better returns than labor. As a result, those with wealth to invest will get wealthier; those without probably won't. Or as William Alden explains, "These markets also tend to attract a class of well-heeled professional operators, who outperform the amateurs—just like in the rest of the economy. Listing a spare room on Airbnb might keep you current on your always-climbing Manhattan rent, but real entrepreneurship (as always) requires real dough."[52]

While wealthier hosts can rent multiple apartments and charge by the night, lower-income residents find that the increased demand for housing in their neighborhood leads to rent increases. In 2018, McGill University researchers released a report suggesting that between 7,000 and 13,500 units of housing were removed from New York City's long-term rental market, including 12,200 frequently rented entire-home listings that were available for rent 120 days or more.[53] A 2015 study by New York Communities for Change and Real Affordability for All noted that as many as 20 percent of the vacancies in parts of Manhattan and Brooklyn were listed as Airbnb apartments. The East Village led the list, with a staggering 28 percent of its units going as illegal hotel rooms on Airbnb.[54] A 2015 Streeteasy report notes, "According to census data, New York City rent prices grew at almost twice the pace of income between 2000 and 2013, meaning that over time rent has taken up a much larger piece of New Yorkers' incomes."[55] *EV Grieve,* an East Village blog, lists East Village residents as spending 56 percent of their incomes on market-rate rent.[56]

New York City has strong renter protections, but renters in other cities aren't as lucky. In San Francisco, rent-controlled residents face the threat of owner-occupied move-ins, where an owner or immediate family member can evict a tenant in order to personally use the apartment. Although the Ellis Law, which allows landlords to leave the rental business, is a legally acceptable reason for eviction, these newly vacant apartments are often turned into Airbnb rentals, making thousands of dollars more profit each month.[57]

A recent *Economist* report on the digital revolution acknowledged the growing divide between a few lucky ones and the rest of society: "In the past new technologies have usually raised wages by boosting productivity, with the gains being split between skilled and less-skilled workers, and between owners of capital, workers and consumers. Now technology is empowering talented individuals as never before and opening up yawning gaps between the earnings of the skilled and the unskilled, capital-owners and labour. . . . [I]t is creating a large pool of underemployed labour."[58] A recent report by the Federal Reserve Bank of Dallas found that the majority of new job growth of the past decade has come from low-skill, nonroutine manual jobs, those that "require few skills and little problem solving." Although some of the new errand jobs may feature high pay—Instacart can pay thirty dollars a hour—no grocery run takes eight hours.[59] Thirty dollars an hour is a decent income if you can get eight hours of work; it's lousy pay if that's all you earn in a day.

The Guardian, as part of its 2017 series on homelessness in America, identified a number of Los Angeles Uber drivers who were living out of their cars.[60] Even *New York Magazine* has pointed out the underemployed-labor problem confronting the new gig economy, noting numerous cases of Handy home cleaners who were homeless and living in shelters.[61] While it's good that even the homeless are able to find work utilizing these platforms, Handy had received $110.7 million in investments as of November 2015—so why are any of its workers homeless?

PARTICIPANT RECRUITMENT AND METHODOLOGY

I drew my data from seventy-eight in-depth qualitative interviews with twenty-three Airbnb hosts, twenty-two TaskRabbit workers, nineteen Kitchensurfing chefs, and fourteen Uber drivers/messengers. These four services were chosen because they illustrate the diversity of businesses within the sharing or gig economy: incredibly successful, well-funded companies worth billions (Uber and Airbnb), an established but somewhat struggling start-up (TaskRabbit), and a relatively new upstart (Kitchensurfing).[62] In addition, these companies were also chosen for their ability to highlight the different components of the sharing economy. For instance, all four services offer consumers access to underused physical assets ("idle capacity"), but TaskRabbit and Kitchensurfing offer consumer-to-consumer or "on demand" services, while Airbnb is about granting consumers temporary or shared access to a home. Uber focuses on the more efficient use of assets by making money from a personal vehicle and offering shared rides through uberPOOL.[63]

Finally, these four firms also illustrate the range of skill and capital barriers that divide services in the sharing economy (see table 1). TaskRabbit, a personal assistant service, has few barriers to involvement: workers complete an online application and attend an orientation; there is no capital investment needed. Other services, such as Kitchensurfing, required a specialized skill set and that prospective chefs audition by cooking a restaurant-worthy meal; as a result, the on-demand, prix fixe Kitchensurfing Tonight service had a high skill barrier but a low capital-investment barrier. The Kitchensurfing chef marketplace service, by comparison,

Table 1 Skill and Capital Barriers to Sharing Economy Work

	Low Capital Investment Barrier	High Capital Investment Barrier
Low Skill Barrier	TaskRabbit	Uber/Lyft
High Skill Barrier (auditioning/marketing)	Kitchensurfing Tonight	Airbnb/Kitchensurfing Marketplace

required high skills and high capital-investment—workers need dependable transportation, food storage tools/facilities and cooking equipment. Airbnb and Uber involve high levels of capital investment: Airbnb requires a space that is desirable enough that other people will pay to rent it; Uber necessitates access to a relatively new car that meets Uber requirements and New York City licensing requirements that cost thousands of dollars (high-capital investment).[64] However, whereas Uber skills are fairly minimal (being able to pass a driving test and background check), successful Airbnb hosting requires a level of communication with guests; successful hosting also requires creating a listing that will appeal to travelers (high-skill requirement).

BACKGROUND ON SELECTED SHARING ECONOMY SERVICES

The following section provides a short history on the four services chosen and their presentation of an entrepreneurial ethos.[65]

Airbnb

Founded in San Francisco in 2008, Airbnb was created by two roommates who couldn't make rent that month. In an oft-repeated story, they literally tossed down several air mattresses the weekend of the Industrial Designer Society of America Conference and rented them out to people who were

Figure 5. With messages like "Welcome Home," Airbnb presents prospective guests with the idea of an open and accepting community. Screenshot by author.

unable to get hotel rooms.[66] By November 2015, Airbnb provided access to more than two million rooms, and by July 2017, the number exceeded three million. The website allows hosts to list their home or extra space online and rent it out to guests. The company operates as a listing service and escrow account: payment for the host is held until the guest arrives and ensures that all is as expected.

The entrepreneurial ethos is best highlighted by comparing the bookings pages of Airbnb's website with the pages for hosts. The opening page of the Airbnb website (see fig. 5) emphasizes sharing and community: the text announces, "Welcome Home," and the company's tagline is "Belong Anywhere." According to the company's website, Airbnb is "your home, everywhere." There's even a video on "how Airbnb hosts create a sense of belonging around the world."

The section targeted at hosts, "Earn money as an Airbnb host," is focused on the financial- and personal-control aspect of hosting (see fig. 6). Workers are assured that "no matter what kind of home or room" they have available, Airbnb "makes it simple and secure to earn money." For those who remain hesitant, Airbnb assures them that "you're in full control of your availability, prices, house rules and how you interact with guests." The same web page also helpfully notes how much a host can earn—in New York, that's apparently more than thirty-two hundred dollars a month.

Airbnb takes the stance that it is a marketplace, and that control—and risk—fall on the hosts and guests. It's believed that the earliest docu-

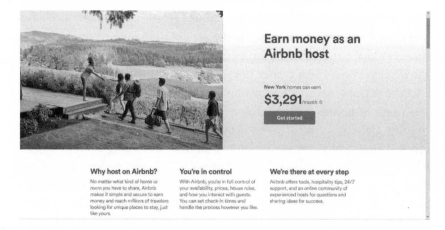

Figure 6. As part of the entrepreneurial ethos, Airbnb targets hosts with messages about the income potential of listing on the platform, and there is much less emphasis on community. Screenshot by author.

mented case of an Airbnb disaster was listed on a host's blog in June 2011.[67] The female host returned to her San Francisco apartment to discover that it had been ransacked by her guest and a team of accomplices:

> They smashed a hole through a locked closet door, and found the passport, cash, credit card and grandmother's jewelry I had hidden inside. They took my camera, my iPod, an old laptop, and my external backup drive filled with photos, journals . . . my entire life. They found my birth certificate and social security card, which I believe they photocopied—using the printer/copier I kindly left out for my guests' use. . . . Despite the heat wave, they used my fireplace and multiple Duraflame logs to reduce mounds of stuff (my stuff??) to ash—including, I believe, the missing set of guest sheets I left carefully folded for their comfort.

As illustrative of Airbnb's hands-off approach, the host reported that it took fourteen hours and outreach to an acquaintance associated with Airbnb for the company to respond to her complaints. The story was soon publicized in *TechCrunch, Slate, Time,* and other publications. Airbnb later implemented a twenty-four-hour emergency helpline and a one-million-dollar insurance policy that applies to eligible accommodations within the United States, Canada, and many westernized countries.

However, the policy is secondary insurance. Hosts are required to file for compensation through their own homeowner's or renter's policy first, even though most insurance companies will not cover damage that occurs in the process of renting out one's home.

A quick Google search for "airbnb trashed apartment" provides numerous cases of homes destroyed and possessions ruined: a drug-induced orgy in Canada, a wild party resulting in a feces-and-used-condom-covered New York City penthouse, and an "overweight orgy" Freak Fest in a New York City apartment.[68] A *Huffington Post* article from July 2014 even provides a handy summary of "Airbnb horror stories" that includes meth addicts, stabbed hookers, hosts being evicted because of their Airbnb activities, and a squatter who refused to leave.[69] Not all of stories are sensational—some are as simple as an Airbnb guest flushing sanitary napkins and causing ten thousand dollars' worth of water damage.[70] Even Airbnb user forums include stories and documentation of trashed homes; and the Abundant Host, an Airbnb listing consultant, has shared a blog post documenting a stay that included broken possessions, rule violations, and generally disruptive behavior in her own home.

While it's true that hotels, too, experience rowdy guests and destroyed rooms, hotel rooms are known for their neutral and often nondescript decor. By comparison, many Airbnb locations are private homes with numerous unique personal effects. Additionally, the requirement that hotel guests provide a credit card and driver's license or passport means that hotel management can identify the perpetrator or at least who should be held financially responsible for destruction. Airbnb hosts don't have the same access to personal information and, instead, must go through Airbnb customer service to plead their case and get relief. Likewise, when a hotel room is wrecked, incoming guests can be assigned to a different room; when the same occurs in a personal home or apartment, hosts don't usually have a backup home for themselves or their next guests. Hotels have security, and the rooms are often smaller than those of the average apartment or house, especially in New York City. To host a raging party or orgy, one generally needs the larger space and privacy offered by an Airbnb rental. Finally, there's also the trust component: hosts who hew to the community message of the sharing economy end up being especially broadsided when the trusted strangers they let stay in their homes act like perfect strangers.

In an effort to reassure hosts that they won't face problems, Airbnb is quick to declare, "You're in control. You set the price for your listing, your availability, and reservation requirements for your guests." The company also notes that its "trust and safety tools help you accept a booking only if you're 100% comfortable." However, this "control" and becoming 100 percent comfortable require that hosts decide who they will rent to—the responsibility for screening guests falls on their shoulders. Airbnb has a strict antidiscrimination policy, explaining, "Airbnb is an open marketplace. . . . [W]e prohibit content that promotes discrimination, bigotry, racism, hatred, harassment or harm against any individual or group, and we require all users to comply with local laws and regulations." Yet, as mentioned earlier, research shows that guest screening and discrimination remains prevalent.[71]

In order to rent on Airbnb, hosts and guests must create profiles that include a full name, birthday, sex, and contact information. Although the profile process notes that sex and birthday are never shared with fellow Airbnbers, each user is urged to post a profile picture that clearly shows his or her face. Explains Airbnb, "Clear frontal face photos are an important way for hosts and guests to learn about each other. It's not much fun to host a landscape!" Users are also expected to write a short self-description in order to "help other people get to know you." Suggested topics include five things you can't live without; favorite travel destinations, books, movies, shows, music, and food; your "style of traveling"; and a life motto. In addition to the personal profile, hosts post a listing profile, which includes pictures of the space for rent, a list of applicable rules (such as no smoking), and a map with a location "pin" so that prospective guests can understand where the space is in relation to landmarks and transportation.

The majority of my Airbnb interviews were conducted with hosts in the East Village. As with many New York City neighborhoods, the specific borders are open to debate and discussion. I use the *New York Times* real-estate section's definition of the neighborhood, which states it is "bounded by 14th Street and East Houston Street, the Bowery / Fourth Avenue and the East River" (see map 1).[72]

The East Village is known as one of the more affordable downtown areas in Manhattan. In her work on gentrification, sociologist Sharon Zukin describes the East Village as "an area where protest is a way of life

Map 1. The East Village is often described as being bordered by East Fourteenth Street, East Houston Street, Fourth Avenue (also called the Bowery), and the East River. Map data © 2018 Google.

and history is important. These are the sources of the neighborhood's reputation for authenticity, and they have been preserved in the low rents and social spaces of a sometimes shabby, often funky locale of tenements and small stores."[73] The neighborhood is particularly appealing to potential Airbnb hosts: according to the New York City Population FactFinder, which draws on data from the 2012–2016 American Community Survey, slightly more than half of the housing stock is composed of small tenements (built before 1939).[74] As a result, on-site building superintendents are rare and doormen are generally nonexistent. In most situations, a lack of on-site building personnel is considered a negative point: on-site supers, doormen, and porters are considered an amenity. But for Airbnb hosts, the lack of supervision is often described as a "perk" that provides the requisite level of anonymity.

Owing to this neighborhood popularity, I attempted to target Airbnb hosts in the East Village, and nineteen of the twenty-three hosts (83 percent) I interviewed had locations in the East Village; five of the hosts with listings in the East Village maintained multiple apartments that also included listings on the Upper West Side, in the West Village, and in Brooklyn. I also interviewed three hosts who lived outside of the East Village and rented their personal homes in Midtown West, Queens, and Brooklyn. One host, in an effort to hide his location, described his apartment as being in the East Village, although it was in Gramercy, a neighborhood on the north border of the East Village.

Respondents were overwhelmingly white (83 percent), with one individual identifying as black, two as racially mixed, and one declining to answer. The population of white respondents was composed of a number of white ethnics, including immigrants from Armenia, Israel, Germany, and Ireland and two from Canada. Roughly half of the participants were female (48 percent), and about half were male (52 percent). Their ages ranged from twenty-three to sixty, with nineteen between twenty and thirty-nine years old; the average age was thirty-two. Their education levels were especially high: 48 percent had a bachelor's degree; 22 percent had a graduate degree, and an additional 22 percent were enrolled in or had completed some graduate education. Only two participants listed their educational level as "some college," and one of those individuals was currently enrolled at a local college. Illustrative of the high cost of living in New York City, twelve of the participants listed their household income as $100,000 or more, and seven described their income as between $25,000 and $49,999. Two respondents identified their income category as $75,000–99,999, with the remaining two respondents reporting an income of less than $25,000 a year.

Uber

The Uber creation story has several versions. According to the Uber website, "on a snowy Paris evening in 2008, Travis Kalanick and Garrett Camp had trouble hailing a cab. So they came up with a simple idea—tap a button, get a ride."[75]

True to its high-end roots, the first iteration—UberCab—was a black car service that allowed a user to call a car by pressing a button on a smartphone or sending a text. The price hovered around 1.5 times as much as a typical San Francisco cab.[76] The service ran into regulatory issues almost from the start. After an October 2010 cease-and-desist letter from the San Francisco Metro Transit Authority and the Public Utilities Commission of California claiming they were operating an unlicensed taxi service, UberCab removed the word *cab* from its logo and started to operate under the brand name Uber. On its Facebook page, the company commented that it was "more uber than cab."[77]

When Uber began in New York, it also billed itself as an app-driven dispatch service catering to people who were willing to pay more. Early articles describing Uber's entry into New York included one by CEO Travis Kalanick explaining that Uber's cost was about 1.75 times as much as a taxi, and that the appeal would lie primarily in the app's "efficiency and [the] elegance of the experience."[78]

In 2012, Uber announced a cheaper version—only 10 to 25 percent more than a cab—that used hybrid cars.[79] Later that year, Uber announced a taxi partnership that allowed cabs to use its smartphone app to find potential customers. Within days of the announcement, the New York City Taxi and Limousine Commission reminded drivers that taxis were limited to street hails, and that drivers were not supposed to be using cell phones while driving.

Not to be thwarted in its efforts to gain market share, Uber increased its efforts to recruit drivers of cabs and car services. In addition to offering recruitment bonuses, Uber began advertising for drivers on the rear of Metropolitan Transit Authority buses—the better to reach people sitting in traffic. The ads guaranteed drivers anywhere from five thousand dollars a month to thirty-five thousand dollars in six months. Other ads promised workers the opportunity to be their own bosses, drive without limits, and escape dispatcher favoritism (see fig. 7). Lyft, Gett, and Via soon followed with their own ad campaigns.

The advertisements were successful—nearly two thousand for-hire vehicle licenses were issued each month during the 2015 fiscal year (July 1–June 30), a 63 percent growth in the for-hire fleet after Uber entered the New York City market in 2011.[80] By March 2015, the *New York Post*, citing numbers from the Taxi and Limousine Commission, reported that Uber alone had more than 14,088 black and luxury car affiliates operating

Figure 7. Uber advertisement on the back of a Metropolitan Transit Authority bus in New York City. Photo by author.

in the five boroughs, compared to 13,587 medallion cabs.[81] Uber's own projections estimated that the service would add another ten thousand drivers in the next year. By January 2017, the *New York Times* reported that 46,000 vehicles in New York City were connected to Uber, out of 60,000 black cars, and that Uber vehicles outnumbered the 13,587 yellow cabs by almost four to one.[82]

In the summer of 2015, concerned about the unchecked growth of Uber and other for-hire car services, City Council Transportation Committee chairman Ydanis Rodriguez of Manhattan and Brooklyn councilman Stephen Levin proposed legislation that would limit the number of for-hire licenses issued while the city studied congestion.

Figure 8. Protest organized by Uber in response to Mayor Bill de Blasio's proposed limits on the number of for-hire vehicles. Photo by author.

As UCLA sociologist Edward Walker explained in a *New York Times* opinion essay, Uber quickly went on the offensive, mobilizing its customers into a "populist social-media assault, all in support of a $50-billion corporation. The company added a 'de Blasio's Uber' feature so that every time New Yorkers logged on to order a car, they were reminded of the mayor's threat ('NO CARS—SEE WHY') and were sent directly to a petition opposing the new rules. Users were also offered free Uber rides to a June 30 rally at City Hall (see fig. 8). Eventually, the mayor and the City Council received 17,000 emails in opposition."[83]

In addition to the social media campaign, as part of its entrepreneurial ethos, Uber launched a series of television ads highlighting the company as a "champion of racial equality and an indispensible tool for economic mobility in the working class."[84] Meanwhile the mayor, who accepted hundreds of thousands of dollars from yellow-taxicab interests during his 2013 campaign, was accused of being in the pocket of "Big Taxi."

The mayor's proposed limits on Uber and other car companies were quickly tabled in favor of a four-month study on the effect of Uber and other for-hire vehicle operators on New York's traffic. The agreement required Uber to release a trove of data the city had been seeking for its analysis. The city's analysis was released in January 2016, six weeks later than expected, and although it noted that for-hire vehicles contribute to congestion, the report did not recommend a cap on for-hire vehicles.

In much the same way that Airbnb divides its website into distinct sections for potential workers and potential consumers, Uber's main website, uber.com, is marketed to separate groups. The section for clients features a large banner noting, "Your Ride, on Demand: Transportation in Minutes with the Uber App" (see fig. 9). The careers section of the website lists only corporate jobs, such as those for account executives and account managers. Clicking the "Become a Driver" button brings the visitor to a new website: https://partners.uber.com/drive/.

Whereas the main Uber site focuses on convenience (one tap to ride, reliable pickups, cashless payments), the driver-partner site is all about the service's income possibilities and entrepreneurial ethos. Drivers are told that "Uber needs partners like you," and that they can "be your own boss" (see fig. 10). Other sections of the website note that the "app lets you earn money with the tap of a button" and "get paid automatically." And once a driver is approved, he or she is "ready to start earning money." Uber's billboard advertisements to drivers focus on the entrepreneurial ethos by emphasizing monthly or weekly income guarantees for new drivers; noting that driving for Uber means "no shifts, no bosses, no limits"; and advising potential drivers seeking a bright future to "consider us the headlights."

Approximately half of the Uber drivers I interviewed were immigrants. An equal number of drivers identified as white (21 percent) and black (21 percent), while 14 percent described themselves as Hispanic and one driver was racially mixed.[85] In the same way that a high percentage of cab drivers in New York are male (estimates range from 90 to 97 percent), all Uber and Lyft participants were male. Their ages ranged from twenty-two to fifty-nine, with 60 percent falling between twenty and thirty-nine years of age; the average age was thirty-six. Of those who answered education questions, 50 percent had at least a bachelor's degree. Two participants listed their educational level as "some college," one individual was currently enrolled in a local college, one had an associate's degree, and one had a GED. Four of the participants described their incomes as between

Figure 9. Uber's client-focused webpage. Screenshot by author.

Figure 10. The bottom text reads, "Drive with Uber and earn great money as an independent contractor. Get paid weekly just for helping our community of riders get rides around town. Be your own boss and get paid in fares for driving on your own schedule." Screenshot by author.

$50,000 and $74,999, and three described their incomes as less than $25,000 per year, with one respondent making between $75,000 and $99,999 and one making within a range of $25,000 to $34,999 a year.

TaskRabbit

In the origin myth of TaskRabbit, founder Leah Busque developed the idea when she and her husband realized they were out of dog food for their one-hundred-pound yellow lab. Busque was certain one of her neighbors must be at Safeway, a grocery store chain, picking up food for their own dog. Wouldn't it be great if she could get in touch and ask them to pick up food for her dog too? The ethos of friendly neighborhood help continues today. The TaskRabbit website describes itself as "an old school concept—neighbors helping neighbors—reimagined for today." The company allows people "to live smarter by connecting you with safe and reliable help in your neighborhood," and it does so by outsourcing "your household errands and skilled tasks to trusted people in your community."

TaskRabbit started as a bid-focused marketplace, almost an eBay for personal-assistant work. Clients could post tasks, and "rabbits" (as they were then called) bid on the work, giving short marketing spiels about why they were the best worker for the task. The marketplace model allowed for a wide variety of tasks, including creative projects such as making a short video or taking a headshot, in addition to cleaning, errand-running, and handyman work.

In July 2014, TaskRabbit retooled its business model, shifting from an open-bidding market to more of a temp agency format. Instead of bidding, workers provided their availability in four-hour chunks of time and were shown, via an algorithm, to prospective employers. Potential employers chose a job category (cleaning, delivery, Ikea assembly, etc.), clicked a time window, provided a job description, and picked from an algorithm-selected listing of up to fifteen potential workers. Taskers were then required to respond in thirty minutes or less, regardless of time, or lose the task, at which time it was up for grabs by other Taskers. The categories for creative tasks were also phased out at this point.

Workers who didn't respond within the thirty-minute time limit often enough found their profiles were temporarily deactivated. In addition to the problem of being on call at all hours, the new system meant that Taskers didn't get to choose which specific job they were interested in—they just received notifications that they were needed in a preset category. The sense of freedom and of being one's own boss quickly dissipated. "'Anyone left working for TR is an indentured servant,' wrote one commentator on a popular TaskRabbit Facebook group. . . . 'You are not growing your own business, you are growing TR as a business.'"[86]

In the summer of 2015, TaskRabbit increased its service fees from 20 percent to 30 percent, tacked on an additional 5 percent trust-and-safety fee to be paid by the consumer, and offered a fee reduction to 15 percent for any repeat business from the same client. A task that had previously cost the client $100 and netted the worker $80 now cost the client $105, and the Tasker received $70, before accounting for taxes and expenses. Even as many TaskRabbits watched their incomes drop, they were told that the change was intended to "incentivize entrepreneurship" so that workers would obtain repeat clients. In 2017, TaskRabbit changed the trust-and-safety fee to a trust-and-support fee and increased it from 5 percent to 7.5 percent. The change meant that for every $107.50 spent by a customer, TaskRabbit received $37.50 and the worker earned $70.

The TaskRabbit listing on Peers.com, a now defunct nonprofit created to support the sharing economy, further highlighted the company's entrepreneurial ethos. Before the Peers.com website content disappeared, the site noted that, "as a Tasker, you can use your skills and free time to become a microentrepreneur and build your business." The TaskRabbit Tasker resource site even included a link to print-quality logos so that workers could "create your own marketing materials to promote your business on TaskRabbit," along with the suggestion that Taskers "build their business" by customizing their TaskRabbit URL.

However, research suggests that there were limits to the type of small business formation supported by TaskRabbit. Juliet Schor's graduate students at Boston College found that Taskers had generally positive views of the service before the first pivot, and several respondents were using it as an entrepreneurial opportunity. As noted in a *Work in Progress* blog post, "One TaskRabbit with good linguistic skills started a small translation business, and outsourced jobs to digital workers on other platforms. Another who specializes in virtual assistant work was also outsourcing tasks from the platform."[87] Later follow-up interviews found that the pivot—partnered with a TaskRabbit crackdown on such outsourcing—led to an end to those fledgling companies.

My interviews with TaskRabbits occurred between March and November 2015. Roughly half of my respondents had been active on the platform before the first pivot (from bidding marketplace to temp agency) and all of my participants were active during the service fee change.

Study participants were generally diverse, with 48 percent identifying as white; 24 percent describing themselves as black, 14 percent as

Hispanic, and 10 percent as Asian. The remainder identified as multiracial. Sixty-four percent of participants were male, and 36 percent were female. Their ages ranged from twenty-one to sixty, with 66 percent falling between twenty and thirty-five years of age.

In 2013, the TaskRabbit company reported that 70 percent of its marketplace workers held a bachelor's degree, 20 percent had a master's degree, and 5 percent had a PhD.[88] The education levels of my respondents, too, were high. Forty-one percent of respondents listed their educational level as including a bachelor's degree, and 29 percent were currently college students. Eighteen percent of the sample had a graduate degree, and one person had a PhD. The majority of my sample described their household incomes as below $50,000 (68 percent), while 18 percent reported incomes between $50,000 and $74,999. One participant had a household income of $75,000 to $99,000, and two participants declined to provide income numbers.

Kitchensurfing

Kitchensurfing was started in 2012 as a way to hire professional chefs for home dinner parties. Like TaskRabbit, the platform was originally a marketplace; the service vetted chefs by having them cook a sample meal within the company's test kitchen. Approved chefs were then given the opportunity to post a profile and sample menus (ranging from an intimate dinner to a cocktail party for fifty) and related food images. In addition to providing marketing and advertising, Kitchensurfing processed client payments, serving as an escrow service for chef and client and taking a 10 percent finder's fee.

In 2015, the service pivoted, and while the chef-driven platform remained active, the company launched, and began extensive marketing of, its Kitchensurfing Tonight, an on-demand alternative to eating out or ordering takeout. Kitchensurfing Tonight was launched in select neighborhoods in Manhattan and, eventually, in parts of Park Slope, Brooklyn. Clients picked one of three meal options (which changed daily), and a chef would arrive at a preset hour with all of the ingredients and tools necessary to cook and serve the meal. The cost, which started at twenty-five dollars a head, included labor, ingredients, transportation, tip, tax, cleanup, and even disposable plates.[89] The portions were generous, featured a main dish and side, and often also included a salad and small after-dinner treat. The entire process—from the time the chef arrived to when she or he left—usually took about thirty minutes. Workers were paid sixty dollars for a four-hour shift, even if the shift ended early, and those who worked at least four shifts a week were also given a weekly MetroCard, worth thirty-one dollars.

The increased focus on the on-demand chef service occurred soon after the company's cofounder and CEO, Chris Muscarella, stepped aside and Zynga senior vice president Jon Tien took the reins. The strategy change allowed for one-click bookings—as opposed to emailed negotiations with chefs—and lower-cost meals, and resulted in increased rebooking rates.[90] Eventually, the platform discontinued the marketplace feature and focused entirely on Kitchensurfing Tonight.

The company's entrepreneurial ethos was highlighted from the start. Cofounder and former CEO Chris Muscarella developed the idea for Kitchensurfing after helping a friend open the Brooklyn Italian eatery Rucola in 2010. Although Muscarella met a number of gifted chefs, he realized that many chefs would never open their own restaurants, because of the prohibitive costs. An article in *Mashable* quoted him as saying, "Restaurants are great, . . . but they are bad businesses."[91]

Perhaps because of this founding focus on small-business possibilities, Kitchensurfing's focus on the entrepreneurial ethos was especially high, an emphasis I describe as "entrepreneurialism plus."[92] The main Kitchensurfing website was geared to clients. Just like with Uber, information on available Kitchensurfing jobs was limited to opportunities to work on the back end, such as jobs for product designers and data analysts. But the chef recruitment page, available through a Google search, provided chef testimonials that were quick to promote the idea of Kitchensurfing entrepreneurship as taking the hassle out of small business ownership. "Kitchensurfing is the *perfect tool for me to mimic a restaurant experience* in completely different surroundings *without all of the chaos and uncertainty* that inevitably comes with running a NYC kitchen," said Anthony Sasso, chef de cuisine at Casa Mono (emphasis added). And chef Warren Schierenbeck stated, "Kitchensurfing is a *gift from the food gods*. It *takes all the boring aspects* but necessary evils of the food world, such as PR, advertising and collection of money out of your hands. *It lets you do what you do best:* cook!" (emphasis added).

In case the chef testimonials weren't clear enough, the copy below the revolving quotes further reiterated that Kitchensurfing would allow you to "grow your business" with a "100% free web presence." After pivoting to a nightly prix fixe, on-demand chef service, the company continued to focus on the possibilities for future entrepreneurship. Its ads for part-time-employee chefs noted that the job provided the opportunity to develop "private chef skills," and that it was an "alternative to the traditional restaurant career."

My interviews with Kitchensurfing chefs occurred between March and November 2015, in the midst of the service pivot and multiple other changes. In September 2015, the service announced that on-demand workers would switch from being independent contractors (1099 workers) to being employees. Workers, who had previously been paid sixty dollars for a shift of up to four hours, had their pay changed to fifteen dollars an hour. And although they were to become eligible for health insurance, there was a lack of clarity about when this would happen or the policies related to it. The Secret Diner program, which allowed workers to earn two-hundred-dollar bonuses for meeting service expectations, was also discontinued. Then in April 2016, the service closed its doors.

I recruited participants from both branches of Kitchensurfing. Several marketplace workers also had experience working for the Tonight service, having been tapped by Kitchensurfing to fill service gaps. Participants were split between those who were primarily marketplace chefs and those mostly affiliated with the on-demand service. Five of the interviews with Kitchensurfing marketplace chefs occurred as the service was closing down or soon after it was shuttered.

Study participants were generally diverse, with 58 percent identifying as white, 26 percent as black / African American, and 11 percent as Hispanic. One participant declined to answer. Sixty-eight percent of participants were male, and 32 percent were female. Their ages ranged from twenty to fifty-six, with 58 percent falling between twenty and thirty-five years of age. The education levels of my Kitchensurfing respondents were especially varied. A third of participants mentioned having earned either a bachelor of arts degree or a bachelor of science degree, while three listed a graduate degree and three noted that they had "some college." Two had high school diplomas, two had associate degrees, and one had "some graduate school." Two declined to give an education level. The majority of my sample described their household incomes as below $50,000, while six listed incomes between $50,000 and $74,999, three had incomes between $75,000 and $99,999, and three reported incomes above $100,000.

The sharing economy is often hyped as a solution to many societal ills: inflexible work policies, a lack of social connection, a growing trend of inequality, and even a faulty social safety net. An examination of the lived experiences of workers illustrates the dangers that result from the gig economy's shifting of risk and liability, and it highlights the downgrading of the value of labor in the United States. As the next chapter will demonstrate, rather supplying a solution to modern societal troubles, gig work subjects workers to a technologically enabled early-industrial system with limited workplace-safety measures or options for redress.

3 Forward to the Past and the Early Industrial Age

Donald, a fifty-five-year-old white male, is a perfect example of a Struggler. A finance professional for more than twenty years, he was "eliminated" in early 2008, on the cusp of the Great Recession. "I went up to HR [human resources] for a meeting and I was out the door. I never even got to go downstairs to say good-bye to my coworkers," he said. "Everything went south, and I have not been able to find full-time work since. . . . I've had various jobs. Six months at [a major bank], nine months at [an educational nonprofit], six months at [an insurance company]. I worked for about four months for an interior decorator who didn't pay me. So, you know, I have been trying. . . . I did some work on an eBay business. I was selling on eBay for some people. I'm trying to find things."

Our conversation took place in Union Square, a park on East Fourteenth Street in Manhattan. A tall man with a ruddy complexion, Donald showed his anxiety in his fingers, which were dotted with rusty red scabs from his worrying over hangnails and his habit of picking at calluses.

In order to make ends meet, Donald was in the process of emptying his individual retirement account, paying a 10 percent early-withdrawal penalty in addition to having the funds taxed as income. When he found TaskRabbit, Donald thought he had found a way to staunch the financial hemorrhage. "I wish I knew about TaskRabbit sooner. I just heard about that three months ago," he said, explaining that it took two months to be accepted by the platform. "If I'd known about it seven years ago, maybe I wouldn't be in the situation I am now, desperate for money."

TaskRabbit wasn't just a source of much-needed funds. "When it's dark out [in the winter], it's harder to get out of bed. That's one thing I liked about TaskRabbit. It was getting me out of bed," he said. "You've really got to be available in case somebody contacts you. So it was getting me up, getting me out. There were days in the winter where you just stayed in bed. You know, darkness, depression. It gets serious, and I'm not usually a depressed person."

Most sharing economy workers are relatively young—recent college graduates who are paying off student loans or supplementing starter salaries. MacArthur Foundation–funded research on the sharing economy has focused almost entirely on young people between the ages of 18 and 34 in part because they tended to be early adopters.[1] However, roughly a quarter of the sharing economy workers that I interviewed were adults in their forties, fifties, and even sixties. In my research, I've found that these older adults are more likely to be Strugglers than Success Stories or Strivers. Especially in terms of TaskRabbit work and Uber driving, the sharing economy is an occupation of last resort owing to age discrimination and the reluctance of employers to hire the long-term unemployed.

For Donald, his TaskRabbit work as a Struggler often meant taking on menial tasks such as cleaning and errand running, tasks that may have led to his end as a Tasker. The night before our interview, he emailed me to say, "I am not sure if you still want to meet with me. I received an email tonight from TaskRabbit stating that I have been removed from the Task Rabbit community. The reason is 'unprofessional conduct and behavior.' I do not know what this pertains to and cannot get any answers from them until next week. I have no idea what they are talking about. I have not been able to respond to the (for [lack] of a better word) charges against me."

In our interview the next day, Donald puzzled over what could qualify as "unprofessional conduct and behavior." Maybe a client complained that his cleaning took too long or that quality was lacking? Or maybe it was a client who had asked about paying him outside the platform, a violation of the TaskRabbit terms of service.[2] When we met, he read me his email from TaskRabbit:

> You have violated the following TaskRabbit policy: "Don't display unprofessional or unbecoming communication or behavior in any form. . . ." Due to this we have removed you from the TaskRabbit community. Please do not continue to contact clients or continue with any of your scheduled tasks. If you have started work on any tasks that have not been completed, please let us know immediately. Make sure that all payments owed to you from your account balance will be paid on the next cycle. If you have any questions or concerns regarding this email, the TaskRabbit policy team is available via email and by phone, appointment only.

He had emailed back immediately to ask for the first available meeting and to learn more about the claims against him. But several days after, he was still waiting for a response.

For many workers, human resource departments are a bureaucratic annoyance—mandatory commonsense training sessions on sexual harassment, never-ending paperwork, and the creation of workplace policies that are at best annoying. But for workers in the sharing economy, a human resources office with an open-door policy feels like a luxury.

Workers for many sharing economy services report that it is difficult to contact a person when they have issues. Uber is notorious for providing only an email address for drivers and clients alike. Airbnb's email-only policy led to a public relations disaster with the first reported instance of a ransacked apartment, and its subsequent twenty-four-hour helpline was less than helpful in the case of a guest being held prisoner in Madrid.[3] For TaskRabbit, most issues raised by Taskers have been handled via online service requests and emails, with sometimes weekslong delays in getting a response. The website also offers an emergency assistance phone number; but whereas Taskers can be on call from 8 a.m. to 8 p.m., seven days a week, the service line has reduced hours: 7 a.m. to 5 p.m. PST on weekdays, and 9 a.m. to 3 p.m. PST on weekends and holidays. The reduced service hours on weekends and holidays is especially ironic, given that TaskRabbit offered incentives such as cash bonuses or iPad contests to encourage workers to accept holiday weekend tasks.

Contacting the customer service hotline took on added importance for Donald because of his financial situation. He needed money and he needed work. "I'm very annoyed about the way it was done, that I've got no recourse whatsoever. I'm guilty until proven innocent. I was never asked, I was never . . . Like I said, I've never been told what I did. So yeah, I think it's atrocious the way they treated me, and if I can find something else to do I will. Right now I don't [have anything else], so I need them."

Donald was hoping to be reinstated. But in case that didn't happen, he had already begun looking at TaskRabbit competitors, such as Thumbtack, and at other sharing economy services, such as Kitchensurfing.

TaskRabbit and other sharing economy services claim to be changing the world of work. But rather than freeing workers from the tyranny of bosses, the time-suck of mandatory hours, and even the rigidity of a preset paycheck, sharing economy services often promise a different reality than they deliver. Although many of these services present the "entrepreneurial ethos" and market themselves as bringing entrepreneurialism to the masses, a quick historical review of labor shows that for all its focus on technology, the sharing economy is truly a throwback to an earlier age.

THE HISTORY OF AMERICAN LABOR

In many ways, the history of the United States is the history of the labor movement. Even before the American Revolution, there were small strikes among New York City cartmen, in 1677, and bakers, in 1741.[4] Yet, while the United States was still in its infancy as a colony of Great Britain, labor unrest remained short-lived and isolated. Seeking the "pursuit of happiness" through higher pay and shorter hours, New York printers went on strike in 1794, cabinet makers in 1796, Philadelphia carpenters in 1797, and shoemakers in 1799.[5]

In the early 1800s, when workers tried to use collective bargaining power to obtain increased wages, decreased hours, or just generally improved conditions, they faced the threat of indictment and prosecution for criminal conspiracy. Although the United States did not have specific laws against worker organizing, early American courts followed British common law: when two or more workers plotted the harm of a third, or of the public, they could be indicted on a charge of criminal conspiracy. As a result, two workers could not unite to negotiate with an employer to win concessions that they were unable to earn on their own. In one case from 1805, eight Philadelphian shoemakers were indicted on charges of conspiring to raise wages. The defendants' lawyer argued that the employers were hiding behind the 1349 English Statute of Laborers, which required all able-bodied workers who survived the black plague to work for state-fixed wages in the interest of employers.[6] The shoemakers lost and were fined eight dollars each.

In the first half of the nineteenth century, workers in at least twenty-three cases were indicted and generally convicted for criminal conspiracy in Louisiana, Maryland, Massachusetts, New York, Pennsylvania, and Virginia.[7] Most were found guilty but were given relatively small fines as a "testimonial to the temper of the people," even as the guilty findings demonstrated an intention to "drive unionism out of American life."[8] However, workers continued to organize, and by 1810—less than twenty years after the first trade union was established in America—some unions had already established collective bargaining; minimum wage demands; a "closed," or union, shop; unity between skilled and unskilled workers; and solidarity between different unions.[9]

The economic depression of 1819–1822 destroyed those unions that had managed to survive strikes and conspiracy charges, but the mid- to late 1820s heralded a resurgence of worker organizing. In 1825, Boston carpenters struck for a ten-hour workday, only to be told that the shortened workday was bad for workers, would "exert a very unhappy influence," and expose workers to "many improvident temptations and improvident practices."[10] By 1829, New York City workers had secured recognition of the ten-hour workday, although employers continued to attempt to reinstate an eleven-hour day. In the four years from 1833 to 1837, there were 168 strikes in the country as a whole, with the majority focused on two issues: 103 of the strikes were for higher wages, and 26 were for a ten-hour workday. By 1835, a day's work was ten hours for skilled mechanics in most cities.[11] However, for factory workers, hours remained long. In 1835, children working in textile mills in Paterson, New Jersey, struck for the reduction of their working day to eleven hours for five days a week and nine hours on Saturdays. Although mill owners didn't meet their demands entirely, they did reduce the work week to just sixty-nine hours (a daily reduction ranging from ninety minutes to two hours).[12]

Before the Industrial Revolution in Great Britain began, in 1760, most of the workers considered "unskilled" were those in agriculture or the piecemeal system, quaintly referred to as the "cottage industry," in which work was outsourced to be completed at home. Also known as the "putting-out" or "giving-out" system, such work drew on both artisanal and domestic arrangements. Merchants and village storekeepers distributed raw materials to women, who used them to produce goods that the entrepreneurs then sold. Women were given flax and wool to spin into yarn, which was then woven into cloth and stockings or used in shirts and gloves; straw to be braided into hats; and stockings to seam and shoes to bind. This early work-at-home arrangement was seen as a panacea for poor women, and from 1734 through the War of 1812, charitable benefactors gave needy women spinning wheels as the solution to their financial difficulties.[13]

The enclosure movement in Great Britain—in which land that had been farmed by tenant farmers was enclosed by fences and used for grazing sheep—along with the consolidation of farmlands, displaced large portions of the population in England. Former tenant farmers flocked to the cities, providing a source of labor for the fledgling factories. In 1781, Richard Arkwright established the world's first steam-driven textile mill in Manchester, England, and within a hundred years the area became the largest and most productive cotton-spinning center in the world, producing nearly a third of global cotton goods.[14]

English law prohibited the emigration of skilled textile workers; but in 1793, Samuel Slater, a former British textile apprentice, founded the Slater Mill in Rhode Island. The mill became one of the first successful cotton-spinning factories in the United States and was soon joined by a number of other factories in the Blackstone Valley.[15] At its peak, the Blackstone River and its tributaries, described as "America's hardest-working river," provided power to more than eleven hundred mills along a forty-five-mile stretch between Worcester, Massachusetts, and Providence, Rhode Island. In 1823, a group of Boston investors took advantage of the thirty-two-foot drop of the Merrimack River's Pawtucket Falls to establish the first large-scale, planned textile center, a town they later named Lowell.

Lowell was different from other mill towns. Relying on vertical integration, the mill combined spinning and weaving under one roof. Approximately 75 percent of its workers were women and girls, some as young as thirteen. By 1840, the mills employed eight thousand women. In this true "company town," workers lived in dormitories provided by the companies and were subject to strict codes of conduct. As the Boott Cotton Mills Museum notes, "Intemperance, rowdiness, illicit relations with men, and habitual absence from worship on the Sabbath" were grounds for dismissal from the factory and removal from the boardinghouse. The women worked about eighty hours a week. Six days a week, they woke to the factory bell at 4:40 a.m., reported to work at 5 a.m. and had a half-hour breakfast break at 7 a.m. They worked until a lunch break of thirty to forty-five minutes around noon. The workers returned to their company houses at 7 p.m., when the factory closed.

Public sentiment against women engaging in public activity was strong, but when factory owners in Dover, New Hampshire, and Lowell cut wages in 1834, workers went on strike: seven hundred in Dover and eight hundred in Lowell. A second pay cut in Lowell in 1836 led to another strike, this time by fifteen hundred young women. As they marched, the women sang,

> Oh! isn't it a pity, such a pretty girl as I
> Should be sent to the factory to pine away and die?
> Oh! I cannot be a slave,
> I will not be a slave,
> For I'm so fond of liberty
> That I cannot be a slave.[16]

Even though the Lowell strikes were not successful, they inspired a similar—and successful—strike in Amesbury, Massachusetts, when mill workers were ordered to tend two looms for the same pay. The factory owners soon reverted to their previous policy of one loom per worker.

Although the factory system was common in the Northeast by 1815, it did not become established in New York City, where ground rents were already high and continued to increase as the city became ever more crowded. In the 40 years from 1820 to 1860, the population of New York City increased by more than 550 percent, from 123,706 to 813,669.[17]

Additionally, New York lacked access to fast-moving rivers like those in the Northeast. As a result, no large water-powered factories were built and the putting-out system lingered and grew, further institutionalizing the sex-divided labor market. Although men sometimes worked in the putting-out, or outside, system, they were generally found only in trades that also employed women, such as sewing and shoe binding. By the 1850s, employers in other women's industries had also adopted the outside system. Even female workers inside New York factories often used patterns imported from the outside system to structure work. In a description that is equally apt for the sharing economy today, historian Christine Stansell notes that "by dispersing female workers among thousands of individual workplaces, outside employers made it virtually impossible for women to combat the low wages and exploitative conditions."[18]

Nationwide, workers who attempted to strike were regularly attacked by the police or members of the Pinkerton National Detective Agency or Baldwin-Felts Detective Agency. Particularly bloody battles occurred with miners and railroad workers. For instance, in 1894, workers for the Pullman Palace Car Company went on strike in Chicago. The American Railway Union asked its members not to handle Pullman cars. Since nearly all trains included a Pullman car for passengers, this resulted in a nationwide train strike and led to President Grover Cleveland ordering federal troops to Chicago. After hundreds of cars were burned by strikers, the state militia was also sent to the scene. When the strikers threw rocks, the militia opened fire, killing thirteen people and seriously wounding fifty three others. Before the strike was over, more than thirty people were dead and seven hundred had been arrested. The *Chicago Times* reported, "The ground over which the fight had occurred was like a battlefield. The men shot by the troops and police lay about like logs."[19]

At the turn of the century, strike struggles were multiplying: in the 1890s, there had been about a thousand strikes a year; in 1904, there were four thousand strikes. It soon became clear that "the state stood ready to crush labor strikes, by the law if possible, by force if necessary."[20]

Perhaps the most vicious attack on striking workers occurred in April 1914, in southern Colorado. Before that, in September 1913, when eleven thousand immigrant workers for the Colorado Fuel and Iron Corporation, owned by the Rockefeller family, had gone on strike protesting low pay, dangerous conditions, and their almost feudal existence in the company-owned mining towns, they had been quickly turned out of their company-owned shacks. Assisted by the United Mine Workers Union, the workers took up residence in tents in the local hills and continued their strike, even as the Baldwin-Felts Detective Agency attacked with Gatling guns and rifles.

Eventually the National Guard was sent in, its wages supplied by the Rockefellers. The guardsmen brought in strikebreakers (not telling them that there was a strike) and beat and arrested miners by the hundreds. They also utilized a "death special," an improvised armored car that would periodically spray machine-gun fire. On April 20, 1914, in the mining town of Ludlow, two National Guard companies began a machine-gun attack on a tent colony of twelve hundred men, women, and children. While the miners fired back, the women and children dug pits below the tents to escape the gunfire. Then, at dusk that day, the guardsmen approached the encampment and set the tents on fire with torches. Families fled into the hills, with thirteen people killed by gunfire. The next day, as the remains of the tent colony was removed, the charred bodies of eleven children and two women were found in a pit below one of the tents. This earned the battle the title of the Ludlow Massacre and national attention, including editorials in the *New York Times;* and five thousand people marched on the state capital in Denver in protest. In the end, sixty-six men, women, and children were killed; none of the militiamen or guardsmen were indicted for crimes; and the miner's union was not recognized.[21]

During the First World War, labor efforts were less prominent, but in February 1919 the Industrial Workers of the World (IWW or Wobblies) led a hundred-thousand-worker walkout in Seattle. Immigration quotas established in 1921 and further reduced in 1924 meant fewer new workers to be exploited; and until the stock market crash of 1929, most attention was paid to prosperity, as opposed to continued labor efforts.

During the Great Depression, worker organization was perhaps best described as the original sharing, or bartering, economy. In Seattle, in particular, the fishermen's union traded fish to fruit and vegetable pickers, and food was exchanged for chopped wood. In Pennsylvania, unemployed coal miners dug small mines on company property and then sold the coal for below-market prices, eventually mining and selling five million tons of "bootleg" coal. Nationwide, by the end of 1932, there were 330 self-help organizations in thirty-seven states, with more than three hundred thousand members, although as the economy deteriorated further those organizations, too, collapsed.[22]

In 1934, 1.5 million workers went on strike, including longshoremen on the West Coast, 325,000 southern textile workers, and 2,500 Lowell mill workers. In 1935, the Wagner Act was passed, which established a National Labor Relations Board and gave employees the right to form and join unions and engage in collective bargaining and strikes. Then, in 1938, President Roosevelt signed into law the Fair Labor Standards Act, which banned oppressive child labor, set the minimum hourly wage at twenty-five cents and the maximum workweek at forty-four hours (later shortened to forty hours under the Fair Labor Standards Amendments of 1966).[23]

The Wagner Act was challenged by steel corporations, but the Supreme Court found it to be constitutional on the basis of the federal government's right to regulate interstate commerce, which was hurt by strikes. In 1936, rank-and-file workers developed the idea of a "sit-down" strike, where they sat down on the job and refused to leave. The sit-down made it harder for strikebreakers to be moved in, helped keep workers unified, and provided more pleasant conditions than marching outside. The sit-downs were especially popular: 477 such protests in 1937 alone.[24]

In these grassroots strikes, involving union leadership was often seen as an afterthought, and local unions were often not aware that a strike was brewing until one was well under way. As a result, corporations eventually embraced the Wagner Act as a way of controlling direct labor action. The National Labor Relations Board and the unions "would channel the workers' insurrectionary energy into contracts, negotiations, union meetings, and try to minimize strikes."[25] After the National Labor Relations Act was passed in 1935, the number of workers and the percentage of the workforce in unions grew rapidly, from 7 percent of total employment to a high of almost 35 percent in 1954.[26]

The labor movement was successful in many ways. For nearly fifty years, from the beginning of the Great Depression and until the early 1970s, the trend in income distribution in the United States was toward greater equality. In 1928, the height of the Gilded Age, the top 1 percent of families in the US income distribution held 23.9 percent of national income. By the end of World War II that share had fallen by nearly half, to 12.5 percent, leveling off to around 10 percent by the mid-1950s, where it remained for nearly twenty-five years.[27]

DEVOLVING EMPLOYMENT PRACTICES

Today, many workers benefit from policies fought for by early unions and their striking workers: the minimum wage, a forty-hour work week, and even the simple recognition of unions as representing workers. But for workers in the sharing economy, it's as though none of these labor battles were ever fought, much less won. Gig economy workers are often second-class citizens in the labor world, denied many of the same rights taken for granted by workers in the mainstream economy. For instance, even though the right to organize and form a union was established in the 1935 National Labor Relations Act, most sharing economy workers are considered independent contractors and outside the coverage of the act. As a result, as of this writing, only drivers in Seattle have been granted the right to unionize, under a law approved by the Seattle City Council.[28]

The lack of union or employee status for Uber drivers has led to an ironic twist—a lawsuit alleging that Uber's technology unlawfully coordinates fares and surge-pricing fares as part of a large-scale price-fixing conspiracy.[29] Much in the same way that early efforts to prevent collective bargaining hinged on the idea that independent workers couldn't unite to secure rights that they were otherwise unable to negotiate on their own, the lawsuit argues that drivers don't compete with each other but charge fees based on the Uber algorithm. As a result, the app may violate antitrust law, which prohibits collusive practices such as price-fixing.

Meanwhile, in an effort to prevent further attempts at organizing, Uber has taken proactive actions in New York, one of its largest markets. In May 2016, Uber entered a partnership with the International Association of Machinists and Aerospace Workers to develop the Independent Drivers Guild. As part of the guild, drivers can appeal deactivation decisions and can have guild officials represent them in their appeals. Yet unlike a traditional union, guild members do not have access to collective bargaining: they cannot negotiate fares, benefits, or protections—Uber will continue to make those decisions unilaterally, albeit with more input from drivers. The preliminary agreement is for five years, but in the meantime, the union will refrain from trying to unionize drivers, encouraging them to strike, or waging campaigns to have them recognized as employees. Instead of receiving benefits, drivers will be given information on where to purchase discounted legal services, life and disability insurance, and roadside help.[30]

Offering information on services, as opposed to offering services, isn't a new strategy. Peers, a grassroots organization that aimed to "to grow the sharing economy" was started in 2013 with the support of twenty-two partners, including Airbnb, TaskRabbit, Lyft, and several foundations. While not directly funded by the platforms, donations from "mission-aligned" independent donors, such as platform executives and investors, have raised questions.[31]

Originally, Peers focused on a petition tool that encouraged members to "step up and defend the sharing economy," but in 2014 the organization switched its focus to helping workers. Toward that end, the organization launched an "income discovery" tool that could be used by workers to find platforms that matched their assets, skills, and interests; a review tool for rating platforms; a discussion forum; and a "support marketplace," where workers could access health insurance, accounting businesses, and other services. But the "support center" was a database of services for sale, some of which came from other sharing economy platforms, such as auto repair by YourMechanic, Airbnb listing management by Guesty, and insurance from the Freelancers' Union. And the "income discovery tool" featured ads from companies seeking more workers for their apps.[32]

In its heyday, Peers reportedly had more than 250,000 members, identifying itself as "the world's largest independent sharing economy community" and positioning the tools as a way to "support workers by making the sharing economy a better work opportunity."[33] But by the end of 2016, the organization appeared defunct: its Twitter account hadn't posted a tweet since March 2016, and its Facebook feed had been static since September 2016. At the end of 2017, the website was no longer available.

Peers isn't the only site that has been thought to be in the pocket of sharing economy services. Some have suggested that UberPeople.net, the discussion forum for drivers, is a lurking ground for Uber executives or at least monitored by Uber staff. Discussion threads have even been created to "expose Uber employees."[34]

Most sharing economy services are a far cry from company towns where workers were paid in script and housed in units owned by the company. One notable exception to this was CrowdFlower, a online platform that allowed for data cleaning and was similar to Amazon's Mechanical Turk. Although Mechanical Turk has been criticized for paying low wages, sometimes CrowdFlower didn't even pay workers, instead giving them points for various online reward programs and videogame credits.[35]

While company towns were most common in the United States in the late 1800s, Uber's recruiting playbook reaches back much farther. In 2013, Uber offered a partnership with Santander Bank that promised auto loans with a "low weekly payment" that would be "automatically deducted" from drivers' Uber earnings. In a promotional video released by Uber, the Preferred Financing Program sounds suspiciously like subprime lending, with the voice-over noting, "If you've been turned down for a loan before, even if you have bad credit or no credit at all, we can help you get behind the wheel in a week." As explained by Uber's CEO, Travis Kalanick, the loan program, with payments deducted directly from Uber earnings, meant drivers "have to [keep] working with us a certain amount." But being bound by debt to an employer is essentially indentured servitude, a practice that declined with the American Revolution and was outlawed in 1917.[36]

Uber's program was halted in mid-2015 but then resurfaced later that year through Xchange Leasing, LLC. The Xchange leases offered unlimited mileage and regular maintenance, such as oil changes, tire rotations, and air filter replacement. *Verge* reports that when the lease ended, either through early termination or at the end of a three-year term, the driver owed a final $250. Leases with Xchange did not help build credit, but an early termination also didn't damage a driver's credit score. Yet the rates were high, and drivers who kept a car for the three-year term would pay thousands of dollars above the standard purchase price.[37] In an article written for *Bloomberg*, Eric Newcomer and Olivia Zaleski discussed one driver who leased a 2016 Chevy Cruze, "If he keeps the lease to the end of its term, he'd end up paying Uber about $31,200. To buy the car, he'd need to pay Uber another $6,000 to cover the car's residual value. The fair purchase price of the car, according to *Kelley Blue Book,* is $16,419."[38]

Uber executives expected to lose roughly five hundred dollars per car, a small price for increasing the number of drivers on the platform. But in August 2017, just two years later, Uber executives learned that the actual losses were almost eighteen times higher: around nine thousand dollars, or half the price of a new vehicle. According to the *Wall Street Journal*: "By charging high-lease fees in exchange for the risk, many drivers worked longer hours and returned the vehicles in poor shape, damaging their resale value, people familiar with the matter have said."[39] Additionally, Uber found that established dealers were pushing drivers into leasing more expensive vehicles, lowering their likelihood of turning a profit. As of this writing, it was uncertain if Uber would pursue additional lease opportunities.

Just like the workers in company towns, where the loss of one's job could also result in the loss of one's home and the social safety net was nonexistent, today's sharing economy workers are on their own in many ways. Workers pay for their transportation between gigs and while on tasks or rides; they (or taxpayers, through Medicaid) provide their own health insurance; they must calculate and pay payroll taxes such as Social Security/Medicare; and they must personally finance any time off (owing to illness, vacation, or a lack of work). Workers are also financially responsible for any workplace injuries, a topic discussed more fully in the following chapter. While workers can utilize online discussion boards to chat about their experiences, they remain much more isolated than other low-income workers, such as Caribbean nannies.[40]

It's hard to imagine the National Guard being called on striking Uber drivers or to imagine TaskRabbit workers unionizing. But most worker strikes generally revolved around several broad issues—pay cuts, work hours, and "workplace arbitrariness," such as policy changes and sudden firings—issues that remain particularly salient in today's sharing economy. Much like miners and mill workers, gig economy workers experience considerable pay cuts. Both the erratic hours, where work today doesn't mean work tomorrow, and worker income often seem to be based on the whims and desires of the platforms as much as a worker's effort.

In the United States alone, Uber changed driver payment rates in sixteen cities in January 2014, forty-eight cities in January 2015, and one

Table 2 UberX Rates in New York City, 2014 to 2018

	June 2014	December 2015	January 2016	April 2018
Base fare	$6.00	$3.00	$2.55	$2.55
Per mile	$3.00	$2.15	$1.75	$1.75
Per minute	$0.70	$0.40	$0.35	$0.35
Minimum fare	$12.00	$8.00	$7.00	$8.00

SOURCES: 2014 rates are from Uberdriverdiaries.com, 2015 and 2016 rates are from the *New York Post*, 2018 rates are from Uberestimate.com.

hundred cities in January 2016. Not counting the changes in guarantees and bonuses or weekly promotional rates (such as $2.75 uberPOOL rides between Manhattan and Brooklyn), the company reduced rates in New York in July 2014 by 20 percent and in January 2016 by 15 percent. Although in many cities Uber partially subsidized the cuts by temporarily reducing the commissions it collected from drivers, that wasn't the case in New York in July 2014, when Uber continued to collect 20 percent of the reduced fares. While drivers who utilize both platforms often view Lyft more favorably, Lyft has also cut rates—reducing fares nationwide in April 2014 by as much as 30 percent.[41]

Table 2 shows how some New York City uberX rates have changed. Within four years, uberX drivers saw their per-minute rate cut in half, their mile rate reduced by 42 percent, and their base fare slashed by a whopping 58 percent. The minimum price for a ride decreased by about a third.

In addition to reducing rates, both services have also changed their commissions. When Lyft reduced rates in 2014, it "temporarily eliminated its 20% commission 'to provide our growing driver community with peace of mind' during the price drop." In 2014, Uber temporarily decreased its commission from 20 percent to 5 percent, before returning it to 20 percent in April. Then in September 2014, Uber increased its uberX commission to 25 percent, up from 20 percent for new drivers in select markets, and quickly expanded to additional cities. However, the commission doesn't include platform booking fees, which range from $1.40 to $2.15, or more, depending on market. The rate drops, commission hikes, and booking fees have led the Rideshare Guy website to point out that in some markets, on short trips that are charged a minimum fare, platforms take more than 40 percent of the price of ride.[42]

Adding insult to injury, in May 2017 the *Wall Street Journal* revealed that Uber had been mistakenly underpaying New York City drivers for more than two years by charging the platform's 25 percent commission before deducting sales tax and Black Car Fund fees. The company planned to refund the overage, with interest, which it estimated would result in a payment of roughly nine hundred dollars per driver, although at least one driver expected to receive over seven thousand dollars.[43]

Uber has also experimented with paying some drivers on a tiered commission system. In 2015, in San Francisco and San Diego, Uber increased its commission to 30 percent. The program, described as a pilot, involved new drivers paying a 30 percent commission on their first twenty rides in a week, 25 percent on their next twenty rides, and then 20 percent on any rides beyond that; the San Diego version ran on tiers of fifteen rides. Uber's commission for its premium products, like black cars and SUVs, ranges from 25 percent to 28 percent.

As *Forbes* writer Ellen Huet explained, an increase in rates could be used to increase company coffers: "Uber's CFO Brent Callinicos apparently said that the company saw raising commissions as a valid way to earn more and bolster its valuation, said Fortress Investment Group president Michael Novogratz in a panel on Sunday. He said that Callinicos had described this dynamic to him when Uber was raising money this winter. When Novogratz asked Callinicos why Uber would risk upsetting drivers by raising rates 5%, he said Callinicos didn't hesitate and said, 'Because we can.'"[44] As reported in *The Guardian*, while some have raised questions about Uber's future, given worker discontent, the Uber chief product officer, Jeff Holden, reportedly explained, "We're just going to replace them all with robots."[45]

Generally, pay cuts are used when a company is struggling to stay afloat; or in the case of a pay cut for just one person or portion of the workforce, it's an effort to convince someone to quit. But many of these sharing economy services are fairly well funded. According to Crunchbase, a crowd-sourced database to track start-ups, TaskRabbit had, by August

2015, received $37.68 million in six rounds of investments from thirteen investors, before being bought by Ikea in 2017. In August 2017, the *New York Times* reported that Uber had a valuation of more than $68 billion; and by February 2018, the platform had received $21.1 billion in twenty-one rounds from ninety-three investors.[46]

Outside of the sharing economy, many companies, rather than suddenly reducing pay, rely on layoffs, which is hardly an improvement. But for gig economy workers who have been told that they can determine their own pay, a sudden pay cut—especially when it's marketed as being for their own good—can feel like the proverbial slap in the face.

For instance, when Uber dropped uberX rates in New York City by 15 percent in January 2016, the company issued a statement on its website explaining that the price cut had made Uber more affordable for passengers in the five boroughs: "Drivers will feel the benefits of lower prices too—because when demand increases there's less idle time between trips, and that means more time with a rider in the car. . . . This means higher hourly earnings for drivers. For example when we cut prices in July 2014, the average idle time fell by 42% and average hourly partner earnings increased by 33%."[47]

Drivers were split on the rate changes for Uber. For instance, Gerald, a fifty-nine-year-old African American man who began driving for Uber in 2012, saw an immediate drop in his income: "When they reduced that fare back in July by 20 percent—and this is the thing I'm getting with clients as well, 'Oh, the fare has improved, the tip is included.' I say, 'No, it's not, not anymore.' If you do the math, when they reduced the fare back in July by 20 percent, where do you think that 20 percent came from? Out of their pocket?"

An additional income cut may have resulted from the public perception that the tip was included. CNET reporter Dara Kerr suggests that the confusion comes from Uber's app registration process. When passengers set up a new Uber account, they're asked what percentage of "gratuity for Taxi" they'd like to include with every ride. The drop-down menu includes options ranging from nothing up to 30 percent. "Many people likely believe this choice applies to all rides they take with Uber, but a reading of the fine print says it's only for the company's UberTaxi service. . . . [S]ervice is only available in a few cities, like New York and San Francisco."[48]

The idea that Uber is taking money out of the pockets of drivers was also repeated in an explosive exchange, captured on video in 2017, between Uber's then CEO Travis Kalanick and his UberBLACK driver, Fawzi Kamel. In the video, Kamel confronts Kalanick, noting, "You're raising the standards, and you're dropping the prices. . . . I lost ninety-seven thousand dollars because of you. I'm bankrupt because of you. Yes, yes, yes. You keep changing every day. You keep changing every day."

In the video, Kalanick argues that rates were not dropped on UberBLACK, but on services such as uberX as a way to compete with Lyft, before going on to lose his temper and blame the driver for his own financial woes: "Some people don't like to take responsibility for their own shit. They blame everything in their life on somebody else. Good luck!"

Bloomberg notes that in San Francisco between 2012 and 2017, the per-mile rate for UberBLACK (the premium version of Uber) dropped by 23.5 percent, and the per-minute rate was cut by 48 percent. Drivers such as Kamel, who had purchased expensive luxury cars, banking on the higher rates, found themselves being paid less even as they faced more competition from other drivers.[49]

For some, it's not the fare decrease that has caused them financial problems—it's the policy changes or policies that were not clearly communicated up front. Bryan, a forty-three-year-old married father of four and a former handyman and welder, started driving for Uber in New Jersey thinking that it would serve as a flexible second job and a way to make additional money. When he lost his full-time job, he moved his registration to New York so that he could drive in the city and make more money. He hoped that driving for UberBLACK and another luxury car service would eventually land him a job doing something else; he doesn't expect to keep driving for Uber.

When we spoke, Bryan was receiving emails from Uber advising that he needed to accept more jobs or risk being deactivated. Even though he has a luxury SUV and should be able to command the higher UberBLACK rates, Uber also wants him to take the cut-rate uberX jobs.

> I didn't know that you would have to take uberX jobs, so I didn't think if you sign up with them, and if you refuse a certain amount of jobs, they could end their relationship with you. . . . They are so greedy. You know if you book a

flight in American Airlines and you get upgraded to first class, the airline is paying for that. If you send an UberBLACK to do an uberX job because there is no other car around, and you want to do the same prices, the driver is paying for that.

Bryan thought he was going to be free to make decisions about who he would pick up, like a true "driver-partner" (what Uber calls its drivers). "But then it's like, if you don't like it, too bad, you can leave." he said. "You can't tell people that after they have made that investment."

Likewise, the TaskRabbit service pivot in 2014, when the company switched from operating as a bidding marketplace to functioning as more of a temp agency, similarly caused problems for Taskers. Sarah, twenty-nine, the Tasker profiled in the opening chapter, explained, "There were people complaining and in tears because they were like, 'I don't have any income now. I was your top TaskRabbit and you are treating me like shit,' and [it] kind of felt like a betrayal."

The pivot also introduced strict requirements in terms of response rates and task acceptance. "You know," said Sarah, "they have these performance metrics, which is not a very good way to measure. You have to accept 85 percent of what's given to you. The way that the metrics work is a thirty-day kind of thing, so sometimes it just doesn't add up—and you don't know what you are going to get or when you are going to get it." As a result, Taskers who don't accept several tasks within a relatively short period may find themselves flagged. Sarah explains, "They pause your account, and you have to take some kind of test to say, 'Yeah, I understand the guidelines,' And they kind of talk to you like you are an eighteen-year-old. It's kind of insulting. And they say if this keeps happening then you can be taken off."

The pivot wasn't the only change. In the summer of 2015, TaskRabbit increased its service fee to 30 percent, from 20 percent, and tacked on an additional 5 percent trust-and-safety fee to be paid by the consumer. Taskers were told that the rate change was intended to incentivize them to grow their business and focus on promoting themselves more. But some suggested that the rate increase was TaskRabbit's response to people trying to go off the platform. Natasha, twenty-eight, put it this way:

It's pretty awful. The funny thing is that was exactly at the point when I was trying to be good and diligent about staying within the app. And then they raised the rate, which I think: why not just do 25 percent and gradually raise it? But to just jump to 30 percent for [an] incentive to keep people coming back, that's a terrible idea, because almost all of my tasks are people who are first-time clients of mine. It's very rare that people rebook. And if they do rebook . . . For me it's difficult because consistency in my schedule is not really there. I mean, I usually schedule myself whenever I feel like working, and so if someone wants someone every third Sunday, I'm not going to be available every single month, every third Sunday. I travel. I do other things. So I lost my job. I lose my opportunity for 15 percent, which is stupid because 15 percent is still my money.

As with many TaskRabbit changes, the new pay structure was communicated to workers through email, but a few highly productive Taskers received personal phone calls. That didn't make the news any easier. Richard, fifty, a former finance professional, was one of the few Taskers to get such a call. Flattered that they considered him to be one of their top Taskers, he listened to the representative's "dog and pony show" explanation for the increased commission rate.

I said, "I'm professional." I listened first. [They said,] "Advertising: you're going to see it's going to help you in the community. But your repeat clients' rate is only 15 percent. Did you know that?" I let them finish. Then I said, "Look I've been doing this three months, I can guess-timate that my repeat business is probably around 3 or 4 percent. It doesn't equate. . . ." I said, "You can do what you want because it's a company, but you asked me how I feel so I'm telling you. You just gave yourself a 50 percent increase." She said, " Fifty percent?" I said, "Yes." She should have done the math already. If you're going from 20 percent to 30 percent, you're giving yourself a 50 percent increase.

And I'm pretty good with math, so I was sure of that. So I explained. . . . I said, "If I earned a hundred dollars, I was making eighty dollars; now I'm making seventy dollars. And I'm one of your best, and you're telling me this. So now let's pretend this is not virtual, and you're coming to the office. And you've got a hundred Taskers sitting at desks, and you will say, 'Richard, I'm sorry but we're cutting your pay. You're our best, but we're cutting you.'" I said, "It doesn't make me happy." I said, "You want to know; that's how I feel."

Why not just leave? In Richard's example above, a worker who suddenly has his pay cut might think that the boss was trying to force him to quit. In some cases, workers stay with the sharing economy because of a lack of employment alternatives, whether attributable to the stigma of long-term unemployment, middle age, a lack of experience, or the need for a flexible work schedule. In other cases, workers have invested a good deal of time, effort, or resources (ranging from an Uber-approved car to extra sheets for an Airbnb rental) that increase the opportunity cost of starting over. Finally, in many jobs, even if people aren't getting regular raises—or if, owing to inflation, they're actually making less each year—most people don't quit. Why would gig economy workers be any different?

A second issue previously addressed by early labor reformers is the issue of work hours. Although the sharing economy markets itself to workers as offering a chance to set their own hours, the reality is often much more nuanced. Uber drivers can set their own schedules—but the monthly income guarantees generally require that they accept a certain percentage of rides (90 percent), and often, that they drive during certain hours or for a certain number of hours per week. As of April 2016, Uber's six-thousand-dollar-a-month guarantee in New York City applied only to a driver's first month, and, according to the website, it further required that the driver do the following:

- Be online for at least 50 hours, 15 hours of the 50 hours falling within the peak hours [Monday–Friday 6 a.m.–9 a.m., 9 p.m.–12 a.m.; Saturday 12 a.m.–1 a.m., 10 p.m.–12 a.m.; Sunday 12 a.m.–3 a.m., 10 a.m.–3 p.m.]
- Complete at least 1.3 trips per hour
- Accept at least 90% of trip requests dispatched, including uberPOOL requests

With those requirements, driving begins to seem less independent and more like a regular job, but one without any of the usual protections or perks—especially since the guaranteed income is only for the first month. By January 2018, even the monthly guarantee was gone, replaced by an eight-hundred-dollar credit toward vehicle expenses for new drivers. For other sharing economy workers, there's less focus on working a specific number of hours, but workers are often expected to be on call. Freelance chefs working with Kitchensurfing have just twenty-four hours to respond to potential work. Airbnb hosts have more time, but those who don't respond quickly enough can find their accounts temporarily deactivated.

Gabriele, twenty-seven, rents out her apartment when she and her son go out of town for a weekend. Originally, she left her listing up all the time, but her low-cost rental was popular and she received an influx of emails that she described as "really, really annoying." She said, "Sometimes I can't make it to answer in time, and then Airbnb blocks my access. They do it if you don't answer within, I think, one or two days. They have this specific—I think it's even hours, forty hours or something, then they block. People can't see your apartment anymore. . . . Until you go in and unblock and answer all the emails." As a result, Gabriele opens her listing only when she plans to go out of town or when she really needs the money.

For TaskRabbit, the response requirements are even more arduous. As noted previously, the 2015 policy changes included a requirement for a thirty-minute response time. As TaskRabbit's website explains it, "Taskers are available to respond to task assignments between 8 a.m.–8 p.m. local time." The same page is quick to note that Taskers can "go off duty at any time." But there are consequences: "By doing this, they are not available for direct hire on the platform and will not show in search results."

For Taskers who are known entities, former clients can reach out to them directly to request work. But for most Taskers, showing up in the algorithm research results is key to getting work. At the same time, workers who don't respond to a request within thirty minutes lose that specific task invitation and may fall below TaskRabbit's 85 percent task-acceptance requirement, risking deactivation. Christina, thirty, explained,

[My percentages] were pretty high, but then there was one task—you were supposed to accept the task within thirty minutes. So there was one task that I saw, and I still had time to respond, but then, all of a sudden, that task was no longer available to me. I don't know why that happened. So, [TaskRabbit] took that and said that I had not accepted one task. I called them, trying to explain to them what happened, and they're really bad. Like, they barely listened: they did not try to understand what I was trying to say. They were like, "Well, we see that it took you more than thirty minutes to respond." I was like, "Okay, but I was on my phone, and I saw how much time went by, so that's not true." And they were like, "Oh, okay, we'll just send you a form that you can fill out, and then someone will get back to you." So I filled out the form explaining what happened. Nobody got back to me. And the percentage still looks bad because of that one task. . . . And it's ridiculous, 'cause I think half an hour is not enough time for anybody. Because if you work, you might be at lunch, or you might be in a meeting, or you might be underground. I don't understand why it's only thirty minutes.

Just like the Airbnb host Gabriele, Christina has decided to temporarily remove herself from the platform until she needs it for work: "I also haven't made myself available, 'cause I've been busy with other things on the weekends and evenings the past couple weeks. After that happened, that one task happened, I just changed my availability for the past few weeks, 'cause I didn't want that to happen again."

The response requirement applies even when workers are occupied with an active task or traveling on the subway, where there is often limited cell phone reception. This puts workers in a difficult situation. They can either be on call for as many as eighty-four hours a week (8 a.m. to 8 p.m., seven days a week) or not get any work. Although sending a quick text message or email response to a work request is something that white-collar workers do regularly, even the strictest of bosses generally allows at least an hour for a reply, and taking a few hours to respond is unlikely to cost someone her job. Numerous Taskers mentioned that the thirty-minute deadline adds an increased level of stress. Donald, fifty, said, "[It's] nerve-wracking at times, because you can't always constantly be thinking about TaskRabbit. You know, thirty minutes, I think, is a decent amount of time, because usually, I almost always have my cell phone on. But say I'm cleaning the bathroom in my apartment. I may not realize that thirty minutes have gone by. You can make yourself unavailable, but [then] you're not getting any business. So it's sort of a double-edged sword." Likewise, Jasmine, twenty-three, observed, "I think it's silly. I think it's unnecessary. Because sometimes I'm like, 'Do I want to do this?' Or some-times I just don't see it on my phone. It's like they assume everybody's glued to their phone, or if your schedule says you're available, that you need to respond immediately."

A white-collar worker facing the need to respond to emails promptly is generally paid a higher salary to compensate for such time infringement. TaskRabbits have to put in unpaid time if they want to be paid at all. Eighty-four hours a week of being mentally "on call" is more than double the standard work week, and there is no overtime pay. Michael, forty-nine, explained,

If you add the time that I'm sitting there looking for tasks, then who knows how long. . . . It might be three hours for every hour that I'm billing, but I don't know that I can really count . . . I mean, I'm sitting there looking for tasks while I'm doing a crossword puzzle or having lunch or whatever. Unless I'm misunderstanding the whole thing, one of the biggest problems with the app is: in order to see tasks that are available, you have to hit the refresh button, and it's not self-refreshing. . . . Unless I'm missing some setting that will allow me to enjoy my life, you have to keep clicking. . . . So I spend a lot of time going like this: "click" crossword, crossword, crossword, "click," crossword, crossword, crossword, "click."

The thirty-minute response requirement is only for TaskRabbits—clients are not held to the same requirement. This is especially problematic for Strugglers who need to schedule tasks around odd jobs, or who rely on the service for living expenses and can't afford to hold space in their schedule for work that may not materialize. Rebecca, thirty-four, told me,

So, I'm quick. My average [response rate] is three minutes. But basically, if you don't respond within thirty minutes, they're pissed. I don't know what they do to your stuff, but it drops. But you don't have to accept. Here's the thing: I will respond with a chat right away. Rarely do I just accept. I always want to ask first, "Exactly what time do you need me?" There's always something I need to ask before I accept it, and I'll write that. I'll be very quick with my response—three minutes, two, one. And then I don't hear back from the client for a really long time. And I'm like, "I really need to put this in my schedule. I'm not just floating around waiting at your beck and call. I have things to do. This is marginal. This is not my life. You are not my life. Let's just figure this shit out so I can put you in your two- or three-hour block." But no, they don't just get back to you.

Rebecca's solution so far has been to implement a personal policy in which she allows clients a three- to four-hour window to respond to her. If she doesn't hear back by then, she calls TaskRabbit. "I'm like, 'Hey, this isn't right, you know. I had to respond right away. How come they're not obligated to? Just cancel it because I don't want to do it anymore.'"

Further complicating this on-duty versus off-duty calculus is that the algorithm is particularly opaque. Workers know what will remove them from the search results, but they don't know what makes them appear. As a result, it may take several days of full availability before a Tasker becomes visible in the search results. Once their profile becomes visible, work may arrive in spurts. Natasha, twenty-eight, said,

> Ever since I got the elite status, it has helped in a way. But I think their algorithms are really unfair, because if you decline maybe two or three tasks, they will deny you the opportunity to get more tasks. For example, if my TaskRabbit app is off for a few days, when I come back I won't get jobs for two or three days. Unless I start doing the available tasks, and if I start becoming active again, for whatever reason the algorithms pick up that I'm active. And then it starts swarming me with jobs, so I'm just really overwhelmed. And I'm afraid to say no to some stuff, because if I do, in a way they penalize you.

Similarly, Rebecca, thirty-four, observed,

> I hate to say it, but sometimes this new way, it can be a little bit easier, but I hate that you can't be picky. I hate that about it. I hate that I turn on the thing, and it's like, "Am I going to get hired to do something fun, like an event, or fold underwear and move heavy boxes? I hate . . . that it feels like, once you've been hired, even though you can chat and ask questions before you accept, if you don't accept you kind of get penalized a little bit. Not hugely—it's not like you've accepted and forfeited. But if you decline after you've been picked up, your rating or whatever goes down, and then you're not featured as much. And then you're not chosen as much. It messes with the algorithm or whatever, and people aren't seeing you unless you accept every single thing that's thrown at you. And I don't like that. I mean in times of desperation, when you're like, "Shit, I've just got to work every day and make money," it does work in your favor. Because you pretty much turn it on and you're going to get hired to do something. But it's just like . . . it would be nice if on the phone, I could just be like, "I'm available tomorrow, but only to do this particular thing. I really don't want to do packing and shipping tomorrow." But you can't. It's either all on or all off.

Some workers simply mark themselves as "off duty," but doing so for too long can be problematic. Taskers are expected to remain active on the platform—if they go too long without doing a task, they can be deactivated or "removed from the community," as happened to Will, a thirty-eight-year-old actor.

> It's the most ridiculous thing ever. So I had been working for two years on and off, and I didn't hear anything about . . . I got a random email saying, "If

you don't book a task within the next thirty days, we're going to deactivate you." I called them and I said, "I'm an actor. I haven't turned my app on because I'm on tour and I'm in Austin, Texas, and I can't really . . ." And then the lady was like, "Oh, well, we're in Austin, Texas." And I'm like, "No, I'm acting. Like, dude, . . . I have a tour. I have two shows today, and then I want to sleep and eat at some point. So I'm not going to put together someone's Ikea furniture when I have no way to . . . No. Just telling you that I'm going to be away. I'm not going to be back until January." And she said, "Oh, yeah, okay, not a problem."

And then sure enough, I come back in January, and I think nothing about TaskRabbit—because it's great when you don't have to think about it—and I'm deactivated. And I called them and [a customer service rep] says, "Oh yeah, it's not a problem. We see that you've been a TaskRabbit, but you've been deactivated. So in order for you to become a member, you have to go to this community training program." I said, "Excuse me?" And she said, "Well, you know, you've been away from TaskRabbit, so you need to, you need to," what's the word that she used? It was some horrible corporate-like PR term that was really insulting. *Rehabilitate's* not it . . . *Reorientation.*

Will argued repeatedly with the customer service representative before eventually asking to be transferred to someone else.

I was like, "Listen, man, I'm happy to work for you guys. I like working for you guys. I like helping customers. I like spreading the good word of TaskRabbit, as it were. I just flat-out refuse to go to a second meeting for two hours where you're not gonna pay me and you're not even gonna tell me something good out of it. The nature of my business as an actor is that I'm gone for a spate of time. And I was told when I became a TaskRabbit that that's exactly the kind of person you cater to. Why is this happening now?" And he said, "No, you know what? You're right. Don't worry about it. We'll make you reactivated. Just, you know, if you decide that you wanna go on tour or anything, or you book another job, just let us know." I said, "Well, as a point of fact, I did . . ." So, I don't know. We'll see. I mean, I leave on Monday to go do another job upstate, to go do a show.

Even though TaskRabbit markets itself as offering flexibility—"Taskers set their own hourly rates for work, set their own schedules, and deter-mine their own work areas"—there's apparently a limit to how much flex-ibility workers are allowed to have. The limit also applies to workers who aren't hired for a period of time, even through no fault of their own. For example, Sarah, twenty-nine, explained, "I haven't had any jobs in two

months, over two months. And if you are not working for three months
and they just deactivate you. . . . I've told them, 'When you guys said I am
not active, [it's actually that] I am not getting any jobs. Because I have my
availability on for two weeks straight.' And they were not very helpful.
They were just like, 'Oh well, you know, update your schedule.'"

Finally, the issue of time away from work is not limited just to time off
the clock but also applies to the opportunity to take breaks during the
work itself. Most full-time workers, or nonminimum-wage workers, don't
think twice about taking a bathroom, cigarette, or even lunch break during their workday. But sharing economy workers, in a throwback to the
nineteenth and early twentieth century, don't always have the same
flexibility.

As late as 1890, many stores had at best a single hard bench for workers
to sit on during breaks—assuming they even had breaks. Most shopgirls
ate their lunches standing up, and many of the best stores had no employee
bathrooms: "Workers were encouraged to take care of personal maintenance matters before leaving home in the morning; it was 'their business.'"
Mary Gay Humphreys, a reformer and journalist who focused on the
plight of working girls, "regularly escorted small parades of girls to her
apartment house to 'use facilities.'"[50]

Sharing economy workers, too, are encouraged to address personal
maintenance outside of work obligations. Kitchensurfing chefs were
required to wash their hands when they arrived at a client's home, and
were cautioned against using the bathroom until after they'd cooked, in
order to maintain a hygienic image. Damla, thirty-eight, a Kitchensurfing
marketplace chef who occasionally worked as part of the Kitchensurfing
Tonight program, explained that Kitchensurfing staff suggested that chefs
"just try to not use the bathroom. Because they're only there, I think, a half
hour at a time. So it's possible to not go for a half hour."

It's true that Kitchensurfing Tonight chefs are in a client's home for
only thirty minutes. But a full shift is four hours, which includes cooking
for up to four clients and half an hour for commuting between each gig.
Chefs who are unable to hold their urine for a four-hour shift often turn to
coffee shops or ask favors of staff in the buildings where they cook. For
instance, Francesco, twenty-nine, tried to befriend building doormen,
turning them into modern bathroom benefactors. Even so, the tight time

frame for Kitchensurfing Tonight gigs sometimes leaves workers with few options.

"The worst part is a couple of times when I've had to pee between bookings, and it has been a mess because I do stick by the policy," Joe, twenty-six, explained. "So I have to sort of find some place that's open. Or if it's night, I'll just pee in an alley, if it's available, because I can, and it's there, and nobody [notices]—especially in downtown. In midtown, obviously, that's impossible, because there's just too many people. So sometimes it's a little exciting running around trying to find a place to pee." Joe could ask to use the bathroom after cooking, but he's reluctant to do so and risk losing the opportunity for a tip. "There's always a possibility that they might tip me; it does happen occasionally," he explained. "And I always worry that if I use the bathroom at that last minute, then [I've lost] the opportunity that they might have taken to tip me."

As with many aspects of the sharing economy, one's bathroom difficulties (or lack thereof) are often correlated with status. Airbnb hosts don't tend to have bathroom issues, even when they're sharing with a guest: "Usually, I just talk to the guest and tell them that [my girlfriend] needs to leave early and will be using the bathroom at blank time, and it's not an issue," said Daniel, thirty-one, an Airbnb host. Other workers, who often find themselves on the go—such as TaskRabbits and Uber drivers—tend to have makeshift bathroom arrangements, spending a portion of their day scouting out new bathroom locations. Sarah, twenty-nine, a TaskRabbit, told me about her strategies: "Well, any Starbucks. But also you learn how to get to the bathrooms in the hotels like the Waldorf and the Plaza. And the Waldorf has—you have your own vanity inside the stalls, and it's kind of ridiculous." Larry, fifty-four, an Uber/Lyft driver, explained, "I have an app on my phone, a McDonald's app. A lot of them are open twenty-four hours, and they're pretty reliable. Because a lot of places, like Dunkin Donuts, they don't even have bathrooms. A lot of restaurants, fast food joints, they don't all have bathrooms. But McDonalds is probably the most reliable."

One strategy mentioned by several workers was to maintain a membership to a gym with multiple locations. But Donald, the deactivated Tasker introduced in the opening vignette, suggested that using a gym bathroom might be one of the reasons why he was removed from TaskRabbit:

One day I had to do twelve deliveries, starting downtown and going all the way up [to the Upper West Side]. . . . I stopped at New York Sports Club to go to the bathroom. They may know I did that. They may say, "Well, why did you stop at the gym?" And I'll say, "I went to the bathroom." But yeah, I could see that. . . . You could go into Starbucks. but you could be waiting on line in Starbucks for ten minutes to go pee. So I'm not sure if the bathroom counts as part of your job if you're in the middle of doing it. I didn't really get to that point.

Bathroom breaks are not just a matter of convenience and hygiene. Not relieving one's bladder when needed can lead to health issues, to say nothing of a feeling of extreme discomfort. But just as sharing economy workers are on their own for health care, payroll taxes, transportation between gigs, and sick/vacation leave, they're also financially responsible for any workplace injuries.

As noted in this chapter, American workers have a history of fighting for better pay, shorter hours, and improved workplace conditions. But the 1935 Wagner Act—which established the National Labor Relations Board and gave employees the right to form and join unions and engage in collective bargaining—and the 1938 Fair Labor Standards Act and subsequent amendments in 1966 have long been hailed as having changed the world of work for the better. Yet, for all of these improvements, just eighty years later, sharing economy workers—classified as independent contractors—find themselves without any of these protections. And yet, this is only the start of the workplace troubles that gig economy workers often experience. Like their colleagues in the seventeenth, eighteenth, and nineteenth centuries, sharing economy workers may also encounter unsafe workplaces and on-the-job injuries for which they have no recourse.

4 Workplace Troubles

Emma, twenty-six, is so petite—barely a hundred pounds—that she brings to mind thoughts of Tinker Bell. So when this college graduate tells me that she's done a number of moving and other manual labor jobs as a TaskRabbit, I assume I've heard her incorrectly. Then she starts talking about pain.

"I've actually had back issues; I'm not kidding," she says, catching the look of surprise on my face. "Yeah, I've had back issues for a while; the first time I did it, I had back issues, and more recently I did again, a couple of weeks ago. And I go to the doctor, and they're like, 'Is there anything different that you're doing?' And I was like, 'Yeah, I'm cleaning people's houses.' And they're like, 'Yes, that's probably it.'"

As an hourly contract worker who relies on positive reviews, Emma has to be careful about how she asks for breaks. Although retail workers may be able slow down at times under the assumption that a boss can observe only so many workers at a time, a TaskRabbit who does cleaning tasks is often the only worker on-site and may find herself under the watchful eye of a client. "There's been a few times where I've had to hint to the clients—like, 'Oh man, my back really hurts,'" she says. "I've actually said these things, and they just don't know what I'm trying to say here. They're just like, 'Oh, well, you're doing a great job.'"

TaskRabbit offers workers less anonymity than a traditional cleaning or moving service might. A disgruntled client of Merry Maids may post a negative review on Yelp, but that review will be listed under the name of a corporation, not an individual. Potential clients may assume that they'll get a different cleaner. But with TaskRabbit, Emma is hired directly. The reviews are about her work and personal attitude. As a result, she has to be careful about how she presents issues like discomfort on the job. "[I say,] 'Hey, I'm really in pain,' but kind of in a friendly way. You know, kind of hinting, 'Hey, I need a break. I can use some water,'" she said. "But nothing. It really depends on the client. Sometimes they've been great. Sometimes they've offered me tea or water or whatever. They never have offered [to let] me to sit down. Sometimes it's not a big deal. But with cleaning, it can be really exhausting, especially if you're doing this day after day, back-to-back."

It's not unusual for workers, especially housecleaners, to work without consuming food during their work hours. In *Nickel and Dimed: On (Not) Getting by in America,* Barbara Ehrenreich details not being allowed to eat, drink, or even chew gum while cleaning a house. In a month of working, only one cleaning client, noticing that she was sweating, offered her a glass of water, which she gratefully accepted, "flouting the rule against the ingestion of anything while inside a house."[1]

In detailing her month spent as a cleaner for a national cleaning chain, Ehrenreich describes the experience of her colleagues as a "world of pain— managed by Excedrin and Advil, compensated for with cigarettes and, in one or two cases and then only on the weekends, with booze."[2] Scrubbing floors on hands and knees, strapping themselves into heavy backpack-style vacuums, and engaging in repetitive motions for hours a day gave her colleagues bad backs and aggravated their arthritis and previous injuries. Emma's work for TaskRabbit, too, became a world managed by painkillers. "I'm active, I'm young, I generally don't have health issues, so it is kind of ridiculous," she said. "I take painkillers. I've been to see a chiropractor. I went to see my regular doctor; they didn't help me out very much. . . . It was bad—I couldn't sleep sometimes from the pain."

Emma's pain is similar to what Ehrenreich wrote about, but whereas Ehrenreich's colleagues were hourly employees, covered by workers' compensation policies, Emma is an independent contractor. She is not eligible for workers' compensation, paid sick leave, or health insurance. If she is injured on the job, she has no recourse. Her only option was to quit cleaning, a decision that she made reluctantly. "It made the most money, so that's why I had this inner conflict; but I was like, 'Is this really worth it?'" she said. "So it's really frustrating, but yeah, I took it off and I started doing some exercise, and my back sort of got to somewhat normal now."

Workers getting injured on the job isn't anything new. The neighborhood where I conducted my research was within walking distance of the Asch Building, home of the notorious 1911 Triangle Shirtwaist Factory Fire, in which 143 young women and men perished. The fire was one of the largest workplace accidents in US history and is often considered an impetus for changes to American labor law and for the New Deal.[3]

A SHORT HISTORY OF WORKERS' COMPENSATION

Workers' compensation is hardly a new concept. The first known policy on worker compensation is the Sumerian Nippur Tablet No. 3191, dated to 2050 BCE, which provided compensation for specific injuries, including fractures. Likewise, the code of Hammurabi in 1750 BCE and ancient Greek, Roman, Arab, and Chinese law all provided for specific compensation schedules for the loss of a body part. But while ancient cultures compensated workers for their on-the-job injuries, modern economies have been much less generous.[4]

English common law provided the basis for an American legal framework that persisted into the early Industrial Revolution and included three loopholes that were so restrictive they were known as the "unholy trinity of defenses." These three loopholes were contributory negligence, the "fellow servant" rule, and the "assumption of risk." Contributory negligence meant if a worker was in any way responsible for the injury, the employer was not at fault. If a worker slipped and fell into hazardous machinery that was missing required safety mechanisms, the injury was not covered. Under contributory negligence, the worker was at fault for slipping. The fellow servant exemption provided a loophole for any injury caused by a fellow employee, and, when all else failed, there was the assumption of risk—the claim that by performing a job, employees assumed any risk that was inherent in the job.[5]

Historically, work in the United States was fairly dangerous. In 1904, twenty-seven thousand workers in manufacturing, transport, and agriculture were killed on the job. In one year, fifty thousand accidents took place in New York factories alone. Historian Howard Zinn notes that "hat and cap makers were getting respiratory diseases, quarrymen were inhaling deadly chemicals, lithographic printers were getting arsenic poisoning." In 1914, according to a report of the Commission on Industrial Relations, thirty-five thousand workers were killed in industrial accidents and seven hundred thousand were injured.[6]

Populist support for an organized workers movement began to grow in the first decade of the twentieth century, assisted by the "muckrakers" movement of reform-minded journalists. The most famous of these was Upton Sinclair, author of *The Jungle,* who wrote about the appalling working conditions in Chicago slaughterhouses, the distribution of diseased and rotten meat, and the adulteration of food through the addition of cheap fillers. Sinclair's work led to the development of the Food and Drug Act of 1906, the Meat Inspection Act of 1906, and the creation of the Food and Drug Administration. Sinclair was disappointed by this turn of events: he wrote *The Jungle* to help meatpacking workers, not to improve the quality of meat. "I aimed for the public's heart," Sinclair later wrote, "and by accident hit it in the stomach." Although Congress passed the Employers' Liability Acts of 1906 and 1908, softening the restrictions of contributory negligence, the conditions of workers were still largely ignored.[7]

In early 1911, the states of Washington and Wisconsin passed comprehensive workers' compensation laws, but the true movement toward workplace protections and compensation for injury didn't occur until the March 1911 Triangle Shirtwaist Factory fire.[8] In the year after the fire, nine other states passed regulations, followed by thirty-six others before the decade was done.

In New York, the fire also led to the development of the Committee on Public Safety, headed by Frances Perkins—the future U.S. secretary of labor—and led to new legislation to protect workers, including the "54-hour bill" granting workers shorter hours. The New York State Legislature also created the Factory Investigating Commission to "investigate factory conditions in this and other cities" and to provide "remedial measures of legislation to prevent hazard or loss of life among employees through fire, unsanitary conditions, and occupational diseases."[9] The state commission's reports helped modernize the state's labor laws, making New York State "one of the most progressive states in terms of labor reform," and led to the passing of sixty new laws that granted better building access and egress, mandated the installation of alarm systems and automatic sprinklers, increased requirements for fireproofing and fire extinguishers, improved eating and toilet facilities for workers, and limited the workweek for women and children.[10]

MODERN WORKERS, WITHOUT GENERATIONS OF PROTECTION

In a cruel irony, workers in the sharing economy—hailed as the height of the modern workplace—find themselves without any of the workplace protections enjoyed by their great grandparents. Although workplace protections still exist for full-time and part-time employees, gig workers, as independent contractors, are outside the social safety net of basic workplace protections.

In recent years, the number of workers classified as independent contractors has grown steadily, as businesses have deliberately restructured the work relationship, abandoning the employment model to escape social responsibilities.[11] Independent contractors in the United States do not receive workers' compensation, unemployment benefits, paid vacation, retirement, overtime, disability accommodations, family leave protections, protection from discrimination, or the right to form unions.

The majority of sharing economy services consider their workers to be independent contractors, or 1099 workers, named for the end-of-year tax document they receive that details their income. In addition to freeing companies from the obligation to pay into unemployment insurance funds or to make an employer's contribution to Social Security and Medicare (7.65 percent of the employee's salary), classifying workers as independent contractors allows companies to create a two-tier system in terms of benefits without facing complaints of discrimination. Full-time workers can get 401k contributions, health insurance, and stock options, for which contract workers are deemed ineligible. It's no wonder that in 2011, the

American Bar Association noted that a federal study estimated 3.4 million employees were classified as independent contractors when they should be reported as employees; a 2009 study by the Treasury Department's inspector general estimated that misclassification costs the United States fifty-four billion dollars in underpayment of employment taxes.

The lack of workers' compensation means that any worker injured on the job is not compensated for on-the-job injuries, and workers are responsible for their own health expenses if they are injured. Emma—the twenty-six-year-old TaskRabbit on painkillers—is fortunate enough to qualify for Medicaid, a situation she described as "necessary." But other workers who get hurt while working face a double whammy, gaining medical expenses even as they lose work and income.

For instance, David, fifty-four-year-old Kitchensurfing Tonight chef, was also injured on the job. Kitchensurfing Tonight provided clients with on-demand chefs who arrived in Kitchensurfing uniforms of black chef jackets or aprons, wearing backpacks and dragging insulated bags weighing as much as forty pounds—the ingredients for as many as sixteen servings of steak, fish, and vegetables and all of the necessary pots, knives, and cutting boards. But while the chefs wore uniforms, they were often without shoes.

Proper footwear is required in most professional kitchens, where workers may encounter hot, dripping grease; spills of boiling water; slippery floors; and the discomfort of standing for long periods. As a result of such dangers, absorbent sneakers and open-back shoes, such as clogs, are not allowed at the Culinary Institute of America, one of the top culinary schools in the country.[12] Yet, chefs for Kitchensurfing were instructed to ask clients if they should remove their shoes when entering a home. Kitchensurfing's Secret Diner program, which allowed workers to receive a cash bonus if they followed a checklist of rules, included the shoe-removal offer as one of the requirements, along with explaining the meal's contents and asking how diners wanted their meat cooked.

It was cold and slushy in February 2015 when David arrived at his client's house to cook that evening's meal. It was only his second week of work on Kitchensurfing. Not surprisingly, the client accepted the his offer to remove his wet shoes. His accident occurred after he'd completed the job, as he prepared to leave. "I [had] had snow boots on," he said. "I had my backpack full of stuff, and I hopped to put my boots on that I'd taken off at the door, and I just twisted something. I go to step out of their apartment and my knee just gave out, and I collapsed."

But his shift wasn't over. He still had two more households to cook for. Kitchensurfing used algorithms to assign locations that were within walking distance or along the same transit line, and that evening David had to take the subway to get to his next cooking gig. "It was tough. I was down on Houston Street, and it was a long walk to the last one. If I could have found a cab, I would have taken one," he said with a low chuckle. "And there were a lot of stairs on the subway—that was the killer, all those stairs. . . . I fell down the subway stairs a couple of times. My knee just gave out. I couldn't feel it. It was numb. It was all, 'Aughhhh.' So yeah, that was a long night."

He called Kitchensurfing the next day to let someone know what happened. "She was nice. I was like, 'I have to go see the doctor.' She was like, 'Take as much time as you need.' And, you know: 'The job will be waiting for you,'" he said. "They were really cool, they were really good about that. So that made it easier, that I didn't need to rush back."

The Kitchensurfing administration didn't mention sick pay or reimbursement for the medical expense of visiting the doctor. David missed a full week and a half of work—unpaid—and then returned at three days a week in order to ease in. An MRI revealed what he suspected: a herniated disk. In an effort to stave off the need for surgery, David is going to weekly acupressure and physical therapy—at a cost of about a hundred dollars a week, out of pocket. "I'm hoping [the surgery] is not as invasive as it used to be. I had [a herniated disk] in my neck back in the '90s. I couldn't take time off to do it, because I was raising my daughters. But back then they said it would be a six-week recuperation, and I can't do that right now, either," he said, chuckling softly. "And you know how it is, I'll have to sign something saying that there's a possibility that you'll wake up paralyzed. Anything having to do with your spine. So I'm hoping this combination of physical therapy and acupressure will allow me to not have to do that."

As independent contractors, Kitchensurfing workers are not covered by workers' compensation. They also don't qualify for employer-sponsored disability compensation. "We're just the hired help. We're freelancers,"

David said. "I think it'd be easier, if it happened on the job, to get some sort of worker's comp."

But as hired help, David *was* on the job when he got hurt—he's just not covered under the independent contractor model. He's not the only worker who has experienced long-term health issues as a result of sharing economy work. Shaun, thirty-seven, also experienced a back injury while working as a TaskRabbit. "I have to stop with the moving assignments because I got hurt," he said. "My mind thinks I'm twenty-five, but my body is way older. *[Laughs.]* And I keep telling myself, 'Yeah, let me just lose a couple of pounds, let me just lose the stomach or at least get my flexibility back before doing things like that again.'"

Shaun's injury occurred during a moving task. "I helped lift a dresser. Had to pull it up a flight of stairs. It was two dressers; and even though I had assistance, I'm carrying stuff that weighs about 125, and my current abilities can only allow me to carry 50 pounds. So, yeah, I stretched my back, and I just walked out of there saying, 'I'm okay.' But when I'm out, I'm like, 'Ouch.'"

ADVANCE PLANNING IN AN ON-DEMAND AGE

The stories of Shaun, David, and Emma are not unique. Part of the shifting of risk from employer to worker means than workers are responsible for knowing their own limits—what might make them ill, what might injure them, and how much they can accomplish in a few hours—and plan accordingly. That type of advance planning is challenging enough for people with steady white-collar employment. But for workers who find themselves in a variety of workplaces and dealing with different "bosses" daily, such planning is nearly impossible.

For TaskRabbit workers, especially, this can be a problem. Under the peer-to-peer model, workers are often hired by individuals who may not fully understand what they're asking them to do, or who may downplay the description to avoid scaring off a potential worker. Natasha, twenty-eight, tries to weed out work that she's uncomfortable with, but sometimes clients aren't forthcoming with details.

Recently I had a task where a woman said, "I had construction in my home. I just need you to help me clean." What she really meant is all of these chemical cleaners. She brought gloves. She brought a face mask. She's like, "Well, there's all this dust from the construction, and I need you to take a vacuum; but mostly I need you to dust with rags." And there's this chemical that she got from the contractor, because the contractors didn't want to stay any longer if she didn't pay them. So she got the fluid that they use to clean up the plaster dust. . . and she wanted me to do that. So we did it together for a little bit, and then she's like, "I'm going to go, because I'm getting sick." Well, what the hell do you think I'm doing, you know? I'm getting sick, too.

Same thing with yesterday. I'm getting sick from the dust. I blew my nose and dust came out. Stuff like that, and they just don't care. Those people don't care.

It's hard to believe, but Natasha is actually one of the lucky ones—at least her client provided a mask and gloves and worked with her for a while. Other TaskRabbits have found themselves working alone and without even the most basic safety precautions. Jamal, twenty-five, was hired to clean a small fish pond on a property in the Red Hook area of Brooklyn for a client he described as a movie stylist for feature films.

It was a very nice place, a backyard with a pool. And he hadn't cleaned it out in years, so the pool was just real—oh, it was just—I don't know what it was. . . . I think it was just mildew, and mosquitoes, everywhere. So he wanted me to go into it, scoop the stuff out, and that's pretty much it. And then, add clean water. I guess it was one of those little ponds you put fish in. It had a little flowing waterfall. Kind of peaceful—a little meditation pond. Very small, but it's very deep. It was quite deep, and I had to climb into it, too. I'd say it's probably three feet deep. The stuff came up to right here [he pointed to right below his knees].

"So that's probably the most disgusting thing I ever did in my life. I just had everything through my toes, it felt slimy. I literally have a visceral reaction to that," he said with a laugh. Fortunately, the pond wasn't full, but Jamal doesn't know what he was standing in, barefoot. "He hadn't put water there in year. It was just stuff—I don't know what," he said. "It was green. It was green and slimy. I rolled up my jeans. I took off my shoes and socks. . . . I just got into it and did it. Yeah, so I have nightmares about that." The experience was so disgusting that Jamal photographed his feet

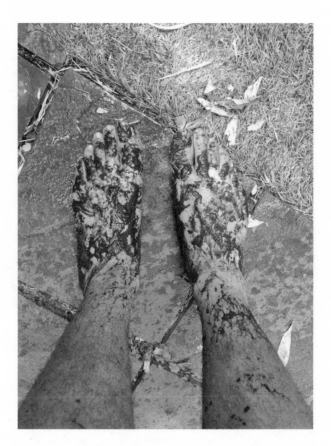

Figure 11. Jamal's feet after he cleaned a fish pond in Brooklyn. Photo by respondent.

afterward, showing them covered with a thin layer of brown and green muck (see fig. 11).

Small ponds are usually cleaned out with a pump or vacuum—not by a person standing in the pond. When people do have to step into a pond, it's usually recommended that they wear tall rubber wader boots to protect their legs and feet from whatever may be in the water and mud.

Perhaps it's not surprising that TaskRabbit's newest advertising materials have veered away from "neighbors helping neighbors" to: "We do chores. You live life" (see fig. 12). This new motto further emphasizes how the service makes it possible for clients to outsource unpleasant work to others, a

Figure 12. TaskRabbit advertising campaign noting, "We do chores. You live life." Photo by author.

concept that Juliet Schor refers to as the "servant economy."[13] It's true that Natasha and Jamal could simply refuse to do the work. Numerous TaskRabbits noted that TaskRabbit orientation emphasizes worker safety, and that Taskers are told to leave any task where they feel physically uncomfortable. But such policies ignore the reality of TaskRabbit work for many Strugglers and even some Strivers: if you are financially dependent on an afternoon of work, you may feel like you can't really afford to walk away from the task. By the time a worker arrives at a location, he's likely spent at least an hour on traveling and on communicating with the client— further decreasing the appeal of such an unpaid "choice."

DANGEROUS WORK DELIVERED VIA APP

Many workers probably encounter work that they'd rather not do at their full-time job—whether it's a white-collar worker fixing a jammed copier, a plumber squeezing into a crawlspace to fix a pipe, or even a teacher grading research papers. TaskRabbit and Kitchensurfing are a far cry from the dangers offered by fishing, logging, or even general construction work. But the sharing economy claims to be "fundamentally changing the way we live and work."[14] Shouldn't that fundamental change involve getting rid of unpleasant work, or at least making it less dangerous?

Others have suggested that peer-to-peer platforms may make it possible for workers to "earn considerably more and have more autonomy over which jobs they accept."[15] But instead of improving workplace freedom, the sharing economy is returning to many of the workplace practices of the early industrial age, when workers found themselves with few protections. Why?

In some cases, the physical dangers of the work are simply inherent in the work itself. According to the Bureau of Labor Statistics, taxi driving, with eighteen fatal injuries per hundred thousand workers, was one of the ten most dangerous jobs in the United States in 2014—more dangerous than the jobs held by police and sheriff's patrol officers (ranked fifteenth) or electricians (ranked nineteenth). A 2010 Occupational Safety and Health Administration fact sheet notes that taxi and for-hire drivers have a homicide victimization rate that is between twenty-one and thirty-three times higher than the national average for all workers. Although drivers for Uber, Lyft, Via, and other car-sharing services do not carry large amounts of cash, they do carry valuable smartphones, tablets, and GPS systems. Additionally, for-hire drivers using their personal vehicles lack many of the physical controls that could prevent dangerous situations, such as security cameras, silent alarms, and improved lighting inside the vehicles—all of which are recommended by OSHA.[16]

Partitions between drivers and passengers are an important tool for reducing assaults. In Baltimore, researchers found that assaults on drivers decreased by "56 percent the year following a citywide mandate requiring partitions between taxi drivers and passengers ... [, and that] between 1991, when only 5 percent of cabs had shields, and 1998, when all taxis had shields, assaults decreased 90 percent."[17]

The lack of barriers between drivers and passengers has also been blamed for documented cases of drivers being attacked in Arlington,

Virginia; choked in Chesterfield County, Virginia; assaulted in Augusta, Georgia; slapped and hit in Orange County, California; and abused in St. Charles, Illinois; and Miami. In Boston in January 2015, an Uber driver was attacked by an off-duty police officer.[18] Research comparing the experiences of for-hire drivers in New York and Boston found that a number of Uber drivers carried weapons, in violation of Uber policy, or employed neutralization strategies, such as refusing to engage with passengers, to protect themselves.[19]

Many of these physical assaults were caught on camera and posted to YouTube, quickly going viral and drawing public outrage. A Miami doctor who assaulted her Uber driver was fired from her hospital, and an Orange County Taco Bell executive who beat up his Uber driver was also fired. But these are only the incidences that are caught on tape. Cameras are not required by Uber or Lyft, and many drivers, whether owing to the expense or to concerns about the legality of the cameras, don't have them. It doesn't help that Uber has lobbied for weaker insurance protections for workplace injuries.[20]

Uber has not entirely ignored worker risks—it's just that any costs associated with protecting drivers are borne by workers or customers. During Uber's 180 Days of Change campaign, part of an effort to improve the company's public image and driver morale, Uber announced Driver Injury Protection insurance offered via Aon. The program provides accident disability payments for lost earnings, accident medical expenses, and survivor benefits. Uber increased rates by five cents per mile in order to have customers finance the pilot, and drivers who choose to participate were charged 3.75 cents per mile. Originally piloted in eight states, the program was available in thirty-two states by April 2018. The cost to drivers, while minimal, may serve as a participation disincentive.

In addition to the documented physical assaults, three Uber drivers were murdered in March 2016: two drivers were killed in Detroit and another in Los Angeles. Police identified robbery as the motive.[21] Also in March, two Uber drivers were robbed by their passengers in Boston.[22] A livery driver in Brooklyn whose vehicle still featured an Uber sticker was murdered in June 2016, and several cases have arisen of people being found dead in cars with Uber stickers in Los Angeles and West Covina, California.[23]

When there's no visual evidence, there tends to be less outcry. In November 2015, Maggie Young, a Seattle Uber driver, was sexually assaulted while driving on the interstate, later publishing her story in *Bustle* magazine. Her passenger was charged with assault and harassment with sexual motivation—a misdemeanor. Young is not the only female driver to be assaulted—a driver in Menomonee Falls, Wisconsin, was assaulted in February 2016. Given that sexual assaults are among the least-reported crimes, the number of assaults on drivers is likely higher. Indeed, in her *Bustle* essay, Young notes, "That passenger was not the first man to sexually assault me. He is just the first one I've reported (I am pressing charges, and a trial date has yet to be set)."[24] Drivers who are attacked may be less likely to report the incident or otherwise publicize it after the experience of Artur Zawada, a driver who was removed from the Uber platform after a University of Michigan student verbally assaulted him with a tirade of antigay slurs.[25]

Of the drivers I interviewed, none had been physically assaulted by passengers. However, several mentioned actively trying to avoid driving on weekend nights in order to avoid dealing with drunk passengers. More than a few detailed experiences of being verbally assailed by passengers. Oybek, thirty-five, is one such driver; he got teary-eyed as he talked about being mistreated by several passengers.

> Yesterday I had five guys from Holland. So they were drunk, and . . . once they get in the car, they start to make fun of me already, you know? They're drunk, what I can do? So I just kept driving and trying not listen to them. But they speak Dutch, right? They're from Holland. Yeah, I can understand a little bit of the Dutch language.
>
> They start to make fun of me; they were laughing. Okay, it's okay. Oh, they start to give me—"Oh, you are African?" I said, "Why you think so?" "Your skin is . . ." I'm still thinking about yesterday, yesterday's riders.

When I met Oybek, he had been driving for just four months, but had already stopped driving on weekend evenings after dealing with an intoxicated passenger who threw up on the door and window of his car, resulting in an emergency car wash. "Every time, I am afraid when the drunk people get into my car. So, I'm afraid they maybe do something," he said. "Yeah, for pee-pee, for throw up."

Not all of the risk is to the inside of his car, either. "I know a lot of people, people on Friday, once you are staying on the red light, they drunk, they kicking your car, my bumper, yeah," he said. "They hold a bottle of water, can of water, they're bumping my hood. They're scratching the . . . so it's really serious. I don't know why so many people like that."

I ask if he ever thinks about no longer driving for Uber or quitting driving entirely. "It's not easy, so sometimes it make you nervous," he says. "So, it's not easy, but I have to pay my bills, I have to pay my rent, finance. It's a lot of bills."

THE RISE OF THE NEVER-ENDING TRIP

Even when drivers are able to avoid altercations with passengers, some dangers are simply inherent in driving. Drivers experience long hours sitting, and the difficulty of finding affordable food with easy-to-access parking means that they often consume a relatively unhealthy diet. Several drivers noted health issues such as weight gain or joint issues that had arisen from the relative immobility of driving for a car service.

For instance, Larry, fifty-four, was a competitive runner until he started driving for Uber. "I used to train pretty hard six, seven days a week, but the driving seemed to make things worse. My legs would be tight after a workout, and then I'd try to go out and drive," he said. "My legs would just be aching, and getting in the car for eight hours just wasn't working out."

These issues are in addition to what medical professionals have dubbed "taxicab syndrome," the increased voiding dysfunction, infertility, urolithiasis, bladder cancer, and urinary infections found among professional drivers compared to the general driving public. These health issues are thought to arise from the lack of ready access to bathrooms, a well-documented difficulty for most cabbies, but a challenge that may be especially salient for app-based drivers.[26]

Although taxi drivers are required to drive within the five boroughs of New York City and to Westchester and Nassau Counties (suburbs of New York City), they are free to decline other out-of-town trips. Uber drivers have no such restrictions and, although it's not a regular occurrence, can find themselves on epic rides, such as from Scranton, Pennsylvania, to

Buffalo, New York, or from Santa Barbara to Palo Alto, California. As of early 2018, the longest recorded ride was Williamsburg, Virginia, to Brooklyn, New York, a "grueling 397-mile, 7-hour-42-minute jaunt" for a fare of $294.09. Factoring in the round-trip drive of fifteen and a half hours, and spending $32 on gas and tolls, the driver calculated that she made around $9 per hour.[27]

Thanks to a 2.75x surge, or a rate that was nearly three times higher than usual, Larry, the former runner, once found himself on a seven-hun-dred-dollar-drive from downtown New York City to the suburbs of Philadelphia. Although the trip was only about ninety miles, most of it was spent in traffic. "I was right by the Holland Tunnel east," he said, "but the traffic to the Holland Tunnel was just terrible that day because [the] PATH [train] wasn't running. Everybody must have taken cars. It was bad. It took an hour and a half to get from Christopher Street to the Holland Tunnel, and the whole time I'm like, 'Geez, I hope this guy doesn't cancel.' This is going to be a really good ride. And he stuck with me." While Larry appreciated the fare, long rides are such an uncertainty that Ahmed, thirty-two, an Uber driver and City University of New York student, stops working two hours before class to ensure that he can get to school on time.

In addition to the possibility of longer rides, the rise of uberPOOL and LyftLine, too, can result in a lack of bathroom breaks. UberPOOL and LyftLine—where a driver picks up multiple passengers, acting as an "instant bus line" that spans multiple drop-offs and pickups—have been hailed as environmental godsends for allegedly "reducing traffic, gas use and automo-bile emissions." But grouping multiple rides can also lead to epic journeys. One such trip lasted "nearly an hour and meander[ed] over 10 miles across San Francisco, stopping nine times to pick up and drop off passengers."[28]

Although a never-ending trip makes it easier for Uber to claim an increase in the percentage of time that drivers spend with passengers (as opposed to driving without a fare or sitting curbside) and can increase driver income, it also means less opportunity for a break. Drivers cannot refuse LyftLine or uberPOOL requests when they're already on a ride, fur-ther reducing their control over the length of their workday. Whereas a taxicab can drop off a passenger and then go immediately "off duty," a driver on these "party-line rides" has to finish the journey before going off duty. In August 2017, Uber implemented a long-trip notification, in which drivers are warned that a trip is expected to last forty-five minutes or more and given a chance to accept or decline it accordingly. However, the notification tool doesn't address the Pool problem.

Furthermore, long rides can leave workers in places where bathroom access is especially limited. Even purchasing a product at a shop and claiming customer status may not be sufficient. Oybek describes restricted access to bathrooms as a problem that he has encountered since day one as an Uber driver. "My first day when I came home, I said to my wife, 'Wow, you know what? I would like to use the bathroom.'"

Even when bathrooms are available, parking may not be. "I can't park anywhere. Even to use a restroom," Oybek said. "[I could try a] coffee shop, but the problem is parking. So I have to pay for parking [and, once I] find good parking, park, pay, and go. And sometimes it's only for customers." Although many stores and restaurants feature a prominent "Restrooms are for customers only" sign, Starbucks has been called "the city's bathroom" for both its prevalence across the city and easy access.[29] But even so, company policy gives managers discretion over who is allowed to use the restroom, and the high-end coffee shop is found only in gentrified neighborhoods. "My idea was to visit the Starbucks. So I said I'm gonna buy the coffee, just let me go, and some of them, 'No, no,'" he said. "I took my money, my wallet, and [I] go, 'Give me the coffee please, but I want to use your bathroom.' They said, 'No, no, no.'"

"It's very difficult in Manhattan," Oybek explained. "So, I'm planning. In another half an hour, I have to stop and go. I'm going to Brooklyn, to any gas station. The best thing is gas stations."

DESPERATE TIMES CALL FOR DESPERATE MEASURES, OR "GOING" ON THE GO

Desperate drivers sometimes resort to desperate measures. "For drivers, bathrooms are our biggest problem," said Hector, thirty-one. "There is no public bathroom. If I go to McDonalds—like most places I have gone to— they will have a key; so in order for me to get that key, I've got to buy something. You have to be a customer. So I do spend a lot buying frappes or a small burger. I figure I might as well get something to eat, so it's packing on [the weight]. And then at night, when it's real late and things close, it's even harder to find a bathroom; and that's when you have to use a cup. They tell me Yellow Cabs normally have their cups and they'll just open the door and toss it out. A guy I was driving with yesterday told me his window is tinted so he pees while he's driving."[30]

"How do you avoid spilling on the seat?" I asked.

"It's tough. I don't know. I only did it once, and it was a bad experience," Hector said. "I had a big cup. It was, I think, twenty ounces. I almost overflowed it. That's because there was no bathroom anywhere, and I was in Jersey; and all their places close early over there. I had to use the cup." When he was done, he tossed it out the window. "I only did that once. Now I just . . . Yesterday—not yesterday, two days ago, I held it for like five hours. It was just that busy, that I was like, 'You know what, I'm just going to hold it and just keep driving, not think about it.' But it does become difficult," he said. "I think that's what takes away from my profits, having to stop for the bathroom, look for a place, and then turn off the app so I don't get a ping. But I can't hold it anymore. That can kill a half hour in getting to a place, McDonalds or Burger King."

But while drivers are often holding their urine, their passengers don't always demonstrate the same restraint. Taxis, in New York City at least, have vinyl seats that do not absorb water or stains. Most uberX vehicles, as personal cars, have cloth upholstery, while UberBLACK vehicles generally feature leather-clad seats. Neither of these materials repel water or, more specifically, urine. Private Facebook groups for drivers, and the public Uberdrivers.net discussion site, feature numerous stories of drivers having to deal with passengers exiting their vehicles while their bodily fluids remain behind.

Some critics have suggested that the posts must be fakes; surely no self-respecting adult would pee on the seat of a car. Yet, several of the drivers I interviewed found themselves dealing with the type of bodily fluids more often found in a bathroom or medical office than in a vehicle. In Gerald's experience, he wasn't the only one who ended up encountering more than he expected in his Uber that evening.

I picked this guy up with his wife over on the west side of Harlem. He was in a suit and tie. He didn't say much, but you know, his wife was—she was doing most of the talking. She was a very pleasant lady. I took them . . . Where did I take them? I don't know if it was Connecticut or it was some part of upper New York. It was one of those areas where you drive up the hills, and there's a house on every layer of the hill, and winding roads, and all woods and trees. It's not cheap to live there. It was one of those areas; so it was a good drive. He didn't say anything the whole time, and she was talking most of the time. She would talk to him, and when he wouldn't reply I guess he was falling asleep.

So I get them up there, beautiful house. It was on another part of the hill. So I drive back. I go pick up this girl. She comes out in a minidress—miniskirt—anyway, she's going out for the night. So she gets in on his side. I guess she put her hand down. She said, "This seat is wet." I'm like, "Oh no." In my mind, I'm saying, "Why is this seat wet? They didn't have no bottles with them. They weren't drinking." All this is processing, and I'm like, "There's only one reason why that seat is wet."

I couldn't tell her. I mean that would have opened up, you know. She could have gone after Uber. She could have gone after me. I couldn't tell her. I felt so upset.

She said, "It is really wet." So I said, "Well, just go over to the other side," because his wife sat on the other side. I said, "I had somebody, they had a bottle; must be spilled wine or whatever." I felt so bad I had to lie to this woman because I could not tell her I knew what it was. So she went over to the other side. I was so upset with myself because I . . . I gave her the disinfectant. "Yeah, just clean your hands and whatever you touched, because I don't know if it was wine or you know. I don't want you smelling like liquor or whatever." That's all I could do. I felt so bad. So after I took her to where she had to go, I pulled over. I texted Uber. I emailed them and texted. I said, "This man urinated in my car."

When I went to the gas station—you know, they have those paper towels that you pull down. I pulled out tons of them just to be sure; and when I wiped that backseat, that backseat was soaked. You could see the yellowness, and I said "Damn." Grown man and obviously very successful. . . . I feel bad because I had to lie to this woman about what her hand went into, because if I had told her the truth, we would be in trouble.

Although urine and vomit are not generally considered to be dangerous from a public health standpoint, basic health precautions generally call for gloves and eye protection—items that are rarely available when drivers find themselves cleaning a vehicle at a gas station or when passengers encounter such surprises. Although drivers can contact Uber and file a complaint against the passenger, Uber is notorious for being difficult to contact. Contact is generally limited to email and tweets. And every day with a dirty car is another day of missed work and income. While drivers can file for a cleaning fee of up to two hundred dollars, some feel the hassle isn't worth it—they'd rather clean the mess themselves so they can get back on the road that much faster. In addition to paying to get the car shampooed, Gerald took the rest of the evening off while the car dried: "I was so pissed, because as soon as she got out, you know, I couldn't get nobody else in the car."

PROTECTING WORKERS IN THE NEW ECONOMY

These stories suggest that working in the so-called sharing economy both increases the risk that workers will get hurt on the job and forces them to assume sole financial responsibility for dealing with any such injuries to themselves or their property. But it doesn't have to be that way. Not all sharing economy companies embrace the independent contractor model. Some start-ups have made an active decision to pay workers as employees, with all of the protections that entails—and without destroying their business model.

For instance, MyClean, a New York–based on-demand cleaning service, originally contracted with local cleaning companies that had their own W-2 employees. The company soon moved to hiring workers as employees. According to a blog posting on their website, this move to employees was integral in growing the company from a bootstrapped start-up to a force of more than one hundred cleaners, and it helped the company increase monthly revenue from fifteen thousand dollars to more than three hundred thousand in just three years. Paying workers as employees strengthened the company and its reputation by improving customer satisfaction, leading to reduced customer-acquisition costs. MyClean's CEO, Michael Scharf, explained, "We see [independent contractors] as a legal risk. We also want, for lack of a better word, control—the ability to manage, dispatch, train, have processes in place for what our end service looks like. We wanted MyClean to have one consistent level of service."

Munchery, a food delivery service, also pays workers as employees. Unlike Uber or TaskRabbit or Airbnb, Munchery includes all of its available positions on one page of its website—there's not a separate site for delivery personnel as opposed to programmers. In addition, each listing notes, "Unlike other companies who hire drivers and couriers, you are an employee of Munchery, not a contractor. As Munchery employees, you get all the perks and benefits associated with being an employee!"

Even without making workers full employees, some start-ups are taking steps to protect them from workplace dangers. In July 2014, Postmates, a sharing economy delivery service, announced that it was offering its couriers full access to general liability insurance, auto excess insurance, and accidental occupational liability while on duty. Although most transportation and delivery services, such as Uber and Lyft, offer general liability insurance to protect individuals hurt by workers, the Postmates accidental occupational liability policy is otherwise unmatched by any competitor (as of this writing). The policy, which has a fifty-thousand-dollar limit, covers medical expenses for injuries incurred while on the job.[31]

Fortunately, for Cody, a twenty-two-year-old African American male, he was on a run for Postmates when he crashed his bike a few months before we met. "I was coming down Fifth Avenue and Twenty-Second. So, you know, Twenty-Second is a straight lane. I had to edge out. . . . You know people in Manhattan. They go across even though they're ahead of the light. They think that they've got it," he said, referring to the documented practice of New Yorkers stepping into the street to cross before the walk signal is triggered.[32] "So first I'm yelling, 'Move away!' And the boyfriend of the lady gets over, and the lady just stood there."

Cody tried to dodge her. "I went left, she went left. I went right, she went right. I stopped. By the time I fully stopped, the impact of my bike hit her. And I grabbed her so she wouldn't go into the street. I grabbed her to swing around with her. So I hit the back of my head; but I had a lot of hair, so I didn't get a full impact. But her, she got knocked out."

"There was a car coming, too, next to me. So if I hit her, the car would hit her, too—and it would have been worse," he said, explaining why he swung around with the woman. "So I grabbed her. I hit her, grabbed her, and turned. And so my back hit, hit the floor."

Even though he landed on his back and head—and wasn't wearing a helmet—the most severe damage was to his leg. When he landed, his leg was caught near the wheel and folded backward, tearing a ligament. He was in the hospital for two days and then in a rigid knee brace for two months. The accident destroyed his bike and the brace prevented him from riding—pausing both his livelihood and his main form of transportation to college classes. He had to use a cane to get around.

"I had to take the bus. Hard for me to get into the bus. People were rushing me," he said. He started physical therapy and acupuncture, and eventually he began biking recreationally, ignoring the pain in his leg. "[The physical therapist] was like, 'If you feel pain, just tell me.' And I was like, 'I do feel pain, but I don't want to acknowledge the pain.' He was like, 'This is not good.' I was like, 'Yeah, it's not good, but this is how I've been dealing with my life, because I play soccer.' I go on the field. You're not coming off . . . because of the pain. You're just gonna wait until the game is done."

As a twenty-two-year-old full-time student, Cody was covered under his mother's insurance—and the Postmates policy. The bill for his injuries was split between his medical coverage and the Postmates insurance plan. "Postmates insures you. Like if you get in an accident while working, you have to send them an email. And if [someone is] trying to sue you, they will try to help you with the case and everything," he said. "It's a way of safety for us because we're working for them "

The rhetoric against making workers employees tends to argue that doing so would limit workers' freedom: people might be required to work forty hours a week or report for shifts that don't fit their schedule. But Cody's experience as a bike messenger for Postmates, a sharing economy service, suggests that workers *can* be covered for injuries that arise on the job, while still experiencing the flexibility that is often seen as the prime appeal of this work. Or as Cody put it, "If something happened while we're on the platform, it's basically their job to help us if we need it."

The sharing economy—rather than moving the world of work forward—is returning us to the workplace of the early industrial age, where workers had minimal workplace-safety protection and individuals injured on the job had no recourse for physical impairments or the loss of income.

Likewise, just as workers had no recourse for on-the-job injuries, they have no protections from sexual harassment. While "sharing is caring" is often bandied about as one of the reasons why people participate in free or low-cost sharing economy services,[33] it also lends itself to antiphrasis when workers find themselves in sexually uncomfortable situations, or when others incorporate sex into their understanding of customer service.

5 Sharing Is Caring

"Do you want to go back to my place?"

Homes are generally considered to be private, intimate locations. Inviting someone to your home can be a signal of friendship, sexual desire, or familial closeness. We rarely let outsiders into our bedrooms or onto our couches. We teach children to never open the door to strangers and to lock the door when their parents leave for work. At the same time, the sharing economy, with its focus on peer-to-peer service, often relies on unknown people entering the home of a fellow unknown either to cook (Kitchensurfing), or to sleep (Airbnb), or to clean, make minor repairs, or assemble furniture (TaskRabbit). Meanwhile, Lyft and Uber and other app-driven car services involve people getting in a stranger's vehicle—violating one of the first "stranger danger" rules that many children learn.

In response to many people's leeriness of strangers, sharing economy companies often promote their background screening mechanisms. For example, TaskRabbit's website notes that Taskers must pass an identity check, are screened for criminal offenses, and must attend an orientation. Uber drivers in New York City are required to undergo the same background checks and fingerprinting as taxi drivers. Drivers in other cities and states, however, may undergo only a background check that looks for criminal records within the last seven years; critics have alleged that even such minimal background checks have been easily sidestepped.[1] Airbnb relies on Facebook or LinkedIn identity verifications, while the Kitchensurfing marketplace's background checks for chefs seem to have been limited to a test meal audition in the platform's corporate kitchen.

In addition, most companies promote the idea that their workers are insured and bonded. If something does go wrong—if a TaskRabbit drops a flat-screen TV, or if a passenger is injured in an Uber—the damage is covered. For instance, TaskRabbit's website notes that every task has guaranteed insurance coverage of up to one million dollars, before quickly noting that this "is secondary coverage to any insurance or policies you already have in place. These would include medical insurance coverage, renter's insurance, homeowner's insurance or an umbrella policy."

Even though workers are screened and insured, clients are not. The terms of service ostensibly prevent clients from setting up multiple accounts, but as long as one has access to multiple email addresses and credit cards, it's very easy to create numerous identities. Worker profiles are often much more complete than those of clients and include a photo and short biography. TaskRabbit, in particular, requires workers to supply additional information for their profiles before it allows them to "pass" orientation. As a result, clients can generally rest assured that they have a fairly good idea of who they're hiring or letting into their homes, but workers don't have the same luxury. In addition, to protect identities, TaskRabbit provides only the first name and the first initial of a customer's or worker's last name. Unless there is an unusual spelling or additional details, Googling for more information is nearly impossible.

Illustrative of the possible danger of entering a stranger's abode, several TaskRabbits told me that one Tasker had accepted a gig to clean a man's boat, but that their follow-up conversations led the Tasker to become suspicious of his task description. The woman looked her client up online and learned that he was a convicted sex offender. She quickly cancelled the task.

Although it's impossible to determine if this story is a true account, even if it is an urban legend, the fact that it was repeated to me several times suggests a sense of discomfort with the imbalance of background checking and resulting risk in the sharing economy. As Jasmine, a twenty-three-year-old worker, put it:

Well, I don't know how they do it now; but before, I felt like they would let anybody get on the website as a client. But it was so strict to be a Tasker. And I didn't like that, because sometimes I would get people who wouldn't have a profile picture [and] they would have no reviews. They would basically have nothing on their page, but they want to hire you. And I'm like, how is that fair that we have to basically give them blood, and then they will let anybody come on the website? I just feel like you can't say you're worried about our safety if you allow any type of person to be on the website. . . . I think they should definitely go through a background check, too, or something. They need something to verify that they're a real person. . . . Just because I haven't had any [bad] experiences, doesn't mean someone else hasn't. I have no idea what other people might have been through. Or, even if they didn't go through the task and it was sketchy, maybe they thought it was sketchy before they got there and wanted to cancel. I don't know. I just think for the safety aspect, it should be verified on both ends.

"THEY LOOK FOR OPPORTUNITIES EVERYWHERE"

None of the workers I interviewed, for any of the services, had been sexually assaulted on the job. But even though my interview guide didn't include any questions on sexual harassment, a surprisingly large number of workers mentioned sexually uncomfortable situations. Jasmine noted that some TaskRabbit clients were especially generous when she was in their home: "'Have some wine. Do you want to smoke [marijuana]?' Like, 'I'm okay. Thank you. I have a job after this. I have to get home.' Those are usually the guys."

Jasmine also noted that she sometimes was hit on, often through a text message after the task. And then there was the cleaning task where she wasn't exactly hit on, but there seemed to be a invitation of some sort on the table.

I had one job where, [when] I went the first time, he wasn't there. He left his key. I cleaned the house. He had his lotion on the side of the table, soiled sheets, like obviously there was some rough-and-tumble before. Okay. So that was, I think, the first test. The second time I went, he wasn't there again. I did this job three times. It was always the same situation—you know, same dirty-sheet situation, lotion next to the bed, box of condoms, wine on the table. Like, you know what's going on. So again I'm just like, "Whatever." I clean it up. I have my gloves. Blind eye, I'm here to help.

Third time, he was there. I don't know how the conversation came up; but he was like, "Does anyone ever hit on you?" All awkward: "Anyone ever hit on you?" I'm like, "Sometimes it gets really uncomfortable." I'm just speaking as myself, so I'm not thinking of the context. "Yeah, sometimes it's uncomfortable when I clean for some men and they hit on me or . . ." And I said something to that regard. He's like, "Okay."

And two minutes later he's like, "I got all my stuff. I'm going to go to the café across the street so I'm out of your way." I was like, "Oh, okay." And I thought to myself, "Oh my God, was he trying to . . . ?" I think he was testing me those last two times. I don't know—like they look for opportunities everywhere.

Getting hit on while working isn't limited to female Taskers. Twentysomething Austin was the only Tasker outside of New York City whom I interviewed. A full-time engineer, he was a true example of a Striver. Married, with a relatively high income, he took on TaskRabbit work only in the evenings and on weekends, which served as a source of "quick easy money for beer or whatever." In three weeks of tasking, Austin completed more than twenty tasks, ranging from picking up and delivering pillows to a home to installing 250-pound storage shelves on the ceiling of a client's garage, directly above a Porsche and several Range Rovers—a project he described as "a little bit intimidating."

> I would say out of the twenty tasks I've had, most of them have been—it's different—it's different clients. So some of them are older women that just physically can't do it. Some of them are lazy people, some of them are guys, whatever, middle-aged guys that just don't have the ability. But there definitely have been several younger girls or women that, I think, if I was single [chuckles], I think I probably could have gotten a date.
>
> In all honestly it almost seemed like that was what they're looking for. . . . It seems like they definitely were looking for something, but when I said I was married, they're like, "Oh, okay." So yeah, I can definitely see it being like a sort of pseudo-dating service. Because a good-looking guy comes in and he's handy.

Another male Tasker, Shaun, found that a fairly standard task—packing and moving boxes—took a rather unusual turn when he found himself privy to a private conversation that he was "trying my best to forget about."

It was an older woman and younger man. I was packing, and then they were having this argument, not in front of me, but in the bedroom. I heard a few things which kind of sounded off, but I didn't really pay too much attention. And then it turns out that the people I thought were a couple were actually mother and son. And they were talking about incest behavior. . . . The son just came out and looks at me like, "You didn't hear anything at all, did you?" I was like, "Nope." He's like, "Okay."

When we were done, the son stepped out and his girlfriend came into the apartment. They were speaking, and she was speaking to the mother, all normal. And so I left, and the girlfriend came by, and she's like, "Oh, I saw you earlier." I'm like, "Don't mind me, I'm just moving help. I'm leaving." And then she said, "Just so you know, my boyfriend has this close relationship with his mother." And then I said, "I don't want to know, I'm just leaving." You know: Just let me go, I really didn't want to hear anything about it anymore.

And then she's like, "You know they're moving," and I said, "Yeah, I understand." She's like, "I always want to get revenge," and I'm like, "No."

And my mind is like: "No, I shouldn't entertain this conversion any further." It gets to a point where she started having this kind of fetish, and then I'm like, I don't like where this conversation is going. So I say, "I have to see someone about a horse," and then I just excused myself and left. I felt very uncomfortable.

Many Taskers provided errand-running services or were hired as one-day temps with local companies; as a result, Taskers found themselves in people's private homes, with the clients, only a fraction of the time. Kitchensurfing chefs, by virtue of the service's focus on providing a chef-created meal in the comfort of one's home, almost always found themselves in people's homes and interacting with their customers one-on-one. Perhaps unsurprisingly, they also reported more interactions with sexual overtones or other situations that simply made them feel uncomfortable.

For instance, Roxanne, twenty-seven, a Kitchensurfing chef with colorful hair and assorted body art, had several clients ask to take selfies with her, including one client whom she described as "weirding" her out:

So this guy wanted to take a selfie with me. He was helping me cook. Then he tried to invite me his rooftop to have dinner with him because his girlfriend didn't show up, and I was like, "No, I'm going to leave." This is too much. *[Laughing.]* This is too much. *[Laughing.]*

I was like, "No, I hope you enjoy your meal and everything." He was like, "Yeah, it's really good; you should like stay." 'Cause he apparently just moved to that apartment, so he's really ecstatic about it. But the same time, I was like, "I don't really want to go have dinner with you on your rooftop." *[Laughing.]*

I just make excuses. I'm like, "Oh, unfortunately I have another booking, so, you know, maybe some other time, maybe I'll see you around again." I try to leave it civil and that stuff; I try to make sure the situation doesn't end up coming off badly, just try to leave it like: "No, you know, thank you anyway, but I'm going to head out," or something to that extent. I don't just plainly say, "No, you weirded me out. Now, good-bye."

Just as workers have to be careful about how they convey pain or injury on the job, sharing economy workers also need to be cognizant of how they come across when a client is hitting on them or otherwise suggesting something that makes the worker uncomfortable. Roxanne is careful to be polite as she turns down what sounds suspiciously like an offer for a romantic rooftop dinner date.

Kitchensurfing workers were not usually shown their client reviews, but the company solicited and reviewed feedback from clients. No one suggested that they would lose their sharing economy gig work if they declined an invitation, but such invitations often created uncomfortable situations for workers and sounded suspiciously close to sexual harassment.

BACKGROUND ON SEXUAL HARASSMENT

Under Title VII of the Civil Rights Act of 1964, sexual harassment is considered a form of sex discrimination. The US Equal Employment Opportunity Commission states that "unwelcome sexual advances, requests for sexual favors, and other verbal or physical conduct of a sexual nature constitute sexual harassment when this conduct explicitly or implicitly affects an individual's employment, unreasonably interferes with an individual's work performance, or creates an intimidating, hostile, or offensive work environment."

Sexual harassment is hardly a new concept. Sexual coercion or unwanted sexual relations imposed by superiors on their work subordinates was a regular component of slavery.[2] Likewise women who worked in domestic service or in mills or shops often reported sexual advances from their male employers.[3] In the late nineteenth century, the Women's Christian Temperance Union attempted to reform the laws protecting women from sexual predation, but their efforts were primarily focused on a national campaign to raise the age of consent in statutory rape.[4]

Even after the 1964 Civil Rights Act, the courts often refused to recognize sexual harassment, sometimes deciding that it was a personal matter, simply an assault that occurred at work, or even that it was "natural and inevitable and nothing that the law could reasonably expect to eradicate from work." In regard to the claim that sexual harassment was discrimination on the basis of sex, the courts often argued that it could happen to men or women, and that even if women were the ones harmed, it was "not inflicted on all women, only those who refused their supervisor's advances." The court case *Barnes vs. Costle* (1977) included the comment by Judge Spottswood Robinson that a bisexual supervisor's efforts to win sexual favors did not count as gender discrimination, since those efforts were not focused solely on one sex, and again, the discrimination was not on the basis of sex but on the refusal to perform sexual acts.[5]

SHARING ECONOMY WORKERS AS MODERN-DAY TEMPS

A number of writers and researchers have studied how sexualized conduct and sexual harassment are used to maintain workplace segregation. For instance, economist Barbara Bergman has detailed how sexual harassment of a woman focuses on insults and "mock propositions to engage in sexual relations" as a sign of contempt and "out of a hope that she will be made sufficiently uncomfortable to abandon the job."[6] Lin Farley, who coined the term *sexual harassment* in 1975, suggests that "the function of sexual harassment in nontraditional jobs is to keep women out: its function in the traditional female job sector is to keep women down."[7] Other models for understanding sexual harassment in the workplace suggest that inequities in structural or formal power within an organization may lead bosses to abuse their position by harassing workers.[8] Yet research also shows that harassers may be more likely to be coworkers, and that harassers may at times be subordinates.[9] In the sharing economy, which prides itself on the idea of peers hiring peers, hiring one's peer can still lead to an asymmetrical power situation, which may further increase the incidence of sexually uncomfortable situations.

Researchers have focused on how the "gendered processes of organizations" and "doing gender" are related to the organization of work and sexual harassment.[10] For example, temporary workers must often be deferential owing to the feminized and powerless status of their job. As a result, this increases workers' vulnerability and potential for experiencing sexual harassment by magnifying an asymmetrical power relationship. Temps are often on the jobsite for a full day, if not several weeks or months, and their transitory nature has often been seen as the explanation for their isolation or for employers' failure to remember their names.[11]

The temporary workers of the 1990s do not merely resemble today's sharing economy workers—in many ways they are exactly alike. In parts of the West Coast, such as Seattle and San Francisco, companies even have specially marked doors for "runners," as the temporary workers are often called. *Wired* described TaskRabbit as "particularly addictive for executives at the pathologically understaffed startups of San Francisco, where the phrase 'we can get a runner to do that' has become common parlance."[12] Although originally marketed only to consumers, for about a year, TaskRabbit expanded to include a business-to-business tier, TaskRabbit for Business, which targeted corporations in need of short-term workers for street-team marketing (workers who "hit the streets" to market a product or service) or supply delivery, as well as event staff. *TechCrunch* reports that the goal was to make it easier for companies to quickly staff short-term jobs, with a product that was "more reliable than online classifieds and less costly than traditional temp agencies."[13] At one point, TaskRabbit for Business had sixteen thousand businesses signed up and began handling compliance paperwork, including payroll taxes, workers' compensation, and unemployment insurance for corporate workers who were hired as temporary employees (known as W2 workers).[14]

In addition to the transient nature of their work, temporary clerical workers also shared several other strong similarities with sharing economy workers. Workers at one agency were told to think of themselves as guests rather than as laborers and "were reminded that a polite guest neither challenges nor otherwise risks offending his or her host."[15] Aside from helping enforce the emotional work of smiling and being cooperative, the guest role also "enforced passivity by rendering any complaining or self-assertion by temporary workers on assignment as inappropriate."[16] One can't help but be reminded that workers experiencing an on-the-job injury or who simply need a break also must also be careful of how they present the request or their discomfort. Sharing economy workers have to contend with the risk of clients posting negative reviews and reducing these workers' marketability; likewise, temporary workers who don't show the correct level of deference can also find themselves out of work when clients complain to agency staff. The temporary component of the work may also free clients to behave badly—if they don't expect to see the worker again, they may brush aside the social expectations of polite and professional behavior.

ANYTHING GOES WHEN "IT'S ONLY TEMPORARY"

Workers being on their best behavior by demonstrating deference and friendliness may be interpreted as responding to flirtatious behavior. In her research on waiters and waitresses at five types of restaurants, Elaine Hall found that while males and females were expected to "job flirt," there were higher expectations for women to exhibit sexual availability as part of their job, and customers seemed to feel encouraged to harass female staff in a sexualized manner.[17]

The risk that friendliness can be construed in a sexual manner is well illustrated by Roxanne's experience in cooking for a couple.

> ROXANNE: I had one [laughing]. I had this really cool couple, and again it was one of the couples that [acted as if] we were all hanging out. They were my last couple, so we were sitting around and talking, sharing stories, blah, blah. They asked about the meal. And I didn't know they were swingers; the wife tried to hit on me and it was very weird. She was really hot, but I was like, "Okay, this is a really random turn; I'm usually going with things, but you guys are married, I'm not, it's not my life."
>
> INTERVIEWER: How does that come up?

ROXANNE: *[Laughing.]* I guess the way we were talking. I guess they thought I was flirting with her. Because, I guess, sometimes it can seem like I'm flirting with people. I'm really not. I'm just really friendly. *[Laughing.]* I really don't flirt with anybody. I'm just really just friendly, and I guess they thought that's what was going on. Then they went to go talk, and then the wife comes back. She's sitting next to me.

ROXANNE: She's like, "So how do you feel about, blah, blah, blah," and I'm like, "I don't care; it's your life. Live it." And then the questions starting getting a little more personal. I'm like, "Are you hitting on me—is this what's happening right now?" I'm like, "Your husband's right there, number one. That's the number one thing; number two, no. I'm very flattered, but no, I'm sorry. I'm going to go now, thank you for the drinks. I'm glad you guys enjoyed the food.

INTERVIEWER: I mean, how personal were these questions getting . . .

ROXANNE: They were getting to like, "Are you into certain bedroom extracurricular type situations?"

Being asked about one's sexual proclivities while at work, or being invited to engage in a sex act with a client, would generally be verboten. But in the sharing economy, somehow anything goes. None of the sharing economy workers I interviewed described these experiences as sexual harassment. This isn't unusual. As Rogers and Henson put it, "Particularly with verbal or hostile environment harassment, temporary workers were likely to ignore the harassment or fail to label it as sexual harassment at all."[18] Workers who ignored the sexual harassment or brushed it off as "nothing major" ignored the behavior because "it's only temporary"—a response that is also prevalent among sharing economy workers. Sharing economy workers often peppered their descriptions of these sexually uncomfortable experiences with terms like "weird" and "bizarro-land" and laughter, suggesting that workers felt the situation was uncomfortable or felt "marked" in some way.[19]

The language of the workers highlights one of the challenges of working in the gig economy. Owing to the focus on community, trust, and peer-to-peer work, workers face heightened expectations in terms of emotional work. Part of the appeal of the sharing economy is that individuals are hiring "real people" and there's an expectation of "authentic" interaction. The other issue is the home-based nature of much of the work. Homes are places of intimacy, and there are different standards for behavior when someone enters a home. I am unlikely to spend much time interacting with a maintenance worker who changes the fluorescent bulbs in my office, but if that same worker comes into my home to change the filter on my air conditioner, I will probably offer him or her a glass of water and make a comment about the weather. The private-home aspect also changes the equation. As the work happens behind closed doors, behavior that would not be acceptable in a workplace—such as asking about one's sexual interests—appears more acceptable.

Additionally, the male-dominated environs of Silicon Valley seems to have a particular issue with sexual harassment. "In the same way that female engineers and start-up founders struggle to report harassment for fear of retaliation or lost funding, gig economy workers are in precarious positions," says Sam Levin.[20] Workers who report sexually uncomfortable situations risk being viewed as problem workers and often note their own concerns about the possibility of being deactivated for complaining.[21] Finally, because of the lip service paid to community and trust, when workers experience situations that appear to be sexual harassment they don't identify it as such. Instead, the focus is on feeling "uncomfortable." This actually makes sense when one revisits the idea of community and trust—we expect to feel comfortable in a situation that promises these two ideals.

Although Roxanne told Kitchensurfing about her selfie-taking, dinner-inviting client, she did not discuss the sexual invitation from her swinging clients. Describing herself as usually situated in midtown Manhattan, she noted that the clients lived uptown and she was unlikely to see them again. "I don't think they knew you could request your chef. I'm glad they kind of don't, because I don't know how I'd feel if I went back there. I would probably just be like, 'Hey, what's up, guys?'" she said in an awkward tone.

Perhaps because Kitchensurfing chefs are almost always in direct contact with clients, they find themselves exposed to sexual behavior more often than other sharing economy workers. For instance, asking Randall, forty-three, a Kitchensurfing marketplace chef about "really memorable experiences" revealed a gig cooking for what he first described as a "sex club" before clarifying that it was a "swingers, wife-swap-type party. Very bizarro-land."

Much in the way that clerical temporary workers are sometimes urged to dress more sexily and present a specific image, Randall was required by his client to wear a specific style of dress—his first sign that the event would be different.[22] "It was just going to be passed hors d'oeuvres, and he requested that I wear my chef's coat, which I don't wear any more. I'm refusing. I don't want to wear it any more. I wore it for twenty-five years. He was like, 'I want you to wear a chef coat.' And he was specific. 'I want you to wear . . .' Normally I would say, 'No, I'm not going to do that.' And then I was like, 'Fine. What the hell. Why not? Let's see if it fits,'" he said, laughing. "And then he was like, 'Make sure you have a waiter who wears specifically this.' 'Okay.'"

Except for the clothing requirements, Randall said he didn't really get "the vibe" of what the party was going to be through his emails or other conversations with the client.

> So I get there, and it's one of those UWS apartments. It's one of those classic prewar ones, and it's very gothic inside and everyone seemed kind of cool. It was probably twenty-five people, and they're talking; and then I hear negotiations. They're negotiating the sexual [activities that'll be] happening, and I'm thinking, "Huh. Swingers club."
>
> And there's different rooms and different playrooms and swings and the whole thing. And then I'm, like, going, "Should I be wearing gloves working in this kitchen?" [Laughing.]

When his staff seemed incredulous, Randall was quick to remind them not to get involved, no matter what happened. Describing it as "an experience," he was quick to note, "They were great. They tipped great. They were friendly. It was fun."

The speed with which Randall explained away the experience, and even his laughter, brings to mind Marvin Scott and Stanford Lyman's work on accounts. They describe an account as "a statement made by a social actor to explain unanticipated or untoward behavior—whether that behavior is his own or that of others.[23] Randall noted that he didn't know that the party would involve swingers (an appeal to defeasibility) but, at the same time, was quick to justify the experience by focusing on the fact that the partygoers were great, good tippers, and friendly.

SERVING AS A "STRANGER IN THE HOUSE"

In addition to the temporary nature of the work, sharing economy workers—digital records and background checking aside—are essentially strangers and, unless specifically requested, are unlikely to be seen again. Randall suggested that his status as a "stranger in the house" is part of his appeal to clients.

> RANDALL: Another favorite thing is for me to go to the house and they go and screw while I'm there.
>
> INTERVIEWER: Seriously?
>
> RANDALL: Yes. Very popular. Say a couple is having their ten friends over, and they're not there yet. So I usually get there two hours before. So, say someone hasn't showered yet, and they're like, "Hey, the kitchen is over here. I have to go take a shower." And then they both disappear. And then you hear the shenanigans. And I'm like . . . First, I thought it was like, "Oh, okay." But now I think it's a thing, too.
>
> INTERVIEWER: Really? Like an exhibitionist thing?
>
> RANDALL: Like a thing.
>
> INTERVIEWER: How do you feel about that?
>
> RANDALL: I'm okay with it. Whatever. Who cares. I don't care. If that's what they need. Cool. Whatever. It has happened on multiple occasions. The first time, I was with [a colleague], and I was like, "I think they're fucking in there." And he was like [said sternly], "They are."

The experience has become common enough that Randall now takes bets with his staff about what will happen while they're on-site. His bet? That the couple will be "doing it." "I usually win. Most of the time it's yes," he said, laughing. "Maybe it's something that people think about, they fantasize about. Strangers in the house or something, and I provide that. I have to be kind of confidential anyway. They probably think I'm going to be confidential because I'm cooking for them or something. I guess it provides them anonymity to a degree. It's great. It's great."

As much as Randall stressed that these experiences are "great" or that he didn't care, the fact that they came up so readily in our conversation suggests that perhaps a part of him did care. In the United States, very-high-income employers tend to utilize "an American version of the 'upstairs, downstairs' segregation of master and servant" that involves a level of distance.[24] Yet Randall is a professional, not a servant, and his sense of uncertainty about the rules of secrecy and familiarity came up when he discussed how the clients "probably think" their behavior warranted confidentiality owing to the cooking relationship.

It should be noted that not all of the sexually uncomfortable interactions involved the workers directly. Randall explained that sometimes his services were combined with Airbnb and used for the seduction of others:

RANDALL: Usually the younger guys, they'll get an Airbnb of a loft down here in SoHo. Pawn it off as their place. Have me come in as their chef and cook . . . to get the girl. But see, I'm always against it, because that's not the long-term thing.

INTERVIEWER: How often does that happen?

RANDALL: A lot. A good amount of time.

INTERVIEWER: And they tell you what's going on?

RANDALL: No, I figure it out within a few minutes. First of all, it's an Airbnb, because there's nothing there. And you can tell no one's lived there—there's no pictures or nothing. And he comes in, and he's probably a second-year on Wall Street or some finance guy. And then she comes in, and he's like, "This is my place, blah, blah, blah." And my favorite is when she's not into him, or she's into him because "I just applied to the country club down in Delaware or down east. I just came back from Washington on Amtrak" or some bullshit. And as soon as he goes to the bathroom, she's calling her girlfriends. "Uhh, yeah . . ." I love it. . . .

INTERVIEWER: So when do you leave?

RANDALL: I'm usually like, "Is there anything else I can get for you?" [And the guy says,] "Uh, no." Sometimes I know, too, that I need to get her out of there. . . . Because it's not going to go any further. And sometimes a girl needs an escape hatch. "Is there anything else I can get for you?" She's like, "Oh, yeah, I have to go too."

INTERVIEWER: And does she talk to you on the way out?

RANDALL: I'm like, "How did that go?" And she's like, "Oh my God." *[Laughing.]* I'm thinking he probably paid five hundred dollars for the Airbnb. He paid me five hundred dollars, so he's into this a thousand dollars and you ran out. There are times when it works. But 80 percent [of the time] it doesn't.

Randall's calculation of the funds spent on the date without a sexual return on investment, may sound callous, but it's actually a fairly common perspective. As Marina Adshade notes in her book *Dollars and Sex: How Economics Influences Sex and Love,* research by psychologists Susan Basow and Alexandra Minieri suggests that while female participants in the study did not feel that paying for an expensive dinner entitled a man to sex, they did feel that his entitlement increased with the price of the date. And men felt more strongly than women that an expensive date increased the obligation to have sex.[25]

Finally, sometimes workers find that they're involved in tasks where the task itself is sexually uncomfortable. When I asked Cody, a twenty-two-year-old black male, if he'd had any weird deliveries in his work for UberRUSH (Uber's delivery service) and Postmates, he told me about accepting a 10 p.m. pickup that needed to be brought to midtown Manhattan, about forty blocks' distance. He expected that the run would take him less than twenty minutes, even if he went slowly, so he quickly accepted the gig. As with many tasks offered by Postmates, UberRUSH, and TaskRabbit, time is truly of the essence, and workers who hesitate and read the whole description of a task before accepting often find that someone accepts it before they get the chance. "I had to go to a dildo store," Cody told me. "I'm not against nobody's sex or nothing. I'm just like, when I got it: 'The way I see it, it's a store." So I'm like, 'Okay. That's an easy run." So I went to the store. I didn't even read the bottom line [of the request]. The only thing it said: 'Long black dildo.' So I look at it; I'm like, 'Did I read what I read?' There's 'long black dildo.'"

Embarrassed to say the words, he tried showing the request to the staff member.

I'm like, "Can I get this?" The guy was like, "Oh, so I see you want a long black dildo." I'm like, "No! I have one. I don't need an extra one." So he gave it to me. He wrapped it and put it in a bag. And the other one, at the bottom, was: "I need an eating . . ." It was some eating thing. Some sexual eating . . . I don't . . . I'm sorry about what I'm gonna say. You put it on the vagina of the girl. And you eat.

So, I was like, are you serious? Like, this is the weirdest delivery I had. And I got this? Surprise and surprise. It's a girl. And she looked at me. She was like, "Are you Cody?" I'm like, "Yes." She looked left, looked right. "Do you have my stuff?" "Yes, ma'am." "Can I . . ." I give it to her. I'm leaving.

She was like, "You don't wanna come and see what's gonna happen?" I'm like, "I'm not . . . I'm not going in there." It was a sex party. . . . I'm like, "Excuse me, I'm out." That was the weirdest thing I ever did.

Like other sharing economy workers who have found themselves in sexually uncomfortable situations, Cody is careful to be polite, saying "excuse me" as he declines the offer of sexual activity and leaves the client's home.

SEXUALLY CHARGED EXPERIENCES FOR WORKERS

As with many aspects of the sharing economy, there is not just one side to the story. Even though many of these experiences suggest an awkward encounter for the worker, there are also times when the sharing economy seems to provide a sexual buffet to the worker, as illustrated by the experience of Yosef, twenty-seven, an Airbnb host and self-described hotelier.

Most Airbnb hosts that I interviewed were hesitant to tell me about where they lived. Our interviews were usually conducted at various coffee shops in the East Village, and mentions of their apartments were often somewhat vague—they lived in a building on Tenth Street or "around the corner" from our chosen coffee shop. Sometimes these descriptions were accompanied by a vague wave in one direction. No one ever told me their specific address or apartment number.

So when Yosef responded to my interview request by suggesting that we meet in his West Village apartment, promising me a tour of his Airbnb rental, I was surprised and more than a bit concerned. Meeting a stranger in the privacy of his home seemed like a bad idea. I was also confused about his mention of a West Village apartment—I'd deliberately focused my recruitment efforts on the East Village, which has one of the highest numbers of Airbnb rentals in Manhattan.[26]

I dug around online and learned that Yosef had been actively and publicly involved in Airbnb's public relations efforts in New York. With that reassurance, I told my husband where I was going to be and gave him strict instructions on how and when to check in—and what to do if I didn't respond promptly.

When I arrived at the apartment several minutes early, Yosef wasn't home, but he soon rounded the corner with a bag of juice and cookies for our interview. Upstairs, he gave me a short tour of his apartment, noting that the two-bedroom rent-stabilized walk-up was his home and his first Airbnb listing—he was responsible for up to twenty-five Airbnb guests per evening. With plans to one day become a professional hotelier, he wasn't letting his age or lack of degree deter him in the meantime. With assistance from his family, he rented two three-bedroom apartments in Manhattan's Upper West Side neighborhood that he listed for thirty-night stints as quasi-hostels, with up to two people per bedroom. He also managed ten listings owned by associates.

Since it was one of my last Airbnb interviews, I thought I'd already reached theoretical saturation—until I asked my standard last question: "Is there anything I haven't asked you that you think I should ask you?"

Yosef's response came quickly: "You didn't ask me about any, maybe, romantic stories that happened through Airbnb."

"Have you had romantic stories?" I asked.

He had. The first story was the tamest: Yosef told me about "clicking" with a young female guest whom he spent time with for three weeks—they cooked meals together, she met his friends, and they even visited his parents for a Shabbat dinner and attended an Airbnb conference. "And the romantic side was the fact that we slept together, cuddled. But I still saw her as my baby sister, because she was twenty, and my sister is—she's two years younger than me, but I see her as nineteen. And, yeah, I felt, definitely, affection, and a very tense vibe in the air. But in a way, I saw her as my guest and someone that I'm supposed to take care of, that she was like a baby sister."

There was something about his story that suggested he wanted to tell me more. I asked if he had slept with any of his other guests. He told me there were two incidents.

The first woman was a few years older and had broken up with her boyfriend of seven years shortly before renting Yosef's spare bedroom. Not realizing that he had a chance with the woman, he had taken two different women to bed during the course of her stay.

> And on her last night here, we went to a lounge or dance bar, and she told me, "You're very active," and she said what she found in the trash [condoms], and I told her, "Yeah, I'm sorry." And she said, "No, that's nice."
>
> And we came back home, and she—yeah, fuck it—so I put a condom on in like ten seconds, and then she said, "Whoa." Because, I mean, we already started, and I'm a very giving person. And once we were ready, I guess I just put it on too quick, and that was just what scared her. So she said, "Okay, wait, wait." And then I fell asleep.
>
> Woke up in my bed by myself, I'm like, "Oh my God, this is bad. This is really bad. What is she thinking?" And she said it was a fine sleep with me. And I had to ask her if we had sex, because I didn't know what happened.

As I was getting ready to leave, Yosef asked if I had time for another story, what he described as one of his "craziest experiences."

> YOSEF: A couple booked—actually, I saw only the guy's profile. And I thought, okay, it's a couple, cool. And they came in. He's in his forties, she's in her twenties. Attractive, kind of avant-garde kind of girl. You know, blue highlights, piercing, some tattoos. I'm like, well, cool, lucky guy; he's hanging with a young, attractive chick. After five days, she tells me, "Oh, we're not together. He just wanted to go to New York, and he offered to pay for my ticket, so I came with him." I'm like, "But you're sleeping in the same bed," and she's like, "Yeah, but he's disgusting, ew, you think I'm—" I'm like, "Oh, so you're not a couple."
>
> And then I'm like, oh, so she's not those kinds of girls that hang out with older guys that came with them or sleep with. So it always happens on the last night. I had work at 7 in the morning, but I stayed up until 4 a.m. They had a huge fight. She was mixing beer with Monster, the energy drink. I was just drinking some random Coke, and every time he went to smoke a cigarette upstairs, we made out. And I'm like, this—I just said, "This guy is going to kick the shit out of me if he knew what's going on."
>
> Eventually, he picked up on it, and he just told her, "That's the kind of girl you are: you just screw around." And I just stood up,

and I'm like, "I'm really sorry. She just said you guys are not together, so . . ." I just told him, like, "I'm sorry, I don't want this to be a part of, whatever." He's like, "No, no, that's fine," and he went to sleep. And then once he went to sleep, love, love, love. And it was fine.

INTERVIEWER: How were the reviews from that couple?

YOSEF: *[Laughter.]* [The first woman] gave me great reviews. She's like, "Yosef is the best host you can get." I wish she had written, "He gives good head," but she didn't. And, damn, what's her name . . . A—, A— or E—. I think they left an okay review, they didn't write any bad thing. They either didn't leave a review, or left an okay review. If it was a bad review, I'd remember.

Yosef's Airbnb sexual exploits aren't just about being a young man in a large city. He dreams of writing a book called *Sixty-Nine* that will detail his adventures. "So, like, I wanted to ask women that I've been with to write about our experience. Kind of like a review about me, but in a story method," he explained. "And then compile it to one book that is going to show the same guy from just sixty-nine different perspectives."

"The perspectives of sixty-nine women who've all slept with you?" I clarified.

"Yes," he said.

Yosef was likely an outlier. He was the only Airbnb host I met who volunteered that he had consummated his host-guest relationship. There may have been more hosts who had become involved with their guests, but if so, they didn't volunteer that information. Although all of my Airbnb host respondents rented their domestic space to strangers—often banking on a combination of intuition, online stalking skills, Airbnb insurance, and social network verification—most Airbnb interviewees were absent when a guest rented their home. Yosef was more open than most to sharing his space regularly.

One considerable difference may also be that Yosef is a Success Story who actively shares his space in addition to managing multiple other "entire apartment" listings. He is financially comfortable and can pick and choose his guests. Airbnb hosts generally prefer to rent their entire apartment because they can command a premium price for doing so, and they can avoid the inconvenience of interacting face-to-face with strangers in their space. For Success Stories and Strivers, renting an entire apartment on Airbnb is a way to finance a vacation, or the apartment serves as an investment property (as I discuss in chapter 7).

But for Strugglers and some Strivers, sharing their space is often a response to a lack of funds. For instance, Gabriele, twenty-seven, a Struggler and an international graduate student, generally preferred to rent her Crown Heights apartment when she traveled outside the city with her young son. "I don't usually do it, because I don't feel comfortable being in the same apartment with other people. But my apartment is big—I have three rooms, and it's just me and my son who live there. So sometimes when huge day-care bills come in and I can't handle them, I rent out a room. But I've just done that twice, I think. I have one room that I can completely shut off that I rent out." For Gabriele, sharing her space with a stranger was done only when financially necessary. Describing herself as "not superattached" to the apartment, she considers it to be a "valuable asset" that can be tapped to help pay bills or provide extra money for vacations.

Although some users spoke about renting out their apartments as shared rentals in order to meet people and be social, for most, doing a shared rental was simply necessary in order to stay in an apartment that they loved or considered a good deal. For instance, Rachel, thirty-eight, rented out her second bedroom on Airbnb after her longtime boyfriend moved out soon after renewing the lease. Likewise, Matthew, thirty-six, started renting his apartment on Airbnb as a way to get himself out of a financial bind. Falling into a depression after a restaurant he planned to open fell through, he was soon so broke that he found himself eating at the local street-meat cart on credit.[27]

Finally, one last characteristic that distinguishes Yosef from other Airbnb hosts is that he is single. Nearly all of my Airbnb respondents were in relationships, and the majority of those couples lived together. However, being single was not always a requirement for "hooking up" in the sharing economy. Muhammad, thirty-three, an Uber driver, had a young daughter and a pregnant wife. When I asked if he had any issues with passengers' behavior, he started talking about his late-night female passengers. "You're going to have some females come out of the club, by themselves, and they might be a little tipsy—meaning a little drunk—but they still control themselves and move around and talk normally. They will try to get you upstairs with them. They will talk to you," he said. "It's like, 'Oh, I had a good time, but I didn't find nobody.' A lot of females are horny."

I asked if he ever accepted any of the offers to go upstairs.

"You can just log out, and you're not working. After you finish the trip, you just log off, and you're not working anymore. You're free," he said. "You do whatever you want. . . . I mean, I look at it, it's okay. You're satisfying yourself, I mean, any person, after work."

Sleeping with a passenger is a violation of Uber rules, but the freedom to do so highlights the flexibility of the app. A driver who rents a yellow taxicab for a shift has a limited amount of time to earn back that cost. The driver of a black car has a dispatcher to contend with and a preset shift. But as the Uber advertisements remind potential workers, when one drives with Uber, this means: "No shifts, no boss, no limits." As a result, drivers can log out of the platform, and then log back in a few minutes or hours later. The flexibility of the app makes sleeping with passengers much more possible than a traditional car service does.

How often do app-based drivers have sex with their passengers? It's hard to say, and it's doubtful that Uber or Lyft will be researching or publicizing such statistics anytime soon. Officials with the Whisper website, an anonymous social media site that allows users to post secrets and confessions, say that they've "vetted accounts of several people who said they have had sex with an Uber or Lyft driver, and of drivers who said they had sex with customers. And based on things such as geo-location of the posts and direct inquiries, they said they have no reason to believe the posts are bogus."[28] When the former CEO of Uber calls the service "boob-er" because it improves his chances with the ladies, perhaps no one should be surprised when drivers or passengers treat a ride as more than a way home.[29]

Although the workplace protections dealing with safety and the right to unionize date back to the early industrial age and the beginning of the 1900s, American protections against sexual harassment are a direct outcropping of second-wave feminism. Some sharing economy supporters suggest that workplace protections are no longer needed—that the laws are outdated or no longer relevant—but even the newer workplace protections are no match for the sharing economy's bulldozing of workplace protections.

This economic movement forward into the past results in an undercutting of sexual harassment workplace protections. Not only is the issue of sexual harassment rarely touched on by the sharing economy companies, but also workers don't expect to *have* workplace protections. Behavior that would be unacceptable in a corporate office is ignored or explained away as "weird" when it occurs in an employer's bedroom or kitchen or when the work is allegedly focused on the egalitarianism of peer-to-peer connections. Instead of feeling free to identify this treatment as sexual harassment, workers who find themselves sexually approached by clients struggle to describe what exactly is going on, using terms like *bizarro-land* to demonstrate a sense of confusion and discomfort.

Sexual harassment is hardly the only illegal activity occurring in the gig economy. Workers sometimes find that their day's work includes a "dirty" element, since the anonymous nature of the gig economy enables the outsourcing of drug deliveries and scams to otherwise law-abiding workers. The gig economy upends our assumptions about work as an alternative to crime by turning workers into criminal accomplices who are hired for illegal or legally questionable activities. As the sharing economy rolls back worker protections, it also creates new opportunities for criminal enterprise.

6 All in a Day's (Dirty) Work

Around six feet tall, with broad shoulders and short black hair, Jamal (introduced in chapter 4) is a graduate from a prestigious university, a school where graduates prefer to think of themselves as creating sharing economy apps—not working for them. A self-described "social media guru," Jamal is soft-spoken and has a slight southern accent. When he gets nervous or feels self-conscious, he tends to mumble slightly, making it necessary to lean in to hear him. His Pinterest page, a tool for compiling online favorites, has dozens of followers, most of them women, and his board with the most "pins" features his ideal apartment layout, complete with a retro Nintendo-console coffee table. Clean-shaven, quick to smile, and a fan of hip-hop, he seems like your standard southern-grown, West Indian boy next door.

The son of a college professor, Jamal grew up down south and returned home after graduation. He spent a year working in Georgia to pay off a small student loan and save money. He planned to move to New York City and start a career in social media marketing. Jamal arrived in New York in February, a cold and wet time to arrive in the city, but a good time to get a jump on early spring job openings.

But New York was more expensive than he expected; and as a black man with a decidedly nonwhite name, he found that his job hunt took a while. His plan to bartend for extra money fell through. "Here in New York, places demand a certain type of person to be a bartender," he said. "He has to already have a bartending license, or he has to be a very attractive female, which I have neither," he admitted, laughing. When bartending and working as a restaurant server didn't pan out, Jamal joined TaskRabbit. He described it as "an opportunity to get some money in my pocket on demand, while being able to continue to apply for jobs and conduct interviews."

Jamal scheduled TaskRabbit gigs around his job interviews and developed a daily habit of checking TaskRabbit each morning to see what kinds of opportunities were posted. The most common listing was for delivery services. "So there'd probably be literally fifty or sixty delivery jobs within the hour," he said. "I'd find myself being able to make between at least twenty to fifty dollars a day, just off the deliveries."

If his bid for a job was accepted, he'd run out and do it. Sometimes his bid wouldn't be accepted, or it would be accepted but was for later in the day. In an effort to get more work, he would take his laptop to a Manhattan public library so he could "be where the action is." This strategy often resulted in his getting two to three tasks each day.

Jamal was fortunate to have relatives in New York; when he moved to the city, he stayed with them for several months, until family drama erupted. A month spent with friends in Washington, DC, wasn't enough of a cooling-off period. When he returned to New York, he discovered that he was essentially homeless: unable to stay with family, too broke to pay for an apartment sublease, and missing the requisite paystubs to show a landlord so he could rent an apartment of his own.

He moved into an illegal hostel that promised free housing in exchange for labor: six eight-hour shifts each week, working from 9 a.m. to 5 p.m. or from 5 p.m. to 1 a.m. Sometimes he worked a double shift of sixteen straight hours. The work included checking people into the hostel, recording their information, and photographing their passports, as well as a good deal of cleaning. "I swept, mopped the floors, cleaned bathrooms, did the laundry and the sheets, cleaned the hair from the shower," he said. "Oh my God, it was disgusting."

Living and working in the hostel meant a roof over his head and a place to keep his possessions, and the constant flux of people coming and going also provided a steady source of food. The hostel was hosted in a house, and in an effort to save money, guests took advantage of the kitchen facilities to cook meals. When visitors left, their extra food often remained. "I would get some of that food," Jamal said. Even so, it wasn't enough:

> I think I lost forty pounds that summer. I came to New York weighing 190-something, and then I went, like, 160, 150. I lost a lot of weight that year. . . . I guess when I look back at it, I did basically live under the poverty line. . . . I didn't eat as much because, literally, the money I made, I had to portion out my food and stretch it out. So I would make some spaghetti and make sure it lasts me five days. I would do whatever I can to try and spend as little money as possible.

Online reviews of the hostel note that it has a certificate of occupancy as a three-family house that has been filled with bunk beds, sleeping as many as ten people per floor in four- and six-person rooms. Reviews mention long waits for the three bathrooms, which were shared between as many as thirty people. Jamal knew that the house was an illegal hostel, and that the crowded home didn't conform to the fire code. "The house actually caught on fire. The whole house wasn't engulfed in flames—just a side of the house around the front door caught on fire," he said. "Well, the people I'm working with called the fire department, even though I told them not to. And you know what, when the fire department of New York comes, they destroy the house. So the house is basically destroyed, not because of the fire, [but] because the fire department destroyed the house with the ax and water damage and all that kind of stuff."

After the fire, Jamal spent a day with a girl he was dating and then began crashing on the couches of friends and distant relatives, eventually renting space for thirty-five dollars a night in another hostel, one he described as "even more disgusting." Without the option of working for room and board, TaskRabbit gigs took on additional importance. "I made sure I did TaskRabbit every day," he said. "So basically it was just some serious home game I played."

Jamal liked the TaskRabbit bidding system. "It felt like I had the power. It's just that I had the power to choose which job that I want to do," he said. "I see what people want, I get to choose. I get to choose for myself; I want to do it for them, and all that kind of stuff."

But in the summer of 2014, TaskRabbit pivoted from a bidding system to a hourly rate (discussed in chapter 2), and Jamal wasn't a fan of the new system. Suddenly it was harder for him to book tasks around his interview schedule. And it became even more important for him to accept the tasks he was chosen for, in order to keep his acceptance rate high and ensure he remained active on the platform. Soon after the pivot, Jamal was hired for what he thought was a standard errand task: pick up and deliver drugs from a pharmacy.

"I'd done it before, so I really didn't think anything of it," he said. But his last prescription pickup task had involved delivering the drugs to a location two blocks away. This one was a little different—while Jamal was on the way to the pharmacy, his customer called to say that she'd just moved to China and had forgotten to pick up her prescriptions before leaving; she needed Jamal to mail her the drugs. Then the woman's credit card was declined because she was out of the country. There was a lot of back-and-forth with the pharmacy. After a two-hour delay, Jamal was finally able to pick up the prescription.

"I got the drugs—and then I realized: this is a lot of drugs," he said. He took a photo of the extra-large pill bottles. "That's when I was, like—wait a minute. Is it legal to mail prescription drugs across the US border?" he said with a laugh. "I was just thinking to myself: don't you have to go through customs?" When he realized that the medicine would need to be mailed through DHL or FedEx, the client told him to hold on to the pills until she determined what needed to happen next.

> So I'm like, "Okay." Then after that, I talked to my friend, [and] she was like: I should call TaskRabbit and tell them what's happening. I was like, "Yeah. because it's been a week that I've carried around all this—not methamphetamine, but amphetamine pills and sleeping pills. And it's a lot—if I were to get caught with it, someone would think I'm running a meth lab."
>
> So I called TaskRabbit, told them what's happening. And at first, the guy said, "Well, it's illegal so you shouldn't do it." Then after five minutes, he puts me on hold and talks to upper management, because he's never had something like this happen before. So then I get a call five minutes later. "So you know what, I think you should do it, because the Tasker does whatever the person needs to be done." But, yeah, so he actually said I should do it anyway, because—even though it's illegal—the client is paying you to do it, [so] you should still do it.

On the advice of his friend, Jamal had recorded the call. He played the recording for me, and I could hear his female friend's voice as she prompted him to clarify whether the TaskRabbit employee stated the task needed to be completed, no matter what. In a slight understatement, Jamal described the situation as "problematic." He explains, "[TaskRabbit is] saying that I should break the law for this person; but at the same time, if I were to get caught, get arrested, it'd be like—who am I working for? And TaskRabbit—here is the problem, because I'm not officially an employee under TaskRabbit's contract. I mean, if contracts are getting worked via TaskRabbit. So if stuff was to hit the fan, I'm not protected."

In the end, Jamal decided that he wouldn't mail the medications. Eventually, the client arranged for him to meet up with a friend of hers and hand over the pills. But until that happened, Jamal carried the drugs with him. For a young black man in New York City, carrying large quantities of someone else's prescription drugs is especially dangerous. Although the New York Police Department's infamous "stop and frisk" program had declined precipitously by late 2013, the city was still conducting random bag searches as people entered the subways. "I know I was taking a risk. . . . Stop-and-frisk was ended by the time I moved to New York. So I wasn't necessarily worried about that. But I was worried about the random bag checks at train stations, which does happen. It's never happened to me, thank God. But I was worried about that. And if that were to happen to me, I could not say, 'I'm a TaskRabbit; I'm delivering this.' Because even if they did believe me, who could I go to? I couldn't go to anybody."

At the same time, between his hostel living situation and need to constantly be on the go for TaskRabbit gigs and job interviews, Jamal didn't feel like he could leave the bag at home. "She didn't give me a time, she just said, 'I'll get back to you,' whenever. So I had no choice."

It feels strange to hear a well-educated young man talk about having "no choice" in the workplace, especially in the sharing economy, where the ability to pick your work, pick your hours, and even set your own income level is nearly sacrosanct. But the freedom promised by the gig economy is often a mirage, and workers may be left feeling as though they have fewer choices than before. As part of the sharing economy's casualization of labor, many long-held assumptions about the American workplace and the redeeming qualities of work are overturned.

WORK AS AN ALTERNATIVE TO CRIME OR ENABLING
CRIMINAL ACTIVITY?

William Julius Wilson, in *When Work Disappears: The World of the New Urban Poor*, writes that it's the loss of manufacturing jobs, along with white flight from cities, that led to the deterioration of African American families and an increase in the crime rate. Without jobs, the logic goes, there are few ways to make money—and little incentive to marry. And without the social stability of marriage and work, there are fewer social controls preventing crime, both in terms of personal deterrents and "old heads" who can talk down the young men who may be considering a life of crime.[1]

The answer, meanwhile, is promoted in every American economic development plan: bring in industry, bring in job opportunities, and the crime rate will drop.[2] The increasing employment levels of the late 1990s are even regularly offered as a reason behind the resulting crime drop. Work by "rogue sociologist" Sudhir Venkatesh further supports this interpretation: the drug dealers he encountered in the projects of Chicago were overwhelmingly poor, on governmental assistance, and living with their mothers.[3]

But in the gig economy, the logic that gainful employment will reduce crime—or prevent someone from engaging in criminal enterprises—is turned on its head.[4] Although workers want to work and avoid trouble, the very nature of the gig economy, with its emphasis on short-term gigs and anonymity, easily lends itself to criminal behavior. Workers receive background checks, but client backgrounds are not checked or monitored in any way. It takes merely seconds to create a fake profile on TaskRabbit or Kitchensurfing, and perhaps a minute or two on Uber or Airbnb.

Unlike workers, clients are not required to provide detailed information in their profiles or post photos. A user could easily set up an account using a burner phone, random email, and a cash card and would then be able to hire workers and delegate tasks to them anonymously. Indeed, members of the criminal element appear to be well aware of the possibilities. In 2015, TaskRabbit announced to its workers that they should not spend more than three hundred dollars out of pocket on a task without company approval. Although the company was not explicit in the reasoning, several TaskRabbits I interviewed mentioned that they thought someone had used a stolen credit card or had otherwise disputed a charge after the fact, leaving TaskRabbit responsible for both the purchase and the cost of the Tasker's time.

Although many TaskRabbits now know not to accept a task that will involve spending more than three hundred dollars out of pocket, these tasks still occur. The TaskRabbit app allows anonymized communication between the Tasker and client and provides TaskRabbit with a written record in case of a dispute. The messaging tool can be used to provide a specific address to the Tasker, to clarify task directions, or even to change the gig after it starts, as Michael, a forty-nine-year-old white male, quickly discovered.

With a doctorate in political science and a strong history of teaching and research, Michael expected that he would be hired for writing and editing jobs. Instead, few materialized. Having moved to New York to be with his significant other, he joined TaskRabbit in the spring of 2015, after the pivot. Heavyset and balding, he found that clients weren't hiring him directly, so he began picking up the emergency tasks—work that other TaskRabbits had rejected or that had to be completed on the same day, usually within just a few hours. Many of these tasks were deliveries or errand-based tasks.[5]

One such delivery task seemed perfectly normal: pick up several bottles of juice from a local shop. But the task quickly grew much bigger than Michael had expected. "Yesterday I was sent a task to pick up some food, and the person changed the order rather dramatically from the description of the task to when I actually got to the place and said, 'Okay, I'm here.' The order had expanded significantly, and the total charge was something like three hundred dollars; and we're supposed to get authorization before we spend that much. I called the support center, and they immediately canceled the task and said, 'Don't do this. We'll be in touch with the client.'"

Explaining that he'd "come to realize some of the scams that are being pulled through TaskRabbit," and that he'd encountered such a scam several times, Michael asked the call center about their decision. "They used the same language that I heard in a previous conversation, where there was another definitely scam task. And I can't remember the language exactly, but it was something like: 'Well, sometimes people misuse the platform to try to work around a situation,' or something to that effect."

Michael was paid for an hour of his time by TaskRabbit, but between the collecting of items and the need to deliver them to the client, this task likely would have earned him more money if he hadn't reported it. At the same time, completing the task against TaskRabbit policy could have cost him his job and even money out of his own pocket. Whereas delivery services like Postmates provide workers with prepaid cards, TaskRabbit expects workers to use their own funds and then be reimbursed. Because it can take a week for TaskRabbit to reimburse workers, many of the Taskers I spoke to rejected tasks that required an out-of-pocket expenditure or accepted only tasks for which the costs were minimal. For Taskers who are living on the financial edge and who have maxed out, or nearly maxed out, credit cards, the reimbursement delay can be problematic.[6]

The low incomes of many gig workers leave them especially vulnerable to making poor decisions. Researchers have found that juggling the many competing demands of poverty can affect a person's ability to focus on other problems, "just as an air traffic controller focusing on a potential collision course is prone to neglect other planes in the air."[7]

It's not enough to be on top of response times and TaskRabbit policies. Workers also need to be smart about which tasks that they take on, being careful not to accept tasks that are outside their schedules or beyond their abilities, and recognizing when a gig is questionable. Workers who are financially more comfortable are better able to evaluate possible tasks and identify possible problems. This concept is clearly illustrated by Brandon's experience. A thirtysomething African American man who had worked in finance for a number of years, Brandon planned to attend law school and had taken a year off to travel. Our interview was conducted during the summer before he started classes. More financially secure than most Taskers, he was not dependent on the app for paying his bills and could afford to be more discriminating when it came to declining tasks that seemed questionable. One client wanted to send him a mailbox key. "They wanted me to go to Westchester," he said, mentioning a town roughly forty-five minutes away. "I would go to the mailbox, get something out, then mail it back to them because they were supposedly out of town for a month." It doesn't take much imagination to suggest that the mystery package was probably not going to help his legal future. He declined the task.

SAFER TO PARTICIPATE THAN TO PROTEST

Aside from the financial aspect, workers whose future employment often hinges on reviews may feel added pressure to engage in potentially criminal activities. It's important to note that no one actually posts tasks that appear criminal. Gig work generally features activities such as helping with moving, standing in lines, cleaning homes, and running errands. There's no option to hire a drug mule on TaskRabbit or a getaway driver on Uber. Likewise, when Airbnb guests want to host wild orgies or ransack someone's apartment, they don't advertise such activities in their communication with hosts. As a result, workers often don't know that they're participating in possibly illegal activities until they're well into a job. In some cases, once they suspect that criminal activity is going on, workers may be in a dangerous situation where it is safer to acquiesce than protest.

This is especially evident with ride-sharing services such Lyft and Uber. New York is one of the few locations to embrace sharing economy drivers as its own: drivers are fully licensed by the Taxi and Limousine Commission (TLC) and undergo the same background checks as taxicab drivers. But in New York, cab drivers' protections include a bullet-resistant partition, security cameras, and a panic button that actives a trouble light near the car's license plate; some of these tools date back to the 1960s. Beginning in 1967, the city required bullet-resistant partitions only in cabs driven at night, expanding the requirement in the early 1970s to all cabs. The partitions were made voluntary in the late 1970s. But beginning in 1994, the requirement was reinstituted after numerous cab drivers were killed as part of the crack cocaine crime wave. In 1997, the partition requirement was expanded to include fleet-owned livery cars. At first, drivers who had their own vehicles were exempt; eventually they were required to use a partition or security camera. Although most New York City taxi drivers keep their partitions open, allowing for easy payment and communication with the passenger, they at least have the option of closing the partition. Ride-sharing drivers don't.[8]

The partition was originally intended to reduce or prevent robberies and can be considered a success: No taxicab driver has been killed in a robbery since 1997. Fidel F. Del Valle, TLC chairman from 1991 to 1995, explained in an interview, "Whatever goes through the brain of somebody intent on physical violence, partitions seem to stop them. The attractiveness of robbing a cab is that it's basically a piggy bank on wheels. You don't want to make the opportunity for crime any easier than it is."[9]

In part because Uber and Lyft drivers do not carry cash and are prohibited from picking up street hails in New York or accepting cash payments, there's an expectation that they're less likely to be robbed. The lack of protections for drivers also appears to be part of the ethos of the sharing economy, where the app-based invisibility of payment, partnered with user profiles, promotes the idea of trustworthiness and small-town safety. When you request an Uber or Lyft, the company is supposed to have your name, credit card number, billing address, and photo on file—a taxicab driver simply has an anonymous figure on the side of the road. Indeed, as noted earlier, when Lyft, with its motto "Your friend with a car," began operating, passengers were even encouraged to sit in the front seat, further reducing a driver's options in case of a dangerous situation.[10] However, as I've pointed out, the app-based profiles may provide a false sense of security—it's entirely likely that the information included is fake or otherwise useless, and drivers can still find themselves in situations that they perceive as dangerous and illegal. It's not unreasonable to suggest that the lack of a camera and trouble light may even increase the possibility that drivers will find themselves with passengers seeking transportation anonymity.

Hector, a thirty-one-year-old Hispanic man, reached out to me in response to a request for research participants that I posted on Uberdrivers.net, an online discussion board for ride-sharing drivers. A college graduate, he was working as an assistant manager for a furniture rental center, working forty-seven hours a week and making $460 a week after taxes, until an Uber ad promising thousands of dollars in monthly income caught his eye.[11] Unwilling to pay the TLC costs in New York City until he knew what he was getting into, he tried driving in New Jersey for a weekend and made $200 his first night out. "That's half of what I made for a week," he said, still sounding impressed several months later. "So I called my boss, 'Listen, I got a better job opportunity. I'm going to go with it.' I knew it was time for a change, so I just went and did it; and in that first week, I made about $1,200. So I was just saying, 'All right, I made the right decision.'"

Like many drivers, Hector drove for both Uber and Lyft, often deciding which app to activate based on the active guarantees and his own experience with passengers and demand. He described Lyft passengers as nicer, but also noted that Uber had more clients. Although his income appears to be higher than his earnings at the furniture rental center, the start-up costs of becoming a driver were considerable: trading in his car for an Uber-approved model, increasing his car note by $8,000: and the addition of roughly $4,000 in fees and insurance prepayments for his TLC license and registration. In addition to maxing out his credit cards, he borrowed his college-student girlfriend's life savings of $2,000, and additional money from his brothers. Even though Uber advertisements guarantee $5,000 a month, money remains a serious concern: between his car payment of $800 a month and insurance bill of $500 a month, he hasn't been able to save.

From the beginning, Hector knew that driving could be dangerous or have legal implications. In New Jersey, where he started driving, ride-sharing was illegal. His first ride was a group of five, technically more than his car could fit, but "they made it work somehow." He dropped the passengers off at a local bar. Later that evening, when they called him back for a pickup, he arrived to find a brawl in the parking lot. "I was about to leave because it was like it was turning into ten guys fighting, and they were right in front of my car," he said. "I had to put the car in reverse to keep them from hitting my car. So I was like, 'Okay, this is getting real bad,' but then I realized I was blocked. They were blocking the exit, fighting."

Fortunately, Hector's passengers left the bar at that time, and he was able to leave with them—just as the police arrived. But Uber's notorious strategies for legalization reassured him that he didn't have to worry about the cops.[12] He explains, "As they do in every state, they just go in, and they're like, 'Don't worry, we'll cover all your legal fees.'"

Even though he's not worried about the police, a recent situation has made him consider getting a camera. Having grown up in Jamaica, Queens, Hector was aware of the difficulty a young man of color has in getting a cab in an outer borough. When he first saw that a young African American man had requested an Uber ride, he accepted. "They put the address as a park. So I'm sitting there, and all of a sudden four dudes get in my car. They're all wearing hoodies. I have a tablet in the back for people to play music; I have a lot of gadgets in my car. And I'm like, 'Am I going to get robbed?' But then they were cool. They were eating all my snacks, 'cause I provide snacks, and they ate all of it. And I provide little bottles of water, and they drank all of it."

The ride went well, until, as Hector puts it, "they wouldn't let me go."

> I was driving them around for an hour, multiple stops. One guy would get out, he would run to wherever it was and then come right back. And then I'd go to another, and then one would get out; or they would swap and pick someone else up; or someone with a hoodie would be waiting outside, and they would meet up and then come back in the car. . . . I think they're doing illegal activity of selling [drugs]. And I was encouraging them to go to college.
>
> One of them was like, "All right, you know, I'm going to go and I want to be a nurse." All the other three didn't say anything. I was trying to make small talk, like: "So why are you stopping here?" Like, "Oh, he's got to get something." They would come back with nothing. So in my mind I was on a drug run.

The experience became even more concerning when he was directed to pick up a fifth passenger. "The new guy we picked up, he was a little older, and then it was like he was running the show. And he was just telling me where to turn, and he wouldn't tell me the address. So he's like, 'All right, turn here, after the light, make a left.'"

Hector followed the man's directions until they arrived at the destination. Then the older man jumped out and approached a man standing outside, someone who "looked like he was up to no good." Hector demonstrated the discreet drug handoff handshake that the men exchanged before the passenger returned to the car, asking to be brought back to his original location.

> So I honestly wanted to say to all of them, "Get out, I'm not doing this," but didn't know if they had weapons or not, and I couldn't tell from their baggy sweatpants or hoodies if they had anything. They could be carrying knives. I didn't even have a pen to defend myself. They could just put a knife to my throat, and what am I going to do? And then there's no photo. I don't even know who was the account holder. It just said A—. I don't even know who was A—.

Hector's passengers may have used a real name. But with only a first name and no photo, it was difficult for him to determine which passenger owned the account. Without a camera, there was no record of who was in the car. Hector believes that ride-sharing services may be especially appealing to drug dealers because the prevalence of Uber and Lyft cars in the outer boroughs of New York City may mean that they are less likely to draw the attention of the police. Hector's assumption may be right: research shows that Uber outperforms taxis in serving the outer boroughs of New York City.[13]

Eventually the young men began talking about traveling to the Bronx, a forty-minute drive without traffic. Hector told them that he was trying to get home to dinner. They agreed to end the ride, but not before one last request. "They're like, 'Okay, give me your number.' They wanted to use me again. And I was going to give him a fake number, but he was just standing there. So I rethought it. I just gave him my real number. And he enters the number, and then he called it. He saw that it rang, and then he left. He was like, 'All right.'"

Hector was called by the young men less than a week later. They wanted him to pick them up in Brooklyn again. He lied and told them he was in Manhattan, too far away. He thinks about alerting Uber; but the passengers have his cell phone number, and he's concerned that if they're deactivated by the app they may take action against him. In the meantime, he's researched cameras for his car, but a TLC-approved camera costs roughly $350, not counting installation. He explains, "I don't want to invest that yet, because I'm still trying to get out of debt."

It would be easy to explain away Jamal's and Hector's experiences as aberrations in the sharing economy or maybe even misunderstandings. Perhaps people really do move to new continents and forget to pack prescription medications; maybe the young men that Hector was driving were looking for a missing cell phone or simply checking in with friends. In conducting nearly eighty in-depth interviews, one is likely to encounter a few outrageous stories. Yet, time and time again, workers told me about situations that certainly sounded illegal.

DISTANCE DOESN'T MEAN PROTECTION

For instance, Christina, a thirty-year-old Asian woman, was hired through TaskRabbit to do research. Although many TaskRabbit gigs are local, this one was "remote," a task that Christina could complete from home. TaskRabbit discourages workers from communicating outside the platform in an effort to keep them from circumventing the system. But while the official system allows for short messages, it's not equipped to handle the file uploads often associated with remote tasks such as researching, writing, or designing websites. As a result, clients and Taskers sometimes share personal email addresses for the delivery of the final product and to more effectively communicate.

Although many TaskRabbit workers admitted to working off the platform, they were also quick to indicate that it was often at the behest of the client. Cutting out TaskRabbit as middleman generally meant lower rates for the client and more money in the pocket of the Tasker, but it also opened up Taskers to the possibility of being stiffed when clients renegotiated payment rates after the fact or simply refused to pay, something several Taskers mentioned experiencing.

But Christina had the opposite problem. Her client kept the task in TaskRabbit, but took advantage of their off-platform communication to learn her email address. It was the same address Christina used for her PayPal account. But instead of underpaying, the client deliberately overpaid.

CHRISTINA: It was just a regular task. Or, it seemed like a regular task. I did research on art schools, putting a spreadsheet together, and then research on something on a website. So I did both for her, and she said I did a really good job. And then she was like, "Oh, can you also help me with learning how to do PayPal?" And that was when she was like, "Oh, I sent you this amount of money on PayPal; can you please send this to the person who did the design for my website?"

INTERVIEWER: It sounds like she knew how to use PayPal if she was able to send you money, right?

CHRISTINA: *[Laughs.]* I was not sure. I was confused when I saw that I had money in there from her. I was like, 'Is she paying me extra for the task?" I thought that is what it was. But then it was: "Oh, send this money over to somebody else."

Christina did as requested and transferred several hundred dollars to the website designer. That was the last she heard from the client. But later, when she met some fellow TaskRabbits, she learned that she wasn't the only one to get such a strange request. "This girl was talking about the same thing, and I think it was the same person who was doing it," she said. "She just found someone else to send the money to."

Christina's experience sounds suspiciously like money laundering or a common overpayment scam where victims are asked to return excess funds, only to later discover that the original payment was a ruse. As of the date of our interview, Christina was not aware of any repercussions; but the transfer was conducted through PayPal, which allows chargebacks within 120 days of the payment. A chargeback is a demand by a credit-card provider for a retailer to make good the loss on a fraudulent or disputed transaction, and it is triggered when a customer disputes a credit card charge. It's unclear whether Christina was inadvertently involved in money laundering or was a victim in an overpayment scheme.

AIRBNB AND THE RISE OF THE ILLEGAL RENTAL

In addition, some gig workers end up in illegal situations of their own doing. Although New York is one of the largest markets for Airbnb, with more than twenty-five thousand active hosts and 30,342 listings, it has been illegal in New York State since 2010 to rent out apartments in buildings with three or more units for less than thirty days.[14] Hosts can get around the law through the so-called roommate rule, which allows hosts to live with one unrelated person if that individual has access to the entire apartment and the host is present the entire time. But most hosts prefer to rent their space when they aren't present. A report in October 2014 from the New York attorney general found that 72 percent of Airbnb listings for entire units offered during the period from January 2010 through June 2014 ran afoul of this and other codes.[15]

Even advertising short-term rentals is illegal. In June 2016, the New York State Legislature passed a measure that forbids landlords and tenants from listing whole apartments for short-term rental on Airbnb and similar sites. The act was signed into law by Governor Andrew Cuomo in late 2016. Violations result in fines of up to seventy-five hundred dollars.[16] As a result, many Airbnb hosts, otherwise law-abiding citizens, are in the unusual situation of actively and publicly working to market themselves in an illegal endeavor.

Most hosts that I interviewed expressed concern that they would get caught, especially when they first started listing. They mentioned strategies to mitigate the risks, such as warning guests to identify themselves as family or friends. Another strategy entailed placing their location identifier pins on the Airbnb map several blocks away from the actual location (see chapter 2 for more details). But a bigger concern was detection by landlords and having to find a new place to live on short notice or possibly losing one's security deposit.[17]

Many Airbnb hosts were not informed about the law. One interviewee, a twenty-three-year-old white female, became markedly anxious about my research when I mentioned the law, and asked for repeated reassurance that I would protect her identity. Those who were familiar with the law against short-term rentals often described it as a remnant of the days of tenements and rooming houses—as opposed to originating in 2010—and hence shouldn't apply. For example, Matthew, thirty-six, told me, "They're still arguing about a law which was designed in maybe the 1940s to protect hotels and prevent landlords from building unlicensed hotels. And it's accidentally now hooked in this new economy." Joshua, thirty-two, said, "There's all sorts of laws that we all violate, probably on a daily basis, that we don't think twice about. The thirty-day law was created in the 1970s, and it was just a completely different world. And laws never keep up with technology."

Interestingly, the illegality aspect of Airbnb was part of its appeal for Joshua, a corporate attorney with a self-described Airbnb "syndicate" on the side. He told me that, when he talks with his partner, "we always use these Mafia terms because we think it's funny. So we talk about the 'scheme' and the 'syndicate.' . . . We've talked about when we make money like it's our 'haul.' In a way it's like we're playing games. I feel in a way like we're playing Mafia, that we're playing some sort of [story] like *The Wire* or something. Just because that's what I like about it: it's kind of exciting. It's like life can be somewhat dull."

An attorney with a law firm in New York City, making well over two hundred thousand dollars a year, can afford to treat his gig economy work as a game. He's not dependent on it. But his "playing Mafia" and treating lawbreaking as an antidote to boredom points to a casualization of criminality within the sharing economy.

In 1982, George L. Kelling and James Q. Wilson wrote about the broken-windows theory in *The Atlantic*. To illustrate their point that disorder begets disorder, they used Philip Zimbardo's 1969 experiments with a car left in the Bronx bearing signs of deviance (hood up, no license plates) and a comparable vehicle left in Palo Alto, California, although without any signs of deviance.[18] Within minutes of being "abandoned," the vehicle in the Bronx was vandalized by a family that stole the radiator and battery. The remaining items of value were stolen within a day, and then "destruction began—windows smashed, parts torn off, upholstery ripped. . . . Most of the adult 'vandals' were well-dressed, apparently clean-cut whites."[19]

The vehicle in Palo Alto was fine for more than a week, until Zimbardo took a sledgehammer to a portion of the exterior. "Within a few hours the car had been turned upside down and utterly destroyed. Again, the 'vandals' appeared to be primarily respectable whites."[20]

Broken-windows theory suggests that any sign of disorder or deviance—such as a single broken window—will lead to more disorder. "Untended property becomes fair game for people out for fun or plunder and even for people who ordinarily would not dream of doing such things and who probably consider themselves law-abiding. . . . But vandalism can occur anywhere once communal barriers—the sense of mutual regard and the obligations of civility—are lowered by actions that seem to signal that 'no one cares.' . . . '[U]ntended' behavior also leads to the breakdown of community controls."[21]

Uber has made a name for itself by asking forgiveness rather than permission and by taking the stance that it's easier to pay fines and penalties than to follow the rules. When Uber enters a new market, as noted by Hector, the driver who found himself on a drug run, the platform tells drivers that it will pay their illegal-taxi fines and summonses as part of the cost of business. Eventually, as the platform's market share increases, localities find themselves effectively strong-armed into letting the service operate.

Airbnb has likewise established itself by breaking laws against illegal hotels and making it easier for people to enter a highly regulated, and taxed, industry without following the same rules or paying the same taxes as established companies. When a company flouts the rules and earns multibillion-dollar valuations as a result, the message sent to workers and customers is hardly one of moral rectitude.

If broken-windows theory suggests that small-scale disorder can lead to wide-scale deviance, then perhaps this is best described as the theory of "dead fish rotting": large-scale illegal efforts, carried out in full public view—such as starting an illegal hotel business by calling it an "accommodations marketplace" or opening an unregulated taxi company by calling it a "technology company"—lead to small-scale deviance by individuals. And when "disruption" and "creative destruction" are sold as ideals to strive for, we see the "breakdown of community controls" so that casual criminality is widely tolerated, hailed, and even laughed about by "primarily respectable whites."[22]

In addition, a major theme of the gig economy is the focus on outsourcing. The companies outsource risk to the workers, letting them assume the costs of insurance and the financial risk of slow periods. The low incomes of most of these workers qualifies them and their families for Medicaid, while those who are marginally better off go without insurance or utilize the state exchanges, effectively shifting the cost of, and obligation to provide, health insurance to the taxpayer and government. Very successful gig economy workers may even manage to outsource their work—at least until the platforms ban such activities.[23] With all of the outsourcing going on, it was perhaps just a matter of time before the criminal element also got involved.

As part of the casualization of labor, work is being returned to the home. Between hiring a Kitchensurfing personal chef, using a TaskRabbit assistant to clean one's home, and booking a driver via Uber, middle-class homes in New York City are beginning to oddly resemble the world of *Downton Abbey,* but with the addition of modern clothing and without the pesky need to personally house one's servants.[24] It's true that for the wealthy, hiring help has long been a part of life, but the app-based gig economy has made it easier and cheaper for the middle class to hire servants.[25] However, whereas an upper-class home with help often had multiple workers simultaneously who could share stories and advice, today's gig economy workers are much more isolated. Often when they find themselves in challenging situations, they're on their own.

As a result of this return of work to the home, even those who avoid inadvertently committing any crimes sometimes discover that they are witnessing criminal activities. Joe, a twenty-six-year-old white male working as a Kitchensurfing Tonight chef, was quick to offer up a story of one of the unusual experiences Kitchensurfing chefs could find themselves in. Hired to cook for a couple, he quickly found himself in an uncomfortable situation, one rarely addressed in culinary school. The woman of the household let him into the home, and they spent a few minutes chatting while Joe set up and began cooking. Then the husband came home.

The couple disappeared to a back room, where it sounded like they had an argument. The husband stormed out in a huff. "I thought that was odd, because I was cooking him dinner and it was about to be ready," Joe said with a laugh. "I think I asked him on his way out, 'Are you coming back for dinner, should I . . . ?' Anyway, he didn't answer." Joe continued cooking. Roughly twenty minutes later, the food was done, and yet the woman had not reemerged from the back room.

> I had the food out on the counter, and I sort of shouted into the bedroom, like, 'I'm going to go now.' And she came out and had a big bruise on her face—not exactly a black eye, but maybe it was a black eye? I don't know how long it takes to develop a black eye, but she had a bruise on her face she hadn't had when she went into the bedroom. And so I said sort of pointedly, "Are you okay?" And she said, "Yes, yes . . ." She told me something about having fallen in the bedroom and hitting her face on the bed frame, and I said that that didn't seem plausible and that I would really like to call the police.

After some back and forth, Joe left and called the police from the lobby. When they arrived, two officers went upstairs to interview the young woman while one stayed behind to interview Joe on the sidewalk. The woman opted not to press charges.

Weeks later, Joe remained conflicted about whether he made the right decision. After a pause, he haltingly explained:

> I think that I just . . . my mother has been involved in domestic violence issues for a long time; she's a social worker. So I have a lot of background in this stuff, and I was always told that you should call the police if there's any suspicion of domestic violence. But on the other hand, this was a grown

woman who had asked me not to call the police. So I just felt like it should not have been my place to interfere. And I decided to interfere, but I'm still not entirely sure that that's what was best for her.

Between the discussion with the woman and the police interview, Joe was unable to make it to his next Kitchensurfing gig of the evening. He contacted the company and used subway delays as an excuse; he says that the missed appointment wasn't a problem.

Weeks later, he still hasn't told Kitchensurfing the truth. After a pause he explains. "As far as I know, they don't have a policy about this. I don't know why they would have a policy about this, because, hopefully, it doesn't come up that often. But I just didn't know what they—you know, it's a sensitive subject, and I am a servant in their house, anyway."

Describing himself as a servant highlights the challenges that Joe experiences with respect to his customers. Historically, servants were expected to keep the family's secrets. In *Not in Front of the Servants: A True Portrait of English Upstairs/Downstairs Life,* Frank Dawes explains that "the upper class relied on the total discretion of those who served them, a trust that was rarely misplaced."[26] The implementation of a modern-day *Downton Abbey* workplace can leave workers uncertain of the protocols. What is expected of them? In modern society, many professionals are mandatory reporters, individuals who are required by law to report abuse. But in a servant economy, discretion rules the day. Where do gig workers fall in this dichotomy?

Joe's discussion of the lack of policies in place also raises interesting issues. Although modern workplaces are often ridiculed for their hefty employee manuals, there's something to be said for the coverture provided by rules and regulations. Although TaskRabbit workers mentioned that the company told them to leave situations that felt uncomfortable or unsafe, of the nearly eighty workers I have interviewed to date, only one mentioned declining an in-process gig that appeared to veer into illegal territory.

"THIS IS NOT IN MY JOB DESCRIPTION": WORKPLACE POLICIES THAT PROTECT WORKERS

I met Cody, a twenty-two-year-old black male (introduced in chapter 5), while walking my dog in a local park. He was sitting on a bench, playing on his phone, while he waited for a new delivery call; his Postmates T-shirt alerted me to the fact that he was a sharing economy worker. When we met for an interview several weeks later, he told me that he also did deliveries for UberRUSH. When I asked if he had ever delivered drugs or questionable materials, Cody told me that Postmates had a strict policy stating that they were not supposed to pick up "any drugs that are not a prescription from the drugstore." Instead, it was the courier's job to contact dispatch and tell them that they had a "drug package" and couldn't complete the pickup. He explained, "If I get caught, even if I have your name, it's still in my bag."

I asked if he had firsthand experience with such deliveries, and he told me he had. The scent of marijuana on one pickup was so strong that he could smell it outside the package. "I handed it back. And I was like, 'Excuse me, I cannot accept this bag,'" he said. "And they asked me why, and I was like, 'This is not in my job description.' And they're like, 'Oh, really?' And I'm like, 'Yeah, really,' and I left. And I when I got downstairs I called dispatch. And I was like, 'Hey dispatch, I'm not doing this job because this is what this is.' And they said, 'Oh, no problem. I'll get you the payout, so just get out of the building.' So I got out of the building." In addition to giving him an out, the company also paid Cody for the delivery and removed the negative rating he received from the unhappy customer.

In 2014, New York State loosened the restrictions on medical marijuana, allowing twenty hospitals across the state to prescribe marijuana for patients with cancer, glaucoma, and other conditions listed by the State Board of Health.[27] However, according to the Drug Policy Alliance, New York City maintains a stringent enforcement of marijuana laws, resulting in nearly 450,000 misdemeanor charges from 2002 to 2012.[28] For Cody, having a clear-cut company policy made it easier for him to reject the illegal task, saving himself from unnecessary risks, and even provided him with the perfect bureaucratic excuse: "This is not in my job description."

It should be noted that I do not consider these workers to be criminals in any sense of the term. They are not seeking jobs in which they deliver drugs, defraud companies, or engage in money laundering. But the structuring of gig-based employment leaves workers in a precarious situation. By deeming gig economy workers to be independent contractors, companies deny them many of the protections often associated with employees. Since their work is temporary and their numbers are many, companies don't seem to pay much attention to policies, training, or even ensuring that they aren't exposed to unreasonable risks. These are workers in every sense of the term, but they have none of the standard protections of the workplace, protections that took literally hundreds of years to achieve.

The outcry over the start-up app Peeple, a self-described "Yelp for People" designed to be used in the anonymous rating of individuals, suggests that people do not want to be judged and rated on a daily basis.[29] Yet gig economy workers are rated by every client, and a canceled task or ride can have repercussions for their continuation on the platforms. In the economy at large, we have at-will employment. In the sharing economy, it can be on-whim unemployment.

The casualization of labor—the transition of the workforce from permanent jobs to short-term, temporary work—results in workers exerting more effort for more uncertain returns. Not only are workers enduring greater job insecurity and receiving lower wages than in years past, as part of a general increase of workplace precarity, but sharing economy companies are not offering any of the workplace protections that Americans have come to expect: health insurance, retirement (or at least Social Security) contributions, and disability insurance. The combination of daily reviews and a lack of dependable income has left some workers feeling as through they don't have many choices, which increases their vulnerability to being used for criminal ends or at least being involved in legally questionable activities.[30]

But not all gig economy workers are without choices. Successful Airbnb hosts and Kitchensurfing chefs find themselves with a surplus of choice: when they'll work, who they'll work for, even how they'll work. These Success Stories are making a comfortable living in the gig economy. Unlike TaskRabbit workers or Uber drivers, who must accept a certain number of gigs in order to remain active on the app, Kitchensurfing and Airbnb workers are much freer to accept and decline work as they see fit. Although their education levels are roughly equal to those of TaskRabbit workers, they tend to bring more specialized skills and financial capital to their sharing economy work, enabling them to live the dream careers promised by the gig economy. In addition, successful workers in these two organizations are much more likely to view themselves as entrepreneurs and to take advantage of the outsourcing opportunities of the gig economy to hire others. Compared to Jamal—the TaskRabbit who felt like he didn't have a choice when it came to carrying around a client's prescription amphetamines for a week—some Airbnb hosts and Kitchensurfing chefs are the epitome of choice in the gig economy.

7   Living the Dream?

I met Damla at a coffee shop in the far reaches of Brooklyn. A dark-haired Turkish woman, Damla was friendly and bubbly. It was easy to see how she would be a positive and welcome presence in a kitchen.

After working for a well-known and prestigious special-events caterer and assisting with a restaurant start-up, Damla was taking a career break when she discovered Kitchensurfing. She wasn't looking for an entrée into the food realm of the sharing economy—she didn't even actually believe that the service was a real opportunity. "I stumbled on it somehow, I guess, looking at either cooking sites or job sites, and something popped up saying, 'Are you a chef, and do you like to work from home?' or something along those lines. I clicked on the website, and it asked me to create a profile. And I did, but very vague. I kind of just put my name and not a ton of other information. And then the following day someone called me from Kitchensurfing."

Damla was surprised to get a response. She was invited for an interview and asked to provide a sample meal for ten people in Kitchensurfing's corporate office. The platform offered to cover the cost of ingredients for her cooking audition.

The address in Brooklyn that Damla was given gave her pause. It wasn't a commercial location. "I was a little bit weirded out by that part," she said. But she gave the address to her roommate and boyfriend and told them she would text when she arrived. "So I got there, and immediately I was so comfortable, and knew they were totally legit," she said. "And I texted them. I'm like, 'This is totally cool; so I'll tell you all about it later.'"

Damla's Kitchensurfing interview happened in 2012, and by the time we met in the summer of 2015 she described herself as working "full time" with Kitchensurfing. It was the first time I'd ever heard someone talk about their gig economy work in such a way, and I asked what she meant by *full time*. "My first job came through someone actually reaching out to me. . . . And it was a cocktail party for thirty or so. I did that, and the customer was very happy. And, still thinking to myself—and talking [it] over with my husband—I said, 'I'll give it six months or so; we'll see how it goes.' If I see that I'm not carrying my end of the deal here, I'll find a real job—or, of course, regular job." With the holiday season beginning, her schedule was soon full of catering work. But she was hesitant to commit to doing Kitchensurfing as her sole source of income, explaining, "I didn't know if I could make a reasonable decision based on those three months. But then January came along, and I was thinking to myself that it would be dead, because I know no one really throws parties in January, February. But January ended up being one of my busiest months. . . . So after January, I was like, 'Okay, I'm going to focus on this full time and I won't bother finding another job; this makes me totally happy.'"

Damla enjoyed working with clients directly and getting to cook her ethnic food, but she also appreciated the flexibility of the work and the opportunity to pick and choose her hours.

It's very flexible, in terms of the gigs that you can accept or don't accept. So it was kind of perfect for me. I mean, I have been in the food industry before, and that was the main thing about it. It's a ton of work, and you do get a lot of gratification; but when you're working with somebody else, that's not directly to you. Not to sound selfish or anything, but I like the gratification to come directly to me, and the compliments to come directly to me, and with Kitchensurfing, they do. And along with that, the money, so it's just a dream job, really.

SKILLS AND CAPITAL ARE CRUCIAL TO SUCCESS

The sharing economy promises freedom, flexibility, and equality as everyone works peer-to-peer. At the same time, it's hard to imagine a TaskRabbit errand runner or an Uber driver describing her work as a "dream job." This is one of the issues at the forefront of the sharing economy. While the platforms promise equality and opportunity, there is still a rigid hierarchy to the work that can be traced back to the divide between skills and capital discussed in chapter 2. Simply put, those who succeed in the gig economy, and especially those who view themselves as entrepreneurs, are often those who have the skills and capital to succeed outside the sharing economy. TaskRabbit and Uber have low skill-barriers and are open to virtually anyone, while Kitchensurfing Tonight has high skill-barriers, and Airbnb and the Kitchensurfing marketplace have high capital- and skill-barriers.

Just as in the mainstream marketplace, the work that requires higher levels of capital and skill is more remunerative in terms of financial and psychic rewards, but it also allows for a greater level of professionalization and creativity. Working as a chef or running a bed-and-breakfast is often a daydream job, a career that an upper-class professional briefly considers after serving his family a particularly elegant meal, or ponders as a postretirement career. The platforms themselves also contribute to this divide—on Kitchensurfing and Airbnb, workers can highlight their experience and include multiple photos of themselves and their product (food or housing). Marketing is much more important. TaskRabbit allows profiles and information about one's experience, but with a rigid character limit. While Airbnb and Kitchensurfing have response-time requirements, they are much more generous than those of TaskRabbit and Uber (twenty-four hours, compared to thirty minutes or a matter of seconds). This additional time lends a sense of calm professionalism to the endeavor, as opposed to promoting a mad scramble.

A STIGMATIZED OCCUPATION OF LAST RESORT

Perhaps one of the biggest signs that the gig economy is not as it appears to be is the stigmatized nature of the work that TaskRabbits and app-based drivers do. Erving Goffman defined *stigma* as a "process by which the reaction of others spoils normal identity."[1] Although stigma is more commonly thought of as affiliated with overt or external deformations, such as scars, disabilities, or medial conditions such as leprosy, stigma can also arise from deviations in personal traits, such as unemployment, welfare dependency, or teenage parenthood. Stigmatized individuals often feel different and devalued by others, and many experience psychological distress.[2]

Richard, a middle-age white male TaskRabbit, opened an interview by telling me that his girlfriend of two years had broken up with him owing to embarrassment over his TaskRabbit work. Rebecca, thirty-four, a TaskRabbit with an advanced degree and a side job as an adjunct instructor at a local college, admitted that she often lied to her mother and friends about her work—telling them that she was temping in an office, not tasking in people's homes. The embarrassment wasn't limited to TaskRabbit workers either.

Even though I assured participants that their identities would be hidden, one Uber driver emailed me after an interview to reiterate the importance of not mentioning him by name. He explained, "Uber for me is a feeling like 'when you get really drunk and regret whatever you did last night.' That's exactly it. I really don't want to be associated as an Uber driver at any point of my life. I really don't want it to come up when people search my name on Google." Another driver—who had previously worked as a professional gambler—said that his embarrassed wife told him not to tell people that he drove for Uber.

Although research suggests that stigma is sometimes associated with entrepreneurship, such stigma is usually associated with entrepreneurial failure.[3] Stigma associated with one's work is much more common among sex workers and those working in minimum-wage fast-food jobs or in blue-collar fields.[4] The embarrassment associated with working within the gig economy suggests that this may be an occupation of last resort for some workers.

MAKING ENTREPRENEURSHIP "EASY"

For Damla, however, Kitchensurfing lived up to the entrepreneurial ethos promised by the site. She soon turned a spare space in her apartment into an office to store her catering supplies, including large coolers and bins. Her health insurance and a good deal of her household income came from her husband's unionized job, so she was financially stable. Her Kitchensurfing work essentially paved the way for her to start a de facto catering company, and by 2017 she had incorporated her business. Kitchensurfing simplified the entrepreneurial process to the point that while she identified as an entrepreneur, she also noted that she felt like she was "cheating a little bit."

She explained, "[It's] just because they make it so easy. This might have been in the back of my head—a dream for years and years—but the fact that I could just go onto this website, and put in my information and my menus, made it really easy. Because otherwise, I'm not really a techy person to try to set up my own website, or I wouldn't be able to reach the marketplace like they're able to reach. So I do feel like an entrepreneur, but at the same time I feel like they made it really easy to do that."

Damla wasn't the only chef who used Kitchensurfing to branch out and get away from the cutthroat nature and daily grind of traditional restaurant work. Randall, the Kitchensurfing chef who found himself catering a sex party, described in chapter 5, and Allen, who closed his restaurant after a landlord-tenant dispute, both found that the Kitchensurfing marketplace opened up new entrepreneurial possibilities by providing them with a marketplace in which to promote themselves. This further illustrates McAfee and Brynjolfsson's point that the Internet creates and strengthens platforms over products because the platform takes on a huge role in the reach and success of the product.[5]

Kitchensurfing allowed established chefs to pursue the flexibility offered by gig work and assisted potential chefs in getting a toehold in the food world. For instance, Ashaki, thirty-five, a full-time financial planner for a major retailer, had dreams of opening a West African restaurant. Working through the Kitchensurfing marketplace as a chef for hire allowed her to test recipes for her upcoming restaurant and gave her an opportunity to meet and market to prospective diners.

> Since I love to cook and I love to educate people about my culture through my food, I decided I wanted to start a company. For me, I knew Friday and Saturday [are all] that I can fit into my schedule right now. So it's a great

testing ground for me, to test: "Do people even like the food?" Because people have heard of African food, they've heard of Ethiopian food—but not
sub-Saharan African food, . . . and I cook sub-Saharan African food, which
is the West African part of it.

For me, it's just a way to test the ground and see what people are reacting
to. Because as I create my company, I want to be able to have data on the foods
that they actually react to the most, or this is what they don't like, so that when
I eventually package the food, I actually have results. Like proven data. . . .

My whole thing is, I want to build a brand. . . . I want to be at the beginning of it, as well, so I can leverage it as it grows.

In addition to testing out the market for West African food, Ashaki's
Kitchensurfing work served as a springboard to get her started on her
marketing efforts. During Thanksgiving one year, Ashaki recruited
her family to assist in staging and photographing the food she listed in her
Kitchensurfing menus. She explained, "It dresses it up. It makes it more
presentable, more appetizing. You want to try it. It's not just cooking. It's
just the presentation of it. It's everything."

The gig-based nature of Kitchensurfing also helped her test-market
descriptions of her food to see which explanations made sense to clients
and had sticking power. She explained,

My whole thing is trying to make connections about African food for people.
Kind of: "You might have tried tamales before. We have *moi moi* that is
Nigerian—that's almost similar to tamales, but they're not the same." The
process of cooking them is the same, because you put them in plantain leaf.
It's black-eyed beans versus corn. You put different seasonings. So they are
from the same family, but they're just a different flavor.

That customer made that connection. When she did my review, she basically did a lot of that, like, "When me and my husband tried it, it reminded
us of tamales. When she cooked this, it reminded us of this."

I love that.

GIG WORK AS A MARKETING OPPORTUNITY

Using Kitchensurfing as a way to establish or grow a business was not limited to those using the marketplace version of the service. Even Kitchensurfing
chefs working for an hourly wage for the prix fixe Kitchensurfing Tonight

service were more likely to view themselves as entrepreneurs overall, and to consider their work for the service to be part of a larger marketing strategy for their entrepreneurial ventures. For instance, Laura, twenty-nine, a self-described cheesemonger, used Kitchensurfing Tonight as a way to literally get her foot in the door to talk about her cheese-tasting-party company. She explains,

> I figured it would be a good way to network with my potential clientele, or at least my target market, and get comfortable speaking about my services. Because, honestly, sometimes the hardest thing is just talking about it, just pitching yourself. And when people ask me, "How much do you charge?" it's a really difficult conversation for me. [Laughs.] It's my own thing, and it's my baby. . . . So this has given me a chance, too, in a very, very low-key way, because obviously I'm here to cook, and they are not—I'm not expecting anything from the interaction, but when people ask me, "Oh, so what else do you do?" it has given me so many opportunities to just refine what I say that I do.

Likewise, David, fifty-four, a personal chef and tutor who wanted to grow his clientele, also saw Kitchensurfing as way to introduce himself and become a known quantity, explaining, "The hope is I can build up some clientele or get some opportunity. . . . My ideal job would be to be a family's personal chef and tutor their kids as well."

I want to caution here that Kitchensurfing was not some idyllic oasis of entrepreneurship in the midst of the sharing economy. For one, the service shut its doors, with little notice to workers, in April 2016.[6] For some workers, Kitchensurfing Tonight was simply a means to an end. They had full-time cooking jobs that took up most of their time, but had evenings open and wanted to supplement their salaries on a part-time basis. Or they were students who wanted to make additional money without the obligations of long hours or a boss-set schedule. While the fifteen-dollar-per-hour pay was roughly on par with that of other cooking jobs, Kitchensurfing shifts ended by ten o'clock each night, virtually unheard of in the food world.

Kitchensurfing was not the only service with a large number of Success Stories or workers who identified as entrepreneurs. Successful Airbnb hosts who had multiple units, or who felt that they treated their listings as a company—often by hiring others, incorporating as a business, or otherwise professionalizing their work—also described themselves as entrepreneurs. The most notable of these included Yosef, twenty-seven, the self-described "hotelier" discussed in chapter 5; and Joshua, who described his Airbnb hosting as part of a "syndicate" in chapter 6; and of course, Ryan, twenty-seven, featured in the opening chapter. Yet, the entrepreneurial mind-set isn't limited to male Airbnb hosts or to those with large-scale Airbnb operations.

Jessica, thirty, began her Airbnb hosting as a way to reduce the waste of an empty apartment while she traveled for work as a consultant. Realizing the income potential, she soon professionalized her Airbnb hosting.

> Once I saw the potential, I got real serious and basically turned it into a part-time business. I hosted over fifty people last year.... [I]t paid for my entire rent.... I was like, "Oh my God, I need to really get serious about this." That's when I hired a key person and a cleaner. I made an official guidebook, got a whole separate set of linens that are just for my Airbnb people, and started thinking about the guest experience, like buying wine or other little small things for my guests to make it feel personalized.

A recent job change meant that Jessica wasn't traveling as much, but she continued hosting on occasion. "My rule is: I never want this to make me crazy; it's not worth the extra money to feel like your life is an inconvenience," she said. "It enables me to feel like I can travel anywhere for free, kind of. I went to Morocco for Christmas and New Year's Eve [a high-demand and high-profit time for New York Airbnbs]. It more than paid for my whole entire trip to Morocco. So it's crazy not to do it."

When we met, she hadn't yet expanded her Airbnb hosting by adding a second site. But she was considering it, and she identified her concern about the future of Airbnb in New York as part of her hesitation. She didn't want to take on the risk of committing to a second apartment if the city was going to increase its efforts to crack down on violators of the illegal hotel laws (for more on this, see chapter 6).

Jessica has the financial capital to rent an additional apartment, but she also has the needed cultural capital. She knows how to market the apartment, such as by talking about the exposed brick walls and the neighborhood, in a way to make it appealing to prospective guests. But, as in the case of Kitchensurfing chefs, not all Airbnb hosts identified as entrepreneurs. And as noted earlier, many hosts were Strivers and a few would fall within the category of Strugglers. There are also a few notable differences between the sort of people who become Airbnb hosts and the sort who work with Kitchensurfing. For instance, while some Kitchensurfing chefs engaged in their food work full time, few Airbnb hosts only hosted. Most had full-time occupations or identities outside Airbnb, whether as students, lawyers, writers, or small business owners, and their Airbnb work was a side hustle or part-time effort. Part of this divide derives from the fact that while Airbnb hosting can require multiple emails or being on call part of the time, it is often less labor-intensive and time-consuming than creating a menu, shopping for ingredients, and cooking for clients. Additionally, while Kitchensurfing chefs often hired assistants to help with large events, they were still expected to show up for such events. Airbnb hosts often seemed to be free of the same personal expectations as long as the apartment or home was roughly what people expected. They could pass off a potential or future guest to a "key person" or assistant without causing any issues. The "star" of the interaction was not the host but the apartment.[7]

SKILLS, CAPITAL, AND CHOICE

But aside from these differences, what sets Airbnb and Kitchensurfing apart from the other gig economy services described in these pages? Three words: skills, capital, and choice. As noted in chapter 2, Kitchensurfing and Airbnb present higher skill or capital-investment barriers. While the Kitchensurfing Tonight service didn't require capital investment—the service provided the food to be cooked, clients, and the necessary equipment—both forms of Kitchensurfing necessitated a high level of skill and obliged prospective chefs to audition by cooking a restaurant-worthy meal.

And while Airbnb doesn't require much in regard to skills, success on the platform demands that one have a rental space desirable enough (in terms of location and amenities) that potential guests will be sufficiently interested to request a reservation. It also requires that hosts have the requisite cultural capital to make their space seem appealing. Hosts talk about highlighting the architectural components of their apartment, the convenience of their location in regard to transportation or landmarks, or amenities such as designer bath products or outdoor space.[8]

For instance, James, thirty-six, noted that he took "probably forty shots" for the apartment's listing on Airbnb and then chose the best twelve to feature. He explains, "I was conscious with the opening shot. Everyone else has a picture of their living room. I have a picture with a view from my roof. . . . Because people are looking to come to New York, and here's a picture of the skyline in New York versus a tiny spot. It's like, tiny spots? There are plenty of those. Here's a beautiful view. Then I have a pool on my roof; I feature that too."

In New York, where app-based drivers are governed by Taxi and Limousine Commission rules, driving for Uber or Lyft has presented a high capital barrier. As noted previously, drivers must provide access to a relatively new car that meets Uber requirements (high capital investment). The background check, requisite driving courses, and commercial insurance requirements also constitute a considerable capital investment. However, there are ways around these barriers. In New York City, drivers can lease an Uber/Lyft-approved vehicle from another driver or from a car service. While the cost is high—Baran, twenty-eight, noted that at least two full days of driving each week were needed to cover his rental fees and gas—such rentals can reduce the up-front costs.

Skills and capital aside, there's also another significant difference between Airbnb and Kitchensurfing and the other services: choice. Kitchensurfing marketplace chefs and Airbnb hosts have considerable autonomy when it comes to deciding if they want to work or not and in picking their clients. As former Kitchensurfing chef Damla noted, "It's very flexible, in terms of the gigs that you can accept or don't accept. So it was kind of perfect for me."

The flexibility to pick one's schedule was also echoed by workers for Kitchensurfing Tonight. Laura, twenty-nine, told me, "I got involved with Kitchensurfing because I've been in the process of launching my own business and needed some steady income. I ideally wanted something that involves cooking, and so I found their posting on Goodfoodjobs.com, looking for chefs, and it was kind of the perfect thing because it was flexible. You could choose what nights you're available to work." Francesco, twenty-nine, said, "Part of the reason I wanted to do Kitchensurfing is because it allows me to keep a flexible schedule so I could do what I need to outside of work. And once I leave work I don't have to take it with me; mentally that's it. . . . It's just [that] the flexibility is great, especially over the summer, because I'm planning on going on my camping trip and stuff like that—just like I can take off whatever day I want." And Lucca, twenty-seven, stated, "We do personal chefing, and it's like Kitchensurfing on a more customized level. . . . I'm doing Kitchensurfing now because my upper-end clients are slowing down after Christmas and going on vaca-tion. When people go away, the business slows down; so now I'm doing Kitchensurfing, just until my other thing goes well." Kitchensurfing's flex-ibility was such that Randall, the Kitchensurfing chef who found himself working a swingers' party, often works for three weeks and then takes a two-week vacation—virtually unheard of in any other career.

THE FINE LINE BETWEEN HOST CHOICE AND GUEST SCREENING

Airbnb, too, delivers on the promise of a high level of worker choice and flexibility. Hosts can use the calendar function to choose when they will rent, and the choice to rent to a guest, or not, is entirely theirs. The requirement that all users post a profile with photos and information about their interests, and the recommendation that guests explain why they want to rent a space, leads to a wealth of information that can be utilized by hosts in picking and choosing potential guests. While a good deal of attention has been paid to racial discrimination in Airbnb, less attention has been paid to the ways in which hosts screen their guests according to a number of factors, including education and occupation, photos, and personal messages.[9] James, thirty-six, explained, "Things that I look for: college educated, what is their job? Like if you have a profes-sional job. If you're like, 'I'm a roadie,' I'll probably not rent [the apart-ment] to you. If you're a producer, I'm probably not going to rent to you. If you're a lawyer, doctor, some professional thing, I'm going to rent it to you. If you're thirty plus, I'm going to rent it to you. If you're a couple, I'm going to rent it to you. If you're gay, I'm definitely going to rent it to you."

Aalia, thirty, said, "I don't really approve everybody. I'm very picky of who I chose. . . . I totally judge by the cover. If I don't feel good vibes, or if there's not a long enough message about them that I feel comfortable, I just don't do it." Christopher, forty, told me, "We look at people's profiles and we're hypercritical of the way their initial interaction is. What did they write? If it's something really sort of short and punchy, and they clearly haven't read anything about our listing, we'll, you know, we'll probe a little bit to see if we can sort of coax more detail out of them to get a sense of who they are. And if they're not forthcoming, then we just decline them."

Profile information, in conjunction with the message first received from the potential guest, is used by hosts to determine if they want to rent to a specific individual. In 2017, in an effort to decrease discrimination, Airbnb began experimenting with ways to reduce the prominence of profile photos, which were seen as a prime source of racially identifying information. When a host received a reservation request, a guest photo no longer accompanied the message; it was replaced with a stylized image of the first initial of the potential guest's first name (for instance, a profile for Michelle would have an image of a large *M*). While reducing the emphasis on photos was believed to help decrease discrimination, the individual's first name was still shown in his or her profile, allowing potential hosts to make guesses about that person's race and ethnicity. Additionally, the image of the first initial was clickable as a hyperlink that connected to the potential guest's profile, making the user photo, personal description, and reviews all literally a single click away. Airbnb soon abandoned the experiment, and by mid-2018 user-profile images were again accompanying inquiries from potential guests.

While de-emphasizing the photo is an important step in making overt discrimination more difficult, names can also tell a good deal about a person, even online. An Airbnb audit study found that individuals with "distinctively African American names" were 16 percent less likely to be accepted relative to identical guests with distinctively white names.[10] Similar work on the website Craigslist, often described as an early sharing economy site, found "severe discrimination against African Americans, Hispanics, and Chinese-origin individuals."[11] Studies in Sweden that utilized the Internet as a research platform for examining discrimination in the housing market also found discriminatory behavior against males with Arabic or Muslim male names.[12]

As part of its efforts to fight discriminatory practices, Airbnb recently began to emphasize its Instant Book service. As described by the platform, "Instant Book listings don't require approval from the host before they can be booked. Instead, guests can just choose their travel dates, book, and discuss check-in plans with the host." However, many of the hosts I interviewed were reluctant to let go of control over their listings by using the Instant Book option. For example, Ramona, twenty-eight, told me, "Instant Book is good for when you're looking for a place at the last minute, but that would feel much more like we are running a business. We like the idea of like discriminating and having some sense of control over when people are staying and when we're opening up our home to people, versus Instant Book, [which] feels like they're choosing and you're just open for business all the time." And Joshua, thirty-two, said, "You shouldn't offer [Instant Book] if you have qualms or if you're trying to pick and choose between guests, sort of like I do in the place where we live. I pick and choose, so I don't offer Instant Book."

Part of the impetus behind the host screening is the issue of risk and damage. As noted in chapter 2, there have been numerous documented instances of damage to homes and possessions by Airbnb guests. Screening guests as a risk-mitigation strategy takes on additional importance after bad experiences such as discovering that a guest hosted a party or rifled through one's personal possessions or private paperwork.

James, the Airbnb host with a rooftop pool, rented out his space while he was out of town and returned home to discover that his guests had "basically trashed our place." There were footprints on the walls, empty alcohol bottles left behind, and personal items removed from the closet. Returning to the mess affected his willingness to rent again, and he admits to "Google stalking" now: "Any information I can get. Copy and paste name in Google, go on LinkedIn, and go on Facebook. Stalk as much as possible. I will especially be doing a lot more of that since my last experience, but yeah, that's pretty commonplace before I click "approve." He wasn't the only host to admit to seeking additional information about prospective guests. Gabriele, twenty-seven, lives alone with a young child. After several bad experiences renting to what she described as "young people, partying people that had just left home and whose mommy usually cleans up after them," she began researching potential guests in advance. "I search information on the applicants on the Internet, then usually I pick somebody. I usually go for older people or people that have children, because I know they won't be having parties. . . . I look at what kind of job they have; I try to find their social profile on Facebook. There's always something available—it's kind of scary, actually."

Obviously, screening by Airbnb hosts is problematic and further supports the premise that the sharing economy is falling short of its promise of building trust and community. And, as Ramona notes above, some hosts reject the idea that they are running a business and should be "open for business all the time." Hosts generally prefer to maintain full control over their hosting practices, including the availability of their home and the decision to accept a guest.

It's this worker control that sets Kitchensurfing and Airbnb apart from TaskRabbit and car services like Uber and Lyft. While all four services promote the entrepreneurial ethos and promise that workers can be their own bosses (see chap 2 for a more complete discussion), workers were free to accept or reject as many gigs as they wished on Kitchensurfing and Airbnb. Unlike TaskRabbit or Uber/Lyft, where participants had to accept a certain percentage of gigs or face the risk of deactivation, Kitchensurfing and Airbnb workers were entirely in control of their schedules. While a lack of activity on either site might decrease one's ranking in the search algorithms, it didn't result in site removal or the "reeducation" practiced by TaskRabbit. This type of worker-directed scheduling, which had been more common in the early days of TaskRabbit, is correlated with an increased identification of the work with entrepreneurship and the entrepreneurial ethos.

As noted, not all workers want to be entrepreneurs, and perhaps not all services can—or should—offer the option to select one's clients. For Airbnb, after all, getting to pick one's clients appears to lead to guest screening on a number of levels that traditional race and ethnicity audit studies have yet to address.

For workers who have high levels of social and cultural capital and skills, the sharing economy can offer a dream job with increased flexibility, choice, and control. But for workers who lack these components, the gig economy simply takes already low-level work, adds an app, and increases the precarity factor. This new economic movement isn't equalizing the entrepreneurial playing field so much as it is highlighting the role of capital—both financial and cultural.

But there is a solution. As case studies of MyClean, Hello Alfred, and even Instacart show, there are ways to protect workers who are simply looking for a way to earn additional money, while still helping those who are pursuing entrepreneurship.

8 Conclusion

Almost weekly, new app-based services are hailed as the "Uber of . . ."
There's BloomThat, which promises flower delivery in ninety minutes or
less. Dryv and Washio are the "Uber of laundry," and Eaze is the "Uber of
medical marijuana delivery." There's even Iggbo, the Uber of blood, which
sounds like a food delivery service for vampires but is more accurately
described as an app for scheduling and managing "on-demand phleboto-
mists," who can be dispatched to draw blood for medical tests in a client's
home or office.[1]

In July 2016, a new sharing economy service seemed to reach a new
low. Advertised as the "smart alternative to picking up after your dog,"
Pooper was an app-based platform that promised on-demand pickup of
excrement for a small monthly fee (see fig. 13). "Users snapped a photo of
Fido's filthy business and someone in a Prius would come by and collect it
for you."[2] Hailed as the "Uber for dog poop," the service promised potential workers the same perks as many other sharing economy services:
"Work on your terms. Scoop when you want, earn what you want. Set your
own schedule. Scooping with Pooper gives you the freedom to work whenever you want. Scoop as much or as little as you like."

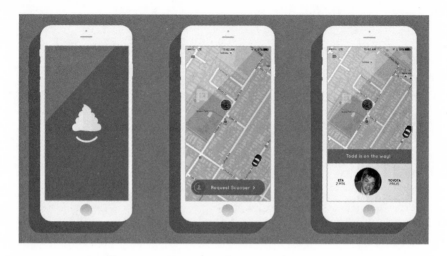

Figure 13. App screens from Pooper media materials. Screenshot by author.

There was just one issue: Pooper was—and so far, remains—fake.

The app was actually an "art project" created by Ben Becker, an advertising creative director, and Elliot Glass, owner of a boutique creative studio in Los Angeles. Friends from Pacific Sound House helped create a custom soundtrack for their website advertising video, something Becker says he thinks helped contribute to the whole aesthetic of the ruse. "Pooper is in fact a piece of art that is satirizing our app-obsessed world. Specifically, the increasing reliance on the gig-based economy to do stuff for us that we could easily do for ourselves," Becker said.[3]

According to Becker and Glass, the target of Pooper's satire was an innovation economy that prioritizes trivial "hacks" instead of addressing genuine societal ills.[4] "What we're doing is more or less just holding up a mirror to culture and society," Becker said. "It also begs the question: What is the gig economy? Is that necessarily a good thing?" The other target: anyone lazy enough to pay an underclass of pooper-scoopers to clean up after their dog. "You don't have to do as much for yourself," Becker says. "You don't have to drive for yourself. You can have someone else do your errands. . . . Do people want to live in a society where [there's] that kind of stratification and division of labor?"[5]

Illustrative of such stratification, as Becker and Glass were disturbed to see, was how popular the app became with potential scoopers. More people signed up to be scoopers than pooper clients. "It's a little bit disconcerting that it's such a demeaning job and so many people were eager to sign up to do it," Glass said.

In many ways, Pooper is a perfect illustration of the trends that led to the sharing economy. Although the start of the sharing economy can be traced back to eBay and Craigslist, the wholesale launch of this new economic movement truly happened during the Great Recession and its aftermath, when the official unemployment rate hit 10 percent in October of 2009.[6] Meanwhile, the "true unemployment rate," which includes discouraged workers who had looked for a job in the past year and those who are underemployed in part-time work, reached 17.5 percent.[7] With rampant unemployment and underemployment, a 2014 Federal Reserve Board study found that a third of workers indicated that they'd like to work more hours at their current wage, and 49 percent of workers with part-time jobs responded that they, too, would prefer to work more hours at their current wage.[8]

The Great Recession also unearthed a savings gap among Americans. According to the Economic Security Index, 20 percent of the American population saw their available household income decline by 25 percent or more and lacked an adequate financial safety net to replace this lost income.[9] Even those who started the recession with savings soon found themselves tapping their reserves: 57 percent of Americans who had savings before 2008 used up some or all of their savings in the Great Recession and its aftermath, and 34 percent reported that they were somewhat worse off or much worse off financially than they had been five years earlier.[10]

Well after the recession ended, nearly half of Americans noted that they would have trouble finding four hundred dollars to pay for an emergency without selling a possession or borrowing money.[11] In many ways, it's almost as if the recession never really ended: in the height of the Wall Street crisis, in October 2008, 57 percent of adults said their incomes were falling behind the cost of living; in 2014, 56 percent of adults echoed the same concern.[12]

The interest in demeaning poop-scooping jobs also highlights another element of the gig economy: workers have such a great need for extra income they will literally pick up almost anything for the promise of extra money.

As I write this, unemployment in the United States is below 4 percent. According to the Bureau of Labor Statistics, the unemployment rate has been 5 percent or less—commonly considered to be "full employment"— since September 2015. Worker incomes, too, have returned to prerecessionary levels, after accounting for inflation.[13]

Even so, research by the Federal Reserve Board points to an ever-increasing number of workers who are working multiple jobs, doing informal work for pay in addition to a main job, or both. In the Federal Reserve Board's *Report on the Economic Well-Being of U.S. Households in 2015,* 22 percent of workers were engaged in such secondary income activities; by the time the 2017 report was published, the number had increased to 28 percent.[14] Nearly one in three American adults cannot get by on just the income from one formal job, even with incomes back to prerecessionary levels.

Part of the problem is income volatility. Described as America's "hidden inequality," income volatility is the degree to which a worker's income varies drastically.[15] The variation can be due to seasonal differences, such as a landscaper facing the winter off-season, or caused by just-in-time scheduling that creates a feast-or-famine situation as work hours vary from week to week.

While income volatility is often associated with hourly workers, it is increasingly affecting large swaths of American society. American household incomes became 30 percent more volatile between the early 1970s and the first decade of the twenty-first century; and recently, more than 10 percent of American households took in half the annual income that they did the previous year.[16] Even though the Great Recession officially ended in June 2009, 32 percent of adults said, in a 2016 report by the Federal Reserve Board, that their income varied to some degree from month to month, and 13 percent struggled to pay bills in some months owing to income volatility. Less than half—47 percent—of adults reported that their income exceeded their spending in the prior year.[17]

As the number of people seeking to supplement their salaries continues to increase, the sharing economy finds itself with a glut of potential workers. Basic economics teaches us that when supply increases, but demand remains static, prices must fall. While the terminology is different when applied to workers, the concept remains the same: having an excess of available workers lends itself to the opportunity to "churn and burn" without fear of losing one's workforce. One can't help but be reminded of the scene in *The Jungle* where injured workers are quickly replaced by those waiting outside the gate, clamoring for an opportunity to be hired next.

Placing the sharing economy in the context of larger social changes demonstrates how the sharing economy is simply the next step in the erosion of the employee-employer social contract. But there are solutions, such as programs and policies that can address the need for workplace flexibility while also protecting workers.

PLACING THE SHARING ECONOMY IN CONTEXT

During World War II, large employers began offering health insurance as a way around wartime wage controls. After the war ended, workers and companies, especially the Big Three automakers (General Motors, Ford, and Chrysler), began to address grievances that had arisen during the 1940s. The so-called Treaty of Detroit was a five-year contract that protected automakers from annual strikes in exchange for extensive health, unemployment, and retirement benefits.[18] Workers also received annual cost-of-living adjustments to wages and increased vacation time. While this was originally an agreement with just three companies, similar contracts soon followed in the steel industry. By the early 1960s, more than half of the union contracts in the United States had copycat provisions calling for cost-of-living adjustments.[19] With labor unions representing roughly a third of all workers, other workplaces soon followed suit in order to keep workers happy and reduce the likelihood of unionizing.[20] Linking benefits to a specific workplace became de rigueur. As noted by the Century Foundation, "The Treaty of Detroit reflected two choices that shaped work over the next several decades: first, a recognition by business that the security and well-being of its workers was in its own interest; second, a decision by labor that it was better off obtaining benefits linked to a specific employer than waiting for government to act."[21]

While the relationship between workers and employers is often thought of in more adversarial terms today, especially in regard to the sharing economy, this was not always the case.[22] Before World War II, employers often followed the scientific management model of Taylorism—which focused on increasing productivity by simplifying jobs into discrete tasks, measuring productivity, and linking pay to performance—in an effort to turn "workers into cogs in an industrial machine."[23] After the war, companies adopted the gentler human-relations perspective, a management philosophy that was propounded by Elton Mayo and other sociologists and industrial theorists and based on extensive studies at Western Electric.[24] Sometimes called the "happy worker model," the philosophy was simple: the best way to increase productivity—and discourage unionization—was to keep workers happy.[25]

The focus on worker happiness took a backseat to the bottom line beginning in the 1980s. A surge in steel and automobile imports, along with the 1981–1982 recession (described as the worst recession since the Great Depression, until the Great Recession) led to the perception that companies needed to be more focused on controlling costs down to the penny. The deregulation of trucking, airlines, and telecommunications, allowed for increased start-ups, but it also affected large, unionized companies. Finally, President Ronald Reagan's firing of 11,500 striking air traffic controllers, and the disbanding of their union, paved the way for other companies to copy such hard-nosed tactics. While the Supreme Court had ruled in 1938 that companies could replace striking workers with permanent replacements, few companies had dared to do so before the 1980s. In short order, striking workers for the timber company Louisiana-Pacific, miners for Phelps Dodge, pilots for Eastern Airlines, and paper workers for International Paper found themselves replaced.[26]

In the 1990s, white-collar workers also found themselves on the losing end of a changing workplace social contract. Job-cutting executives such as "Chainsaw Al" Dunlap, "Neutron Jack" Welch, and "Irv the Liquidator" Jacobs implemented mass layoffs in an effort to save billions of dollars.[27] Workers found that layoffs—once limited to economic downturns and periods of financial duress—became routine, even when companies were thriving. In 1994, Proctor and Gamble reported that profits rose more than 13 percent in its second quarter after a "cost cutting" that included eliminating thirteen thousand jobs and thirty plants worldwide.[28] A *New York Times* analysis of Labor Department numbers found that more than forty-three million jobs were erased in the United States in the period from 1979 to 1995, and that the job losses were increasingly those of "higher-paid, white collar workers, many at large corporations." A poll conducted in conjunction with the paper's coverage of the layoffs found that "nearly three-quarters of all households had a close encounter with layoffs" between 1980 and 1996, and that in a third of all households, a family member had lost a job.[29]

In some cases, the lost jobs were replaced with automation as computers and software made certain jobs and procedures redundant. In other cases, work expectations were simply ratcheted upward as workers, anxious that they would lose their jobs in the next round of layoffs, pushed themselves to do more with less. The layoffs were also used to shed full-time employees, replacing them with outsourced services such as call centers, staffing companies, and perma-temps. The popular business titles of the age are instructive: *The Overworked American, Mean Business, Lean and Mean, The White Collar Sweatshop,* and *The Disposable American.*[30]

This focus on production—and on the expendability of workers—was similar to the early industrial age and the efforts of companies to wring every last minute of work out of their workers. Corporations were no longer using the Pinkerton National Detective Agency to brutalize or intimidate workers, but beginning in the 1990s, software made it possible to track keystrokes of workers and monitor exactly how long it took to complete tasks and whether the workers took unauthorized breaks.[31] And, as computers made it easier to track workers, companies also had an easier time determining when—and if—they needed workers. With the rise of just-in-time scheduling, more and more workers became temps or independent contractors. By the end of 1998, temporary staffing had become a fifty-billion-dollar-a-year business in the United States, with one in five U.S. corporations reporting using temps for at least 10 percent of their workforce. Temping, a short-term solution for students on summer break, retirees, and those between jobs, became a long-term career option. At one point, Microsoft alone employed five thousand temps, including fifteen hundred who had worked for the company for a year or more.[32]

While some temporary workers found themselves in long-term employment contracts, they were still outside the social safety net in many ways. Often hired through a staffing agency, temps did not qualify for the same workplace perks as their colleagues, including retirement contributions, paid time off, and raises and promotions. Even their interactions with peers were affected by their temporary status. In a 1998 interview in *Fast Company*, Jeff Kelly, publisher of *Temp Slave*, described temping as similar to "being an alien. There's such insecurity. No benefits. You never know when your assignment is going to end. Your coworkers treat you as if you're a threat to their livelihood. It's abominable."[33]

As white-collar corporate America began to rely on temps, service and retail work increasingly became part-time work managed via just-in-time scheduling, further increasing the uncertainty faced by employees. During the Great Recession, the number of part-time workers who preferred to work full-time skyrocketed from approximately 4 million to more than 9 million.[34] By 2014, the number had dropped, but still remained almost double (7.5 million) what it was in 2007, before the start of the recession. In addition to working fewer hours than they would like, workers also found themselves with less control over their schedules as employers moved to computerized scheduling systems. Such computer systems allow employers to slot workers into shifts that correlate with times of expected demand, and they lead to shift changes with little notice. The Bureau of Labor Statistics notes that 47 percent of part-time hourly workers ages twenty-six to thirty-two receive a week or less of advance notice for their schedule.[35] Sometimes workers arrived at work only to be told that the computer indicated that sales were slow, and they weren't needed for their shift.[36] Such constantly-in-flux schedules can reduce worker abilities to arrange childcare, take college classes, manage a second job, or earn sufficient income.[37]

Temporary workers, just-in-time employees, massive layoffs—the sharing economy is just the newest (technological) innovation in treating workers shabbily. It combines the no-obligations-attached workforce of temps with the on-demand convenience of app-based on-demand scheduling. For corporations, the sharing economy offers the best of just-in-time scheduling, temp agency outsourcing, and down-to-the-penny accounting. In the words of one CEO, "You can hire 10,000 people for 10 to 15 minutes. When they're done, those 10,000 people just melt away."[38]

More and more of us may "melt away" in the future. In 2013, the global sharing economy market was valued at $26 billion, and some predict it will grow to become a $110-billion revenue market in the coming years, making it larger than the U.S. chain-restaurant industry.[39]

This "new" economic movement is part of a larger trend toward reshaping the employer-employee social contract and changing expectations of what employers offer their workers. While promising innovation, the sharing economy is returning to an earlier industrial age where workers are without a safety net.

GOOD JOB, BAD JOB, OR NO JOB?

In "Why Are There Still So Many Jobs? The History and Future of Workplace Automation," David Autor notes that the rise of automatic teller machines did not decrease the number of bank tellers but allowed them to move into more advanced positions as salespeople who could introduce customers to a variety of new products. The gig economy has also allowed workers to move into sales, as they market and sell their labor on digital platforms.[40] The selling of the self is a continuation of the personal ownership message that Jacob Hacker discusses in *The Great Risk Shift*, where economic risk shifts from businesses and government to the average American worker.

In the new economy, workers are told to improve their market value through training and networking, and to market themselves as a brand and business, "the CEO of Me Inc. . . . willing to temporarily assist other, larger businesses."[41] As a result, "a central concept in this economized, individualized view of the world is 'responsibilization.'"[42] Although citizens demonstrate some autonomy in choosing where to work and live and how to spend their time, there are "no rights without responsibilities."[43]

This message of personal responsibility, part of a neoliberal ideology, gets a further boost with the entrepreneurial ethos employed by the gig economy platforms. The companies claim the sharing economy allows workers to "be your own boss." Work is arranged according to your schedule ("work when you want") and controlled by the worker ("find jobs you love" and "only you decide . . . where to drive" or "who to host"). Workers are told they are empowered to pick their payday ("push a button and get paid whenever you want").

This message ignores the limiting component of choice. Workers are turning to these gig jobs out of a dearth of other options. With stagnating salaries and high levels of income volatility, there are few options for economic stability. Furthermore, the amount of money that workers can make is directly affected by the number of fellow workers who are competing for a limited number of gigs or potential rides. The platforms benefit from having a large, ready, willing, and able stable of potential workers in order to meet the on-demand needs of potential clients. But workers can make more money and have increased control over their own work when there are fewer workers. Decreases in the payment rate, coupled with increased commissions to the platforms, further decrease the "control" workers can exert over their destiny even as they are urged to take a higher level of responsibility for it.

While services market themselves as offering peer-to-peer opportunities, making it easier for a busy parent to hire someone to do grocery shopping, or to hire—and track—an Uber driver picking a child up from soccer practice, the ease with which workers can be hired or discarded has not escaped the recognition of business managers. Numerous TaskRabbits and Kitchensurfing workers that I interviewed noted being hired by companies for everything from making dinners for corporate meetings to assembling Ikea furniture for start-ups. Uber and Airbnb are now being accepted as business travel expenses.[44] In September 2017, Ikea announced that it was acquiring TaskRabbit.[45] One of the ways in which I knew that I had obtained theoretical saturation with my research sample was that several TaskRabbits told me about the same task: stuffing bags for a Brooklyn coffee company that markets itself as offering fair trade coffee. None of workers I interviewed who did gig work for businesses questioned working for an established company, doing the type of manual or service labor that would normally fall under various workplace protections.

In *Good Jobs, Bad Jobs: The Rise of Polarized and Precarious Employment Systems in the United States,* Arne Kalleberg notes that there have been seven major changes to job quality in the past few decades. These changes include increased polarity between good and bad jobs in addition to an overall increase in job precarity and insecurity. Many of the good jobs that have been lost have been replaced with jobs of lower quality and pay, and workplace flexibility policies continue to lag in implementation and usage.[46] Kalleberg also notes the importance of human and social capital, writing, "Transformations in work have underscored the growing importance of skills for labor market success; workers with more human and social capital are better able to take advantage of opportunities created by the greater marketization of employment relations. While more-educated and higher-skilled workers may not necessarily have more job security with a particular employer, their more marketable skills enhance their labor market security, which, in turn, generally provides them with higher earnings, greater control over their jobs, higher intrinsic rewards, and better-quality jobs overall."[47]

In the sharing economy, it's true that higher levels of skills and capital make a difference—Airbnb hosts and traditional Kitchensurfing chefs seem to be more likely to be Success Stories or Strivers than Strugglers and are more likely to identify as entrepreneurs. But the second half of Kalleberg's claim doesn't seem to apply here: in the sharing economy, higher levels of education don't increase labor market security or lead to better quality jobs. If anything, the sharing economy appears to add to inequality by turning even low-prestige, low-education work—occupations of last resort—into part-time positions for the well-educated. As Juliet Schor has noted, the sharing economy makes it possible for college-educated workers to hire college-educated housecleaners.[48] Marriage has long been identified as a so-called luxury good. As the wealthy and well-educated marry each other, those with lower incomes and education levels are seen as less desirable and are less likely to get married. Likewise, the sharing economy turns paid employment into a luxury good that is increasingly accessed by better educated, technologically adept workers with smartphones and dependable data networks.

Arun Sundararajan, author of *The Sharing Economy: The End of Employment and the Rise of Crowd-Based Capitalism,* supports the sharing economy, arguing that it has generated positive spillover effects by putting underused assets to work and expanding economic opportunity. Yet, even Sundararajan has noted that sharing economy platforms blur the lines between the personal and the professional, and between employment and casual work, and may spell the end of traditional employment.[49]

The end of "traditional employment," with its mind-numbing nine-to-five grind, may not be a bad thing: while numerous companies offer flexible work arrangements, their usage is often stigmatized.[50] Work by Pamela Stone demonstrates that the so-called opt-out of well-educated women with children is caused by a lack of flexible workplace policies: flexible hours are important to ensuring the workplace tenure of women with small children and others with child or family care responsibilities.[51] An increase in freelance work, with its focus on deliverables as opposed to face time, and higher hourly wages could be a boon to workers seeking time and location flexibility.[52] Or, the lack of workplace security and dependable income could make "taken-for-granted models for organizing one's life" essentially unattainable.[53]

FREELANCE WAGE OR GIG ECONOMY MIRAGE?

Sharing economy services such as Uber and TaskRabbit argue that their workers also command premium incomes. In 2014, an Uber blog post describing drivers as "small business entrepreneurs" noted that "the median income on uberX is more than $90,000/year/driver in New York and more than $74,000/year/driver in San Francisco."[54] However, tweets from Josh Mohrer, the general manager of Uber in New York City, and statements from Lane Kasselman, Uber's head of communications for the Americas, have noted that drivers earn an average of $25 to $25.79 an hour after Uber's commission. As Alison Griswold points out, "Even at $25.79, $90,000 is a tough mark to hit. You'd need to work 70 hours a week for 50 weeks a year."[55]

While $25 an hour is slightly more than the $22.92 per hour earned by workers in transportation and warehousing in December 2015, the Uber rate doesn't take into account the need to pay for gas, insurance, and vehicle maintenance, and to account for depreciation. The Internal Revenue

Service's standard mileage rate is a commonly accepted tool for calculating the cost of owning and operating a vehicle. The rate is often used when calculating the cost of miles driven when seeking reimbursement on an expense report or accounting for travel costs. The mileage rate was 54 cents per mile in 2016, before dropping to 53.5 in 2017. After accounting for the platform's cut, more than half of every dollar earned by a driver goes to expenses. When vehicle costs are factored in, the actual amount of money earned by a driver decreases precipitously.

Uber seems to know the financial implications of driving for the service. "According to an internal slide deck on driver income levels viewed by *The New York Times*, Uber considered Lyft and McDonald's its main competition for attracting new drivers."[56]

There are stories of super successful drivers, but their high incomes are not the result of just driving. In 2015, *Forbes* magazine highlighted an Uber driver who made $252,000 a year by turning his car into a jewelry showroom and using his profits to purchase a fleet of cars and hire additional drivers. Yet even this "Uberpreneur" made the majority of his money ($18,000 in transactions a month) in jewelry sales. His monthly gross earnings from Uber, in 2014—before the platform began implementing a series of rate cuts—was just $3,000, or $36,000 a year.[57]

TaskRabbit has promoted the idea that Taskers who work full time on the platform can earn $78,000 a year. Jamie Viggiano, a spokeswoman for TaskRabbit, explains, "Some 15% of workers on TaskRabbit work full-time and, of those, many earn $6,000 to $7,000 a month after the commission is deducted.[58] Even at just $6,000 a month, a Tasker would need to work forty hours a week at $45/hour or twenty hours a week at $90. Since client messaging, travel time, and transportation costs are unpaid, a Tasker seeking a premium income would likely need to be working for many more hours. After the platform's most recent service pivot—which increased commissions from 20 percent to 30 percent for first-time tasks—workers would need to work even more hours.

While some tasks do command a price premium, most tasks are one-offs and don't result in the type of steady employment that workers would need to obtain high five-figure incomes. Additionally, earning a high wage for a gig or two doesn't take into account the costs of benefits—sick leave, paid time off, unemployment or health insurance—that commonly equal 20 to 30 percent of compensation.

As a result, the gig economy also raises issues related to inequality and stratification. Even though services market their platforms as bringing entrepreneurship to the masses, the real winners are individuals with capital to spare. In *Race against the Machine*, Erik Brynjolfsson and Andrew McAfee note that rapid technological change is destroying jobs faster than they are created, resulting in a "great decoupling" as productivity increases but employment decreases.[59] Fellow economist David Autor disagrees with Brynjolfsson and McAfee about the robust increase in productivity but acknowledges that not all technological changes have been good. The movement of bank tellers into higher skill sales jobs is an illustration of the "polarization" and "hollowing out" of the middle class as growth occurs with low-level service jobs and high-paying jobs that focus on creativity and problem-solving skills.[60]

The old model of the labor market—whereby workers sell scarce labor to employers over the course of their career—is eroding. As David Autor explains, "It doesn't mean there's no money around, but it's just accruing to the owners of capital, to the owners of ideas. And capital is less equitably distributed than labor. Everyone is born with some labor, but not everyone is born with capital."[61] In the gig economy, the workers who are most likely to succeed are those who have social and financial capital.

This work also has implications for the informal economy, defined as "those actions of economic agents that fail to adhere to the established institutional rules or are denied their protection."[62] Most informal-economy research is focused on illegal markets or examines developing or emerging economies.[63] The concept of the informal economy originates with Keith Hart's study of urban markets in Africa.[64] Other researchers have studied informal work among the middle class, but with a focus on removing activities from economic exchange—for instance, individuals choosing to repair their own machines or mow their own grass in an effort to "maximize the efficient allocation of time."[65] Just like participants in the underground economy, workers in the gig economy—especially when paid as 1099 workers—are engaged in "informal economic activities [that] bypass the existing laws and regulatory agencies of the state."[66] Workers must trust that they will be paid and won't be harassed or get injured on the job.

As this research shows, not all gig work is created equal. When workers in insecure jobs have benefits and workplace protections, worker insecurity and experience of material hardship can be reduced. As Dan Zuberi notes in his study of hotel workers in Seattle and Vancouver, "There is nothing inevitable about the globalization of the economy and rising levels of inequality and poverty."[67]

The gig economy does not have to be the end of stable work or the employment-social-safety net. The sharing economy was born out of an idealism of sharing and community—not gig-based or hourly work. Fortunately, some on-demand platforms on the cutting edge of app-based work still treat their workers as employees and provide access to a basic social-safety net of workers' compensation, health insurance, and unemployment protections.

WORKING AS AN EMPLOYEE—IN THE SHARING ECONOMY

Hello Alfred's Manhattan office fits the stereotype of a tech-enabled start-up. Straddling the border between Union Square and the Flatiron Building, the office is surrounded by expensive exercise studios and upscale home-goods shops. In the center of the brick-walled space, a handful of attractive twentysomethings work on scheduling software, chatting back and forth about changes in worker availability. A copy of their Harvard Business School case study, signatures dotting the margins, is hung in the entry, and a bulletin board features a collection of handwritten notes from clients to their Alfreds, thanking them for cleaning an apartment, making life happier, and generally saving the day.

While the company's physical office fits a stereotype, that's where the similarities between it and other tech-enabled start-ups end. Even the creation story for Hello Alfred is very different from those of Uber or Airbnb. Instead of looking for a way to pay their rent or party more cheaply, cofounders Jessica Beck and Marcela Sapone, while enrolled in Harvard Business School, were thinking about how to balance careers with life. "I just didn't have enough time, and that's the theme that really underlies everything, there's not enough time to do things that you feel like you really want to do," Sapone said.

Their solution, Hello Alfred, is more than an errand-running service. Alfreds are assigned to a client and are tasked with developing the intuition needed to anticipate the client's needs. For instance, an Alfred might note that certain cereals are usually in the cabinet and ensure that they don't run out. Or she may notice that a client has a well-outfitted kitchen but never any food in the fridge, and offer to buy twenty-dollars' worth of fresh vegetables at the farmers' market so that the client can cook.

"The concept of on demand is pretty suboptimal. It means you haven't planned it out. . . . [T]o get to a place beyond demand, where you feel like your mind is being read and your needs anticipated, is actually the same thing as having someone plan for you," Sapone said. "We had to create a relationship with a customer where they trusted that you would be able to do something as well as they would, if not better, and that we were trustworthy people and could be in their home unsupervised."

This "intuitive detective work" isn't easy, but the cofounders have firsthand experience in the challenge—they took a semester off from Harvard to run time trials and work as the company's first Alfreds. Members of the senior management team go out into the field on a regular basis in order to stay informed about the challenges experienced by Alfreds.

Unlike other services that focus on flooding the marketplace with potential workers, Alfred doesn't hire workers until they have sufficient demand in an area to ensure that they can offer at least steady part-time employment. Alfreds are paid sixteen dollars an hour during their two-week training, which is then increased to eighteen dollars an hour. The average pay is roughly twenty-two dollars an hour, and the goal is to get workers to thirty dollars an hour. All workers are W-2 employees, and full-time Alfreds get the same benefits as full-time corporate workers—a standard Monday to Friday work week, health insurance (including dental and vision), disability coverage, and paid time off. There's no 401k yet, but that's company-wide.

Paying workers as W-2 employees hasn't been challenge-free. The company has an added human-resources and legal burden and obviously spends more for labor. They've also received pushback from potential investors who have declined to support their company because they weren't classifying workers as independent contractors. "There was this whole trend at the time because of Uber. 'Uber for anything . . .' It was like heroin for VC [venture capitalists]. . . . [T]hey were all going on to Uber's model, where you put a lot of cash up front to acquire your customers and figure out the economics later," Sapone explained. "All of this stuff about flexibility and extra work, it's all kind of B.S., because what happens is you end up not making enough money or being able to plan for anything or have any benefits."

Sapone admits that their company could have gone either way in terms of hiring workers as employees or independent contractors. But Sapone and her cofounder disliked the high level of customer and worker churn found in the 1099 model, and they were concerned about the quality of the jobs they were creating. In an essay written for *Quartz*, she explains,

> While technology can increase access to new goods and services, it also risks increasing the distance between groups of people being served and serving. . . . There should not be a disconnect between the success of a company and the success of its workers. We believe treating our employees as our primary customer is how we can best satisfy our end users. It can become difficult to achieve this with the 1099 classification, because it inherently distances the worker from the company. There is no onus to provide meaningful work, training, or career advancement. . . . For us, breaking the rules means making people the center of our tech business. It means taking on responsibility to provide good jobs. The relationship companies have with workers is not just about cost, it is about principles. It turns out those principles are good for business anyway.[68]

MyClean, a home-cleaning service started in 2009 by Michael Scharf, Mike Russell and Justin Geller, has also discovered how principles can impact profit. As noted in chapter 4, MyClean began with an outsourced workforce, but then found that the company's lack of commitment to workers led to an equally mercenary attitude among cleaners. Cleaning quality and dependability was spotty, and the customer turnover was high, which was problematic given the service's customer acquisition costs. Additionally, the company couldn't legally require certain things like uniforms or specific work hours.

MyClean now treats workers as W-2 employees. As their mission statement notes, "We employ our cleaners, affording them the rights and benefits that come with that, including paid travel time, paid overtime, payroll taxes, disability insurance, workers' compensation, FLSA protections, health insurance, 401k matching, etc." The expectations of both MyClean and its employees are clarified under the W-2 model—workers and the company know what expectations must be met to achieve success and how workers will be remunerated; and workers can expect regular paychecks. Treating workers as employees has come with an additional, unexpected perk—the company's recruitment costs have greatly decreased, and most of their hires now come as a result of word of mouth, which has its own added benefit of quality control. Few workers want to jeopardize their standing in the company by recommending subpar employees, and as a result those who are referred tend to be carefully vetted in advance.[69]

Treating workers as employees goes beyond the basics of Social Security contributions. It means offering hourly workers access to the same perks and privileges of their salaried colleagues. When I met MyClean cofounder and CEO Michael Scharf, the company had recently hosted a holiday party for staff and their families at a local barbeque joint as a way to thank them for another year of hard work.

MyClean isn't the only company fighting the rise of an independent workforce where hustling rules the day. Makespace, the personal storage service; Munchery, a food delivery start-up; and Managed by Q, an office management service, all treat their workers as employees. Instacart, a grocery service, classifies part-time workers (29 hours or less) as employees.

To be fair, the impetus for treating workers as employees is not generally philanthropic. For instance, the office service Managed by Q views its rejection of the independent contractor model as a business strategy. Shortly before creating the service, the founder, Dan Teran, read Zeynep Ton's book, *The Good Jobs Strategy*. The book, which harkens back to the "happy worker model" of increasing productivity by keeping workers happy, uses case studies of Zappos and Trader Joe's as proof that investing in a workforce can make a company more profitable in the long run. As a result, Managed by Q offers benefits that match, or even exceed, those offered by more traditional companies, including company-paid health insurance, a 401K with match, and paid family leave.[70]

Similar views were echoed by Juno, a "kinder version of Uber" that marketed itself as treating drivers better so that "drivers treat you better." The company viewed drivers as true partners and offered stock options and charged a lower commission (10 percent, versus 25 percent, guaranteed for twenty-four months) than Uber.[71] Drivers were also offered access to 24/7 telephone support with a person, as opposed to Uber's notorious email-based system.[72]

What keeps other companies from also classifying their workers as employees or offering their workers stock options and full company involvement? For one, the cost savings from classifying a worker as an independent contractor can be considerable: after factoring in unemployment insurance, workers compensation premiums, Social Security and Medicare contributions, health insurance, and any additional benefits, the savings can total around 30 percent.[73] Companies that outsource workplace risk to their workers are able to offer much lower prices than companies that commit to paying an actual wage.

The cost savings of deeming workers to be independent contractors creates a perverse incentive for companies to save money on the backs of their workers. It also makes it harder for companies that are classifying their workers as employees to compete equally. "In a world without laws, it would be great to be able to hand someone supplies, train them, and give them 30 bucks under the table," says Ken Schultz, MyClean's chief operating officer. "But we're compliant, and the result is employees who have rights. We'd like to have a level playing field."[74]

"PAY NO ATTENTION TO THAT MAN BEHIND THE CURTAIN"

How did we end up with so few companies playing by the rules and so many companies treating workers like expendable cogs? Why are the platforms and their supporters dominating the public discourse? Part of the issue comes back to the hijacking of language by these companies and the sharing economy. Calling something "sharing" hides a number of sins. Likewise, calling these platforms "technology companies" is a way to brush off the social contract. Describing a company as part of the technology field means that no one can be expected to understand—it gives it the imprimatur of the flashing 12:00 on an old VCR. It's too complicated. It doesn't make sense. There are a lot of buttons, and they're not intuitive. And it's just going to need to be changed again, so why bother?

"I think there's a mistake that happened within the technology community: [the idea] that you could just put technology around anything and it could be a unicorn. And trying to take [a] real-world business like a home-cleaning service and add a tech component, and to just assume that naturally that's going to be a billion-dollar business," said MyClean CEO Michael Scharf. "This is not a social media platform, it's not software, it's a service platform. It's not just a technology business; as a matter of fact, technology is a secondary component. It's a real-world business, and real-world businesses that involve people don't scale at the same pace that true technology businesses do; your growth comes from people, not software."

Sharing economy platforms seem to get a free pass when they identify as technology companies or online marketplaces. Given that technology changes so fast, of course it makes sense that a company will need to shed workers at a moment's notice. Except, this free pass ignores the fact that the argument about being able to shed workers was also commonly used during the massive layoffs of the 1980s and 1990s.

Additionally, because Strivers and Success Stories have other work or interests, they're able to brush off problems within the sharing economy. It's not *really* who they are. It's not what they really *do*. Joshua, the corporate attorney with multiple Airbnb listings, sums this up beautifully:

> So, when I was first doing it, I was spending a lot more time on it. . . . [W]here I was, I did everything. I went and cleaned the apartment. . . . It was weirdly fun to sort of do manual labor instead of being an attorney. So, it's like it was strangely enjoyable to sort of leave the office at one in the afternoon and go down to some apartment and clean it up and welcome a guest, which is so different from the general cerebral work that I do on a day-to-day basis.

A small, temporary change of pace can be interesting. Joshua would probably never consider cleaning houses for a living or working as a hotel's front desk clerk, but as a short-term side hustle it has its appeal. At the end of our interview, he noted that he was moving cross-country and hiring his fiancée's undocumented immigrant mother to manage the key distribution and cleaning. As he put it, he and his business partner "want to do as little manual labor as possible, turn [Airbnb listings] into passive income."

RACE OR CLASS?

Is this brushing off of the social contract an issue of socioeconomic or racial inequities? As noted previously, discrimination has been documented among sharing economy services such as Airbnb, Craigslist, and eBay.[75] However, when it comes to the treatment of workers, it's not certain to what extent the issue is race-based or class-based. There are three main areas in which the experiences of workers may be affected by race: working in the sharing economy, using platforms as a client, and experiencing increased levels of risk and exploitation.

African Americans appear to be less likely to work in the sharing economy. An Uber-funded study found that Uber drivers were more likely to be white, and less likely to be black, than local chauffer-taxi drivers.[76] It's not certain if the "whiteness" of sharing economy services is due to an awareness of such discrimination or to the digital divide. For instance, lower-income minorities may be less likely to have access to the types of smartphones and robust data plans that are needed for successful hustling in the sharing economy. Additionally, African Americans also appear to be less likely to use the sharing economy.

In a March 2016 Pew Research Center survey of 4,787 American adults— a detailed study of the scope and impact of the shared, collaborative, and on-demand economy—Pew found that platform usage varied widely across the population. The survey revealed that 72 percent of American adults had used at least one of eleven different shared and on-demand services, and that approximately 20 percent of Americans had used four or more services. However, the Pew definition is especially broad and includes services that may or may not be part of the sharing economy. For instance, in the Pew survey, 41 percent of adults had "used programs offering same-day or expedited delivery," and 28 percent had purchased tickets from an online reseller—these are hardly concepts that are novel to the sharing economy. While 50 percent of adults have purchased used goods online, there's a sharp drop in the percentage of respondents who have tried a ride-hailing app (15 percent), utilized an online home-sharing service (11 percent), or hired someone online for a task/errand (4 percent).

The Pew study also found racial differences by service platform. Car services, such as Uber and Lyft, have been identified as helping equalize the playing field by reducing the discrimination that racial minorities may otherwise experience in hailing a cab. Latinos (18 percent) and blacks (15 percent) were slightly more likely than whites (14 percent) to have used a transportation service such as Uber or Lyft. But, while 13 percent of white adults had used a home-sharing service, only 9 percent of Latinos and 5 percent of blacks had used such a service. Blacks (36 percent) and Latinos (48 percent) were also less likely than whites (53 percent) to have purchased used items online through eBay or Craigslist, both of which were early entrants into the sharing economy.

Again, there are also distinct class differences at work. Among individuals with incomes of $75,000 a year or more, 61 percent have purchased used items online, compared to 36 percent of those making less than $30,000 a year. Home-sharing services have been used by 24 percent of those with incomes north of $75,000 a year, compared to 4 percent of those making under $30,000.[77]

Finally, it's uncertain if the criminal risks that are experienced by workers are due to race or class. An unpublished joint paper by Isak Ladegaard, Juliet Schor, and myself shows that for-hire drivers in Boston and New York experienced three major categories of vulnerability: legal (e.g., involuntary inclusion in criminal activities), economic (e.g., the ever-present threat of being "deactivated"), and bodily and emotional (e.g., sexual harassment and threats of violence). Additionally, women and minorities experienced enhanced and intersecting vulnerabilities. Likewise, as noted previously in chapter 6 on criminal activity, most of the workers who found themselves in criminally questionable situations were members of minority groups.

Again, however, it's not clear how much this is an issue of race versus class. Work from the Chase Institute found that individuals with lower incomes ($44,800 and below) had a higher involvement in labor platforms (0.6 percent) compared to those with incomes in the highest quintile, $84,900 and above (0.3 percent). A McKinsey Global Institute report also noted that lower-income households are more likely to participate in independent work out of a lack of better alternatives. Forty-eight percent of the earners with less than $25,000 in household income participated in independent work, and 37 percent of such households described their work as being "out of necessity." Meanwhile, one in three high-income earners (defined as those with household incomes of $75,000 or more) engaged in independent work, and the majority of these participated "by choice."[78]

The gains for whites and minorities played out differently after the Great Depression and World War II.[79] While whites were able to utilize government-guaranteed mortgages, African Americans were prevented from accessing such resources, owing to restrictive covenants in neighborhoods and bank redlining. With most of the average American's wealth attributed to a home, the resulting homeownership gap led to a growing wealth gap. By 1994, the median white family had more than seven times the assets of a median nonwhite family; and even among upper-income families, whites had three times the median net worth ($308,000) of nonwhites ($114,600).[80] After the subprime crisis, in which minority homeowners were especially targeted by unscrupulous lenders, the wealth gap has only grown. A 2016 report from the Corporation for Economic Development and the Institute for Policy Studies observed that "in the past 30 years, the average household wealth of white families has grown 85% to $656,000, while that of blacks has climbed just 27% to $85,000 and Latinos 69% to $98,000." Based on current trends, it would take Latinos eighty-four years to accumulate the same amount of wealth as whites. For black families? Two hundred twenty-eight years.[81]

While nonwhite workers were in the minority in my sample for most sharing economy services (for-hire driving remains the exception), minority participants, with lower median net worth, may be especially vulnerable in the gig economy. The workers who found themselves involved in criminal activity were all Strugglers and Strivers—none were Success Stories. It's not certain if they were targeted for involvement on the basis of their race, or if they were more vulnerable to questionable activities because of the nature of the labor platform and the need to hustle for work. All users—regardless of race—experience the same risk of sexual harassment, on-the-job injuries, and sudden deactivation, although these risks are more salient for Strugglers and Strivers than for Success Stories.

Some have suggested that as the economy further improves, gig economy services will have to increase their perks and workplace benefits in order to compete for workers. Yet even as unemployment rates drop, the gig economy continues to grow. Owing to economic volatility and income stagnation, it seems unlikely that employment in the gig economy will decrease all that much. The sharing economy—with its focus on flexible scheduling and opportunity for workers to pick up shifts as necessary—is fulfilling a real need. Indeed, while I was doing this research, one of my family members, seeking to soften a financial blow, began driving for Uber and Lyft. As he put it, driving was helping "make ends meet."

As critical as I am of the sharing economy and its lack of worker protections, if we aren't going to increase incomes overall or implement a universal basic income, then we need a way to help people supplement their incomes as needed without experiencing an undue burden of risk. An easy fix would be to change how gig economy workers are classified by employers.

INDEPENDENT CONTRACTOR (MIS)CLASSIFICATION

While many sharing economy services tell their workers that they are small business owners or independent contractors, the determination of employee or independent contractor is actually based on federal laws, although definitions and interpretations can vary. The Fair Labor Standards Act, the Migrant and Seasonal Agricultural Worker Protection Act, and the Family and Medical Leave Act have broader definitions of *employee*. For instance, under the Fair Labor Standards Act , an employee is "'any individual employed by an employer' and employ is defined as including 'to suffer or permit to work.' The concept of employment in the FLSA is very broad and is tested by 'economic reality.'"[82] Economic reality is composed of six factors, including whether the work is an integral aspect of the employer's business; whether the worker's managerial skill affects his or her opportunity for profit or loss; the worker's and employer's relative investments; the worker's skill and initiative; the permanency of their relationship; and the employer's control over said relationship.[83]

Worker classifications are policed by the Labor Department, the IRS, and local and state tax authorities, but employers manage classification, and it is notoriously difficult to root out violators. Seth Harris, a deputy labor secretary under President Obama, explains that, without worker complaints, "your chances of finding a worker that's been misclassified . . . are worse than your chances of finding a leprechaun riding a unicorn."[84]

As noted previously, classifying workers as independent contractors reduces payroll taxes, including Social Security contributions, workers compensation, and health insurance premiums. Misclassifying workers can also lead to issues when workers file for unemployment, delaying their ability to collect on claims. This misclassification, and the fact that state laws differ, has also led to some Uber drivers in New York and California being considered employees for unemployment purposes, while drivers in Florida are deemed independent contractors (see fig. 14).[85]

Although it may sound as though worker classification is arbitrarily decided by companies, the IRS has released a twenty-factor test (see box 1) to assist employers in determining how to classify their workers. While the idea of a multiquestion test may bring to mind magazine quizzes, the test is not as simple as marking yes or no and then adding up the score. While having control over the work is seen as a sign of employer status, it is not necessary that the employer *actually* control the work— just that he or she has the right to control it. To further complicate the situation, the IRS "emphasizes that factors in addition to the 20 factors identified in 1987 may be relevant, that the weight of the factors may vary based on the circumstances, that relevant factors may change over time, and that all facts must be examined."[86]

The twenty-factor test is especially ambiguous when it comes to the sharing economy. If a worker can be deactivated, is that the same as being fired? If a Kitchensurfing chef must wear an apron (factor 1, regarding following instructions), but is paid a set amount for a set shift, regardless of the number of hours actually worked (factor 12, regarding payment), is he an employee or an independent contractor? If a driver can work for both Uber and Lyft (factor 17, regarding working for more than one firm), but her rates are determined by the services (factor 3, regarding integration), where does she fall? If a TaskRabbit must work in a preset four-hour shift (factor 7, regarding set hours of work), but sets her own schedule (factor 8, regarding whether full time required), is she an employee or an independent contractor?

There's enough disagreement about the difference between an employee and an independent contractor that some researchers have suggested

Figure 14. Not all Uber drivers agree that they are independent contractors. Some drivers attended the June 2015 protest at city hall as part of a counterprotest to raise awareness of their status as 1099 workers. Photo by author.

adding a third category, the so-called dependent worker or on-demand contractor.[87] In Germany and Canada, this option is limited to workers who "depend mainly or entirely on a single employer or client," in some cases making as much as 80 percent of their income through one client.[88] Such a classification in the United States might actually increase worker risks and exploitation. For instance, a worker who was a "dependent contractor" for Uber might not be able to take advantage of special rate

Box 1. Twenty Factors in Determining Whether an Employer-Employee Relationship Exists

The 20 factors identified by the IRS are as follows:

1. **Instructions:** If the person for whom the services are performed has the right to require compliance with instructions, this indicates employee status.

2. **Training:** Worker training (e.g., by requiring attendance at training sessions) indicates that the person for whom services are performed wants the services performed in a particular manner (which indicates employee status).

3. **Integration:** Integration of the worker's services into the business operations of the person for whom services are performed is an indication of employee status.

4. **Services rendered personally:** If the services are required to be performed personally, this is an indication that the person for whom services are performed is interested in the methods used to accomplish the work (which indicates employee status).

5. **Hiring, supervision, and paying assistants:** If the person for whom services are performed hires, supervises or pays assistants, this generally indicates employee status. However, if the worker hires and supervises others under a contract pursuant to which t he worker agrees to provide material and labor and is only responsible for the result, this indicates independent contractor status.

6. **Continuing relationship:** A continuing relationship between the worker and the person for whom the services are performed indicates employee status.

7. **Set hours of work:** The establishment of set hours for the worker indicates employee status.

8. **Full time required:** If the worker must devote substantially full time to the business of the person for whom services are performed, this indicates employee status. An independent contractor is free to work when and for whom he or she chooses.

9. **Doing work on employer's premises:** If the work is performed on the premises of the person for whom the services are performed, this indicates employee status, especially if the work could be done elsewhere.

(continued)

10. **Order or sequence test:** If a worker must perform services in the order or sequence set by the person for whom services are performed, that shows the worker is not free to follow his or her own pattern of work, and indicates employee status.

11. **Oral or written reports:** A requirement that the worker submit regular reports indicates employee status.

12. **Payment by the hour, week, or month:** Payment by the hour, week, or month generally points to employment status; payment by the job or a commission indicates independent contractor status.

13. **Payment of business and/or traveling expenses.** If the person for whom the services are performed pays expenses, this indicates employee status. An employer, to control expenses, generally retains the right to direct the worker.

14. **Furnishing tools and materials:** The provision of significant tools and materials to the worker indicates employee status.

15. **Significant investment:** Investment in facilities used by the worker indicates independent contractor status.

16. **Realization of profit or loss:** A worker who can realize a profit or suffer a loss as a result of the services (in addition to profit or loss ordinarily realized by employees) is generally an independent contractor.

17. **Working for more than one firm at a time:** If a worker performs more than de minimis services for multiple firms at the same time, that generally indicates independent contractor status.

18. **Making service available to the general public:** If a worker makes his or her services available to the public on a regular and consistent basis, that indicates independent contractor status.

19. **Right to discharge:** The right to discharge a worker is a factor indicating that the worker is an employee.

20. **Right to terminate:** If a worker has the right to terminate the relationship with the person for whom services are performed at any time he or she wishes without incurring liability, that indicates employee status.

More recently, the IRS has identified three categories of evidence that may be relevant in determining whether the requisite control exists under the common-law test and has grouped illustrative factors under these three categories: (1) behavioral control; (2) financial control; and (3) relationship of the parties. The IRS emphasizes that factors in addition to the 20 factors identified in 1987 may be relevant, that the weight of the factors may vary based on the circumstances, that relevant factors may change over time, and that all facts must be examined.

Source: Joint Committee on Taxation, *Present Law and Background Relating to Worker Classification for Federal Tax Purposes*, House Committee on Ways and Means, JCX-26-07, 2007.

incentives with competing services or an entirely different gig economy platform.

An alternative category—independent worker—has been recommended by former deputy secretary of labor Seth Harris and Princeton economist Alan Krueger.[89] If US antitrust laws were amended, the independent worker category would allow independent workers to organize and bargain collectively, to be covered by civil rights laws, and to have taxes deducted from their paychecks. Workers would also have the opportunity to pool with other independent contractors to receive certain benefits, such as disability insurance, retirement accounts, and liability insurance, much like workers who join the Freelancer's Union. However, under this model, workers would not be covered by minimum wage requirements, overtime laws, or workers' compensation, and workplace injuries would generally be addressed through the tort system. This option continues to put the onus on the worker to organize and to find and fund benefits such as disability insurance; and the lack of workers' compensation and minimum-wage requirements is especially troubling.

A third strategy is to maintain the status quo but reduce the economic vulnerability of gig economy workers. In 2017, Virginia senator Mark Warner, a former tech entrepreneur, introduced legislation to test-drive a portable benefits plan for gig workers. The bill asked the federal government to set aside twenty million dollars in funding for organizations to use in order to look at the types of benefits programs individual workers could take with them from job to job. Possibilities include an "'hour bank,' modeled on a program used by some building trades, that tracks a worker's hours for a variety of employers and collects and administers training and retirement programs. Or an 'opt-in' that gives consumers the option of adding a nominal amount to their payment that would go to a benefits fund for workers."[90]

"Somebody may be doing very, very well as an Etsy seller and Airbnb user and Uber driver and part-time consultant[,] . . . but if they hit a rough patch, they have nothing to stop them until they fall, frankly, back upon government assistance programs," the senator explained, calling the portable benefits an "emergency fund": "It might be a fund to take care of a disability if you get hurt. It might work with some existing retirement programs. Part of it would be, depending on what happens with Obamacare, an ability to help deal with health care expenses. I think there will be a variety of models."[91]

While the portable benefits plan may be helpful for Success Stories and Strugglers whose main employment comes from the sharing economy, Strivers who have alternative employment may not be as well served under such a plan. Additionally, the "independent worker" model recommended by Harris and Krueger, or the "on-demand contractor" classification, wouldn't provide the workplace protections that all workers need.

THE TIME RULE SOLUTION

A solution for gig economy workers needs to be simple but still account for the variety found within the on-demand economy, in terms of type of work and the opportunities to excel or be exploited. It sounds complicated, but it isn't. My solution doesn't require creating a new category or getting legislative buy-in for a multimillion dollar trial. My solution doesn't require playing an IRS version of the game twenty questions.

My solution is an easy one-step test for determining if a worker is an independent contractor. I call this test the Time Rule. If the hours/times of work are dictated by the employer or market, the worker is not independent.

Having employer-dictated hours is nothing new. Grocery store clerks and retail workers can't just show up whenever they want—they have set hours. Law-firm attorneys, teachers, accountants, postal workers, emergency room doctors, and call center employees have their hours set by an employer and the market: no one wants their mail to arrive at midnight or to get a telemarketing call at 4 a.m. Some of these jobs also have staffing considerations: we want teachers to be present when students are at school and a certain number of doctors to fulfill the needs of a busy emergency room. There's nothing wrong with requiring people to show up to work at certain times, but if you can't do the job whenever you want, you should not be considered an independent contractor.

If work is truly independent, then the worker gets to decide when it will be done and isn't pushed into one time slot or another. For a "true" independent contractor, worker independence is already expected, such as in the case of a freelance writer or novelist or an independent small-business owner. In many cases these individuals have incorporated in order to secure liability protections for themselves.

Uber and other sharing economy services may argue that they offer work-time flexibility as one of their great perks, but for-hire drivers have their hours dictated by the market—workers who don't work rush hours make substantially less money. The platforms also incentivize drivers to work during specific hours by linking bonuses and income guarantees to certain times and days, further reducing worker flexibility. After the 2015 pivot, TaskRabbit workers were prevented from taking gigs outside of the hours of 8 a.m. to 8 p.m. Postmates and FedEx drivers must do their deliveries during a preset window. Airbnb hosts can pick any time of year to host, but the company requires that hosts respond to potential guests within a set time frame; and certain times of year, such as holiday weekends, are more lucrative. All of these workers would be employees.

Under the Time Rule, the default categorization for workers is employee. If you interview and hire someone—or if you provide them with access to your platform and make money off of their work—that person should be considered an employee and have the same access to benefits and protections as other workers for the same firm. A default setting such as this would especially benefit the Strugglers and Strivers who might otherwise find themselves vulnerable to physical, social, and economic risks and exploitation.

THE PAJAMA POLICY

A corollary to the Time Rule is what I call the "pajama policy": work that is truly independent can be done in one's pajamas, whatever those may—or may not—include. The pajama policy is a direct response to the monitoring that arises when work appears to be independent and flexible, but is patently not. For instance, Upwork (formerly known as oDesk and Elance-oDesk) was an early entrant into the online freelance marketplace model. Workers, who include graphic designers, writers, and computer programmers, use the service's desktop app and work diary, which shows work-in-progress screenshots taken six times an hour. The diary also "records the total number of mouse clicks, scroll actions, and keystrokes per segment," and workers are required to use both tools if they want to be covered by the service's hourly-payment protection. Clients can also require that workers take webcam shots of themselves while working.[92] Such "big brother" monitoring is at odds with the concept of allegedly independent work.

While screenshots and webcams are not (yet) being used in the gig economy services I discuss in these pages, monitoring is omnipresent in the gig economy. Whereas a white-collar worker in the mainstream economy can waltz into work thirty minutes late and probably avoid detection by the boss at least some of the time, the app-based tools allow for constant tracking. Thanks to GPS systems, Uber and Lyft know exactly when a driver arrives, picks up a passenger, where he goes, and when he drops them off. With required in-app communication, Airbnb and TaskRabbit track response times and record written communication.

Furthermore, the crowdsourced nature of peer review allows for constant evaluation. While not every client gives a rating score or completes a peer review, workers don't know in advance who will or won't. This leads to internal monitoring as workers know that they must perform satisfactorily or risk a negative review or low rating. The technological panopticon has been outsourced.

While ratings and reviews are marketed as a way to build trust and reduce the unknown for customers, such marketing is fallacious. Platform staff don't examine the reviews to provide one-on-one feedback to workers or to implement additional training procedures. Instead, the rankings allow platforms to screen and evaluate workers en masse. Workers who drop below a certain metric are warned and then deactivated, losing access to the platform. The reliance on rankings and ratings doesn't guarantee a good experience but simply normalizes constant worker surveillance.

WORKER CLASSIFICATION AFFECTS TAX REVENUES

Worker misclassification also impacts tax revenue. According to the Joint Committee on Taxation, the IRS's 1984 Strategic Initiative, an examination of 3,331 employers for the 1984 tax year, found that 15 percent of employers misclassified workers as independent contractors. The IRS also found that "when employers classified workers as employees, more than 99 percent of wage and salary income was reported. However, when workers were classified as independent contractors, 77 percent of gross income was reported when a Form 1099 was filed, and only 29 percent of gross income was reported when no Form 1099 was filed." Even *lower* income reporting was found among owners of sole proprietorships (the simplest and most common business structure), where "net income reporting averaged only 73 percent for Schedule C filers," a reference to the profit or loss form that accompanies a personal tax return.[93]

While employers are generally required to generate a 1099 form for each individual to whom they've paid more than six hundred dollars in a calendar year, sharing economy services such as TaskRabbit appear to be exempt from 1099 reporting requirements owing to their reliance on credit card systems. Under the 2008 Housing and Economic Recovery Act, credit card payments via PayPal or another payment processor are exempt from reporting until they exceed two hundred payments and a twenty-thousand-dollar threshold.[94] Although all income is supposed to be reported to the IRS, income that isn't reported by an employer is much less likely to be acknowledged on personal tax returns.

Worker classification may take on increased importance under the 2017 Trump tax plan, where a pass-through provision allows workers to deduct 20 percent of qualified business income from partnerships, S corporations, and sole proprietorships starting in 2018.[95] According to Patricia Cohen, "The provision will also allow independent contractors, like Uber drivers, to use the same deduction."[96] Under the approved tax plan, companies may classify more workers as independent contractors in order to lower their taxes and those of their workers, at the cost of numerous workplace protections. Implementing my solutions would reduce this risk.

ENTREPRENEURS BY CHOICE

Under the Time Rule and pajama policy, the category of independent contractor would be reserved for people who were largely self-directed. Workers could opt out of employee status and choose to be entrepreneurs by incorporating, which provides liability protection. Such an active opt out would allow workers with entrepreneurial inclinations to pursue those interests. This model would likely be chosen by the Success Stories who bring sufficient levels of skills and capital to their sharing economy work.

A freelancer who enters a contract to create a website or write an article and has a deadline for delivering the project would be an independent contractor. A self-employed accountant with numerous clients, but who can choose to do all of her work between midnight and 6 a.m., would also be an independent contractor. All gig economy workers would be employees. A worker on Upwork, who is monitored via webcam or keystroke software, would not be covered by the pajama rule and so would be an employee.

This model is not revolutionary: even in the tech industry, full-time and part-time workers for Google, Facebook, Apple, and Microsoft are hired as employees with workplace protections and benefits. The default in many fields is to be hired as an employee, with some entrepreneurial individuals seeking to go into business for themselves as independent consultants and contractors. Even workplaces that are part of the gig economy, such as Uber, TaskRabbit, Airbnb, Munchery, and Kitchensurfing, pay their professional workers as employees. Why should frontline workers be treated any differently?

Allowing workers who seek part-time, flexible work to benefit from workplace protections is not unique either. Instacart categorizes workers without cars (or who don't want to deliver groceries) as shoppers or cashiers. Such workers are considered part-time employees and are offered a flexible schedule, but are limited to working up to twenty-nine hours a week (thirty hours a week is a common threshold for obtaining health insurance benefits). Workers who have a vehicle can work as drivers or driver-shoppers with unlimited hours. Instacart notes, "The vast majority of our Shoppers were already picking their own shifts at 20–30 hours a week. So this is right in line with what they were already working."[97]

Some sharing economy companies may argue that the ability to shed employees in a heartbeat is crucial for competition. Yet sharing services that have opted to pay their workers as employees have succeeded in the sharing economy and even experienced great growth. Companies like Hello Alfred, MyClean, and Managed by Q are clear illustrations of how treating workers well—the "happy worker"/"good jobs" strategy—can lead to long-term success. Likewise, history has shown us what happens when workers are without workplace protections.

A BROKEN PROMISE

In *Design: The Invention of Desire* by designer and theorist Jessica Helfand, the author mentions that *hack*, a much-loved Silicon Valley–ism, stands for "horse's ass carrying keys" and is prison slang for "guard."[98] Outside of the technological realm, to "hack" something is to gash, cut, and break it, like a person with a machete. In Silicon Valley, to hack is based on the arrogant view that perceived value is "only in that which you contribute, fundamentally eviscerating the person or process that preceded your intervention. In this view—and it is not insignificant—the idea of hacking comes from a position of arrogance."[99]

Likewise, Silicon Valley's favorite phrase, "let's break shit," is part of Schumpeter's "creative destruction," a theory of economic progress in which new business rises like a phoenix from the ashes of old business.[100] Creative destruction has also been described as an early version of Clayton Christensen's hypothesis of "disruptive innovation," in which economies flourish when start-ups replace established firms.[101] And of course, to disrupt the status quo of established industries is part of the goal of the sharing economy.

When the term *sharing economy* first entered the public lexicon, the sharing economy itself looked like a step forward. Instead of having to compete with the Joneses and step onto in the "consumer escalator," workers could end the cycle of "work and spend" by participating in collaborative consumption in which expensive products, like riding lawn mowers, were shared with the community.[102] By spending less money, workers could minimize their financial needs and increase their leisure time, spending more time with family and friends and reducing the growing trend of "bowling alone."[103] Sharing would replace spending in a newly collaborative world and further reduce the McDonaldization of everything.[104] The sharing economy was a step forward, a way out, a solution to corporate dependency and workers' loss of workplace autonomy.

But the disruption offered by the sharing economy isn't about moving forward. Instead of offering a way out, the sharing economy has simply increased economic insecurity and worker vulnerability. Workers go from gig to gig, ostensibly as their own bosses but subject to the whims of platform pivots and deactivations. The sites say that they promote empowerment and entrepreneurship, but workers are subject to complex algorithms that determine their presence (or lack thereof) in site searches and task assignment. Under the guise of trust, workers undergo background checks, online reviews, and continual monitoring in an online panopticon of worker evaluation, even as they find themselves working for unknown individuals, outside standard workplace protections, and exposed to considerable risks.

Another way to think of Christensen's "disruptive innovation" is "the selling of a cheaper, poorer-quality product that . . . eventually takes over and devours an entire industry."[105] As sharing economy services have grown and proliferated, they've successfully subverted generations of financial gains and workplace protections. Workers have been returned to an early industrial age in which protections were nonexistent, their risks were great, and they were under the control of corporations and the elite. As Jill Lepore puts it, innovation is "the idea of progress stripped of the aspirations of the Enlightenment, scrubbed clean of the horrors of the twentieth century, and relieved of its critics. Disruptive innovation goes further, holding out the hope of salvation against the very damnation it describes: disrupt, and you will be saved."[106]

The sharing economy offers workers a way to "save themselves" through extra work, but the growth of the sharing economy may only continue to subvert workers' rights and protections. Hard-won victories for workers' rights and protections are being hacked and disrupted in the name of a "cheaper, poorer quality" progress that is eviscerating a hundred years of workers' rights. The disruption offered by the sharing economy is simply a hustle.

APPENDIX 1   Demographic Survey

How old are you? _____   What is your sex?   M   F   Other _____

What is your race?   Black   White   Asian   Hispanic   American Indian   Not listed: _____

What is your marital status?   Married   Single   Divorced   Separated

Do you live with a partner?   Y   N   For how many years? _____

Do you have children?   Y   N
      Sex   Age   Sex   Age   Sex   Age   Sex   Age
      M   F_____   M   F _____   M   F _____   M   F _____

Are you a student?   Y   N   Major/Degree: _____

What is your educational attainment level?

GED   High school   Some college   AA   BA/BS   Some graduate school   MA/MS   PhD/MD

Is your live-in partner or spouse a student?   Y   N   Major/Degree: _____

What is your spouse's or live-in partner's educational attainment level?

GED   High school   Some college   AA   BA/BS   Some graduate school   MA/MS   PhD/MD

Do you own or rent your home?   Own   Rent   Other: _____

Sharing economy job: Uber

Hours per week: 10 or fewer   10 to 20   21 to 30   31 to 40   41 to 50   51 to 69   70+

How long have you worked with this group? _____   How many gigs/rides/stays? _____

What percentage of your income?   10% or less   11–24%   25–49%   50–74%   75–100%

Do you also drive for Lyft?   Y   N

Hours per week: 10 or fewer   10 to 20   21 to 30   31 to 40   41 to 50   51 to 69   70+

How long have you worked with this group? _____   How many gigs/rides/stays? _____

What percentage of your income?   10% or less   11–24%   25–49%   50–74%   75–100%

Another sharing economy job: TaskRabbit, Handy, etc. _____

Hours per week: 10 or fewer   10 to 20   21 to 30   31 to 40   41 to 50   51 to 69   70+

How long have you worked with this group? _____   How many gigs/rides/stays? _____

What percentage of your income?   10% or less   11–24%   25–49%   50–74%   75–100%

Have you worked or signed up for any sharing economy companies that you no longer work with?

Company _____   How long were you there? _____

Reason for leaving _____

When did you start working in the sharing economy? _____

Do you have an additional job outside the sharing economy?   Y   N

If yes, what is that job? _____

How many hours a week do you work in your other job?

10 or fewer   10 to 20   21 to 30   31 to 40   41 to 50   51 to 69   70+

Does your spouse or live-in partner work outside the home?

What does she or he do? _____

How many hours a week does she or he work?

10 or fewer   10 to 20   21 to 30   31 to 40   41 to 50   51 to 69   70+

How would you rate yourself in terms of political identification?

Extremely liberal   Extremely conservative

   1   2   3   4   5   6   7

Do you identify as any of the following?

Republican   Moderate   Independent   Democrat   Other: _____

Your total household income is best described as:

Under $24,999 $25–34,999 $35–49,999 $50–74,999 $75–100,000 $100,000+

Your personal income is best described as:

Under $24,999 $25–34,999 $35–49,999 $50–74,999 $75–100,000 $100,000+

How would you describe your income?

Inadequate for needs   Tight   Adequate   More than enough   Excessive for needs

How much have you made from the sharing economy (gross)?

Service _____ $_____   Service_____ $_____

How would you describe your sharing economy income?

Inadequate for needs   Tight   Adequate   More than enough   Excessive for needs

How much profit have you made from the sharing economy (net)?

Service_____ $_____   Service_____ $_____

What are some of the common expenses associated with your sharing economy work?

Expense_____ $_____   Daily Weekly Monthly Annually

Expense_____ $_____   Daily Weekly Monthly Annually

Expense_____ $_____   Daily Weekly Monthly Annually

How do you handle sharing economy work on your taxes?

_____1099/freelance   _____C-Corp   _____S-Corp   _____LLC   Other_____

What do you use your sharing economy income for?

_____ Paying off debt/loans ___ Daily expenses, including rent ___ Special treats/trips ___ Savings

Other _____

Which online discussion boards/forums do you use to discuss the sharing economy?

_____

Three words to describe what attracted you to the sharing economy?

_____   _____   _____

APPENDIX 2   Interview Matrix

How did you get involved with the sharing economy? Can you walk me through your decision process?	___ service is part of the sharing economy. What does the sharing economy mean to you? Is there a better name you'd suggest?	Do you think of yourself as an entrepreneur?	Do you think your race or sex or age affects your gigs or who you work with? Do you get hired for stereotypical work in terms of sex?	Can you talk a bit about community? Do you hang out with guests, have you made friendships? Many of the sharing economy companies talk about how the sharing economy is building up community and connection. Can you talk about what that means to you?
What were you doing before you joined ___ service?	I've been told the number-one reason people stop using these services is because they don't need the money any more. Does that ring true to you?	Where do you stay when you Airbnb your place? OR Bathroom and lunchtime— how do you handle these?	How do you handle it when sharing-economy work falls through or doesn't happen?	Can you tell me about trusting strangers? How did it feel at first to work with a stranger like this? Do you Google people in advance?

What is an average day like in your sharing economy work life?	When you think about your sharing-economy work, which situations or experiences stick out in your mind the most (good or bad)?	Do you use the sharing economy? Do you take Uber, hire TaskRabbit, etc? Why or why not?	How have you been affected by changes in the sharing economy (rate slashing, TaskRabbit change, housing crackdown)? What do you think of the _____ company?	How do you ensure that people can trust you? What do you do in terms of your online profile management (screenshot profiles, clean apartment, started Twitter, etc.)?
What did you expect sharing-economy work would be like? Did you think it would be different (in terms of time, income, etc.)?	Do you buy stuff for riders? Guests?	Tell me about getting reviews . . . how does it feel? Are you a Superhost, TaskRabbit Elite, etc.? Was that important to you?	Is there anyone else who you think might be open to talking to me?	Do you go to meet-ups? How do you meet other members of the sharing economy?

Notes

1. STRUGGLERS, STRIVERS, AND SUCCESS STORIES

1. All names have been changed.

2. Lee (2013).

3. Mathews (2014); Botsman and Rogers (2010).

4. Surowiecki (2013).

5. Smith (2016a).

6. Katz and Krueger (2016).

7. On the real growth rate, see Weil (2014: Kindle chap. 1); on the reversal of real income growth, see Krugman (2007).

8. Bricker, Dettling, Henriques, Hsu, Moore, Sabelhaus, Thompson, and Windle (2014:1–2).

9. Leicht and Fitzgerald (2013:74).

10. Leicht and Fitzgerald (2013:76).

11. Morgenson (2008).

12. Mishel, Gould, and Bivens (2015). Middle-wage workers are defined as median-wage workers who earned more than half of the workforce but less than the other half.

13. DeSilver (2014).

14. The definition of *millennials* is not set by the Census Bureau or any other government agency but, rather, differs by media source. I utilize the definition set by *Time* magazine in the 2013 cover story "Millennials: The Me Me Me

Generation" written by Joel Stein, available online at http://time.com/247
/millennials-the-me-me-me-generation/.

15. Kahn (2010).

16. Bui (2017). According to the Federal Reserve's 2016 *Report on the Economic Well-Being of U.S. Households in 2015,* more than half of adults under age
thirty who attended college took on at least some debt (student loans, credit card
debt, and other forms of borrowing) while pursuing their education. As of 2015,
the mean student debt load was $30,156 (reflecting large debt loads for some
borrowers) and the median was $12,000. See Board of Governors of the Federal
Reserve System (2016).

17. Potts (2015); Farrell and Greig (2016).

18. This categorization, of course, is influenced by the grounded theory work
of Glaser and Strauss ([1967] 1999).

19. Ravenelle (2017b).

20. Weber ([1905] 2002).

21. Although this may seem like an extreme solution for getting children into
a good public school, this type of school-district targeting isn't unusual. Higgins
(2013) reports that New York City parents have been known to target certain
school zones before their children are old enough for preschool or to "borrow" a
friend or family member's home address in order to seemingly fall within the
borders of a better school district. I'm indebted to Phil Kasinitz for noting that
this "borrowing" of an address is illegal and a "middle-class hustle."

22. See chapter 3 for Donald's story, and chapter 6 for Michael's story.

23. See Fleck (2009) and OECD (2017).

24. Oxford Economics (2014).

25. Schor (1992: Kindle chap. 2).

26. Hochschild ([1989] 2002).

27. Bianchi et al. (2012).

28. Hochschild (2012).

29. McAfee and Brynjolfsson (2017:141–42).

30. RentCafe, www.rentcafe.com/average-rent-market-trends/us/ny
/manhattan/.

31. Kalleberg (2009).

32. Ehrenreich (2001).

2. WHAT IS THE SHARING ECONOMY?

Portions of this chapter have been reproduced, with permission, from Alexandrea J. Ravenelle, "A Return to Gemeinschaft: Digital Impression Management
and the Sharing Economy," in *Digital Sociologies,* ed. Jessie Daniels, Karen Gregory, and Tressie McMillan Cottom, 27–46 (Bristol, UK: Policy Press / Bristol

University Press, 2017); and from Alexandrea J. Ravenelle, "Sharing Economy Workers: Selling, Not Sharing," *Cambridge Journal of Regions, Economy and Society* 10, no. 2 (2017): 281–95.

1. Mathews (2014).

2. Schor (2014a).

3. Schor and Fitzmaurice (2015).

4. Zipcar is now owned by Avis, which illustrates how successful platforms are co-opted by corporations.

5. Kessler (2015b).

6. Kessler (2015b).

7. Alden (2014).

8. Nadeem (2015).

9. As of April 2018, Zaarly was available only in Denver, Minneapolis, Kansas City, and northern Virginia.

10. Schor (2014a).

11. Frenken, Meelen, Arets, and van de Glind (2015).

12. Stone (2012).

13. Schor (2014a).

14. Stone (2012).

15. Thompson (2011).

16. Sacks (2011).

17. PricewaterhouseCoopers (2015).

18. For an interesting discussion of distinction and belonging in the sharing economy, see Schor, Fitzmaurice, Carfagna, Attwood-Charles, and Dubois Poteat (2016). For more on entrepreneurship, see Andrus (2014); Friedman (2014); McKinney (2013).

19. Kahn (1987:8); Rybczynski (1993).

20. Kahn (1987:9–10).

21. Simmel (1971).

22. Kahn (1987:11).

23. Tonnies (1957).

24. Tanz (2014).

25. Tanz (2014).

26. Tanz (2014).

27. Cass (2013).

28. Nanos (2013).

29. Eckhardt and Bardhi (2015).

30. Bertrand and Mullainathan (2004); Moss-Racusin, Dovidio, Brescoll, Graham, and Handelsman (2012).

31. Edelman and Luca (2014).

32. Doleac and Stein (2010).

33. Jost (2011).

34. See Greenhouse (2008).

35. Cantillon (1755).

36. Stevenson and Gumpert (1985).

37. *New Shorter Oxford English Dictionary* (1993), s.v. "entrepreneur."

38. Bureau of Labor Statistics (2016a).

39. Hacker (2006).

40. Kalleberg (2009).

41. Standing (2014).

42. Weber and Silverman (2015).

43. Pugh (2015).

44. Knight (1921); Acs and Audretsch (1988); Kortum and Lerner (2000).

45. Schoar (2010:57–58).

46. Hall and Krueger (2015).

47. Whitford (2016).

48. Etsy (2013).

49. New York City landlords generally require that prospective tenants make between forty and fifty times the monthly rent or have a guarantor who makes at least one hundred times the monthly rent. In order to afford an apartment renting for $2,800, this individual needed an annual income of $112,000 to $140,000 when he signed the lease.

50. Alden (2014).

51. Kessler (2014b).

52. Piketty (201); Alden (2014).

53. Wachsmuth, Chaney, Kerrigan, Shilolo and Basalaev-Binder (2018).

54. New York Communities for Change and Real Affordability for All (2015:43).

55. Lightfeldt (2015).

56. *EV Grieve* (2015).

57. Hill (2015b); Poston and Khouri (2015).

58. Avent (2014).

59. Kurtzleben (2015).

60. Green and Levin (2017).

61. Roose (2014).

62. As a further illustration of the aptness of these four services, both Task-Rabbit and Kitchensurfing underwent major pivots or service changes during the course of this study, and Kitchensurfing later closed its doors.

63. Frenken, Meelen, Arets, and van de Glind (2015).

64. New York City app-based drivers face particularly high capital barriers. Drivers are required to follow many of the same license, registration, and insurance requirements as drivers of yellow taxis; but unlike with cabs, all costs are assumed by the individual drivers. Estimates of drivers' costs vary widely and depend on the type and age of the car insured, as well as on the driver's record

and experience. However, new drivers often must pay anywhere from three thousand dollars to more than six thousand dollars in insurance and licensing fees, in addition to a car payment, before ever driving a mile in New York. Moreover, drivers must pass licensing and medical exams, take drug tests, and complete courses in defensive driving and wheelchair accessibility.

65. Ravenelle (2017b).

66. Gallagher (2017).

67. Arrington (2011).

68. See Yuhas (2015); Rosario, Sullivan and Tacopino (2014); Bort (2014).

69. Bradford (2014).

70. Bort (2014a).

71. Edelman and Luca (2014); Edelman, Luca and Svirsky (2017).

72. Gregor (2014).

73. Zukin (2009).

74. New York City Planning Department, Population FactFinder. https://popfactfinder.planning.nyc.gov/.

75. According to a *Business Insider* profile, the idea for Uber actually came from StumbleUpon founder Garrett Camp: "One New Year's not long before, Camp and a few friends had spent $800 hiring a private driver. While Camp had made a fortune selling StumbleUpon, he still felt nearly a grand was too steep a price for one night of convenience. He had been mulling over ways to bring down the cost of black car services ever since" (Shontell 2014). Camp realized that splitting the cost with a lot of people—say a few dozen elite users in Silicon Valley—could make it affordable. The idea morphed into Uber, essentially the equivalent of nightclub bottle service for the taxi industry, a premium service for high-end customers.

76. Shontell (2014).

77. Kolodny (2010).

78. Worthman (2011).

79. Chen (2012).

80. Wright (2015).

81. Licea, Ruby, and Harshbarger (2015).

82. Hu (2017).

83. Walker (2015).

84. Peterson (2015).

85. Not all drivers were willing to answer questions regarding their race, education, or income levels.

86. Garling (2014).

87. Schor (2015).

88. Newton (2013).

89. In October 2015, Kitchensurfing Tonight changed its model to pay workers as hourly employees. As part of this change, the service also increased its

prices—for example, to fifty-nine dollars for two adults (up from fifty dollars)—and began to collect a sales tax of 8.875 percent. The company later offered reduced-rate children's meals, before eventually shutting down in April 2016.

90. Griffith (2015).

91. Fiegerman (2014).

92. Ravenelle (2017b).

3. FORWARD TO THE PAST AND THE EARLY INDUSTRIAL AGE

1. Schor and her team of graduate students are part of the MacArthur Foundation Connected Learning Research Network, and their MacArthur funding mandated the study of eighteen- to thirty-four year-olds. As Schor notes, "They were also the predominant group in the sites we were studying, so it felt like the right thing in analytic terms as well. It also seemed to make sense with our first case—the time bank—because the young and old were quite different in their patterns of participation and motives" (personal communication, October 3, 2017). As they've met additional older individuals involved in the sharing economy, they've included those workers in their sample.

2. The TaskRabbit terms of service note, "Without limitation, while using the TaskRabbit Platform, you may not . . . [a]ttempt to circumvent the payments system or service fees in anyway including, but not limited to, processing payments outside of the platform, including inaccurate information on invoices, or otherwise invoicing in a fraudulent manner."

3. On the ransacked apartment, see Arrington (2011); on the Madrid story, see Lieber (2015).

4. Commons (1918).

5. Bliss (1902).

6. Foner ([1947] 1998).

7. Tomlins (1993).

8. Foner ([1947] 1998:80).

9. Foner ([1947] 1998:80).

10. Foner ([1947] 1998:102).

11. Foner ([1947] 1998:102).

12. In 1828, the child workers of Paterson, New Jersey, were actually the source of the first recorded strike of factory workers in America. This earlier strike was in response to factory owners' attempts to move the dinner hour from noon to 1 p.m. Noted one observer, "The children would not stand for it for fear that if they assented to this, the next thing would be to deprive them of eating at all" (Foner [1947] 1998:105).

13. Stansell (1987).

14. Williams and Farnie (1992).

15. Although most have heard of the "mill girls" of Lowell and other East Coast factories, early mill workers were generally children. "Slater's first nine operatives were seven boys and two girls under 12 years of age. In 1820, half of all the factory workers were boys and girls 'of the tender age of nine and ten years,' who worked 12 to 13 hours a day for wages ranging from 33 cents to 67 cents a week" (Foner [1947] 1998:65). It wasn't uncommon for mill-work advertisements to target large families.

16. Foner ([1947] 1998:110).

17. US Census Bureau, Census History Staff (2017a; 2017b). The numbers came from these two sites; percentages were calculated by the author.

18. Stansell (1987).

19. As quoted in Zinn (1999).

20. Zinn (1999:339, 295).

21. See Zinn (1999); Walker (2003).

22. See Zinn (1999: especially p. 396).

23. The Fair Labor Standards Act applied only to a small percentage of workers. Elder and Miller (1979: 10) note that "only 11 million workers, out of about 33 million nonsupervisory wage and salary workers, were covered by the 25-cent minimum wage when it went into effect on October 24, 1938, and only 300,000 of those were paid less than that amount in September 1938." Additionally, the statute excluded workers in laundries, hotels, hairdressing, restaurants, agriculture, and domestic service. While roughly equal percentages of men and women were exempt from the minimum wage provisions, the majority of exempted women (62.1 percent) earned below the eight-hundred-dollar baseline established by the law, compared to 35.6 percent of men (Metter 1994: 652).

24. Ashby and Hawking (2009).

25. Zinn (1999:402).

26. Weil (2014).

27. Weil (2014).

28. Wingfield and Isaac (2015).

29. Kravets (2016).

30. Scheiber and Isaac (2016).

31. See Leonard (2013a) and (2013b). As noted in the latter, the sharing economy services have not directly funded Peers, but some of their executives and investors have contributed funds.

32. Kessler (2014a).

33. Kessler (2014a).

34. There may be some credence to this idea. I posted an ad on the discussion forum UberPeople.net identifying myself as a researcher and seeking workers to talk to in 2015. When I reposted in 2017, asking about driver rates, my posts were deleted as "spam."

35. In 2015, CrowdFlower settled a class action lawsuit regarding the low pay of workers. Although the original plan was for payment of an additional dollar for every dollar earned, the final class of participants was estimated at 19,992, much larger than the previously negotiated 100-worker class size. As a result, instead of workers being paid an additional dollar for each dollar earned, the settlement provided recovery ranging from forty-seven to seventy-five cents per dollar. See Otey et al. v. Crowdflower, Inc. et al., no. 3:2012cv05524—document 226 (N.D. Cal. 2015).

36. The program was the brainchild of Andrew Chapin, a former Goldman Sachs commodities trader, who proposed that Uber create a finance program where drivers could use their Uber earnings to work around issues with spotty credit. Chapin was familiar with how New York limo drivers, who are often immigrants with limited or nonexistent credit histories, financed their rental arrangements with livery services. See Lashinsky (2014); Tiku (2014); Levine (2015).

37. L. Smith (2016).

38. See Newcomer and Zaleski (2016); L. Smith (2016).

39. Bensinger (2017c).

40. Mose (2011).

41. Mangalindan (2014); Lawler (2014); Huet (2015); Rogers (2016); Roose (2014); *Uber Blog* (2016).

42. Huet (2015); Dickey (2014); Perea (2016).

43. Bensinger (2017a); Bhuiyan (2017).

44. Huet (2015).

45. Green and Levin (2017).

46. Isaac and Benner (2017).

47. Uber uses its "time with passenger" calculation to argue that the car service is more environmentally friendly than yellow taxis.

48. Kerr (2015).

49. Newcomer (2017).

50. Israel (2002:87).

4. WORKPLACE TROUBLES

1. Ehrenreich (2001: especially p. 90).

2. Ehrenreich (2001:89).

3. I'm not the only one to note the proximity of the neighborhood to the Asch Building. On the anniversary of the fire each year, sidewalks in the East Village are marked with chalk messages in front of the apartments where the deceased once lived, noting the name, age, and birth year of each, the date of death, and the fact that they were casualties of the fire. The building, which survived, was

renamed the Brown Building and is now part of the New York University campus.

4. Kramer (1958); Geerts, Kornblith, and Urmson (1977).

5. Haller (1988); Guyton (1999).

6. Zinn (1999:326).

7. Guyton (1999).

8. When the fire started, individuals nearby, hearing the fire alarms, raced to the scene, where they were confronted with the sight of workers leaping from the eighth- and ninth-story windows to escape the flames and smoke. One of the witnesses was Frances Perkins, who later became the first woman appointed to a US president's Cabinet. Perkins later called March 25, 1911, the day the New Deal began. "Before the fire, unions tended to tackle owners individually. Afterwards, they had the law on their side" (*The Economist* 2011). The fire had such a major role in reforming American labor practices that the US Department of Labor's Occupational Safety and Health Administration office actually has a website page commemorating the hundred-year anniversary of the disaster: www.osha .gov/oas/trianglefactoryfire.html.

9. *New York Times* (1911).

10. Greenwald (2005).

11. Jost (2011).

12. Hamlin (1997).

13. Schor and Attwood-Charles (2017).

14. Clifford (2016).

15. Schor (2014a).

16. Bullet-resistant safety barriers, cameras, and silent alarms are standard in yellow taxicabs in New York City.

17. Stone and Stevens (2000).

18. See Collins (2016); Wise and Burkett (2016); James (2016); Puente (2016); Leone (2016); Bever (2016); Tedesco (2015).

19. Ladegaard, Ravenelle, and Schor (2017).

20. Chen (2014).

21. Shaffe (2016); Curran (2016).

22. Ellement (2016).

23. Rocha (2016); Ryan, Hawkins, and Pascucci (2015).

24. Young (2016).

25. See Guerrero (2016); Bohr (2016); Mahmood (2016).

26. Mass, Goldfarb, and Shah (2014); Norén (2010); Plaut (2007).

27. See Koebler (2015); Strandell (2015); Balsamini (2016)

28. Manjoo (2016).

29. Kwon (2005).

30. The vast majority of for-hire drivers—whether they drive yellow taxicabs or through Uber/Lyft or a black car service—in New York City are male.

Estimates vary, but roughly 5 to 7 percent of drivers are female. Norén (2010) has suggested that the exceptionally low number of female drivers may be a result of the lack of bathroom access in New York. Unfortunately, in my recruitment efforts I met only one female driver in New York, and she declined to be interviewed.

31. Dickey (2014).

32. National guidelines recommend that when cities determine crosswalk times, they build in three seconds for pedestrian reaction time, the amount of time it takes for a pedestrian to step off the curb and begin moving once a walk signal activates. But Diniece Peters, a New York City Transportation Department project manager, found that New Yorkers had a reaction time of negative three seconds. Whether they had waited patiently on the sidewalk or had already stepped into the crosswalk, New Yorkers watched the traffic light—not the walk signal—and charged out as soon as it turned in their favor, several moments before the walk signal flashed (Peters, Kim, Zaman, Haas, Cheng, and Ahmed 2015).

33. Belk (2010, 2014); Böcker and Meelen (2017).

5. SHARING IS CARING

1. Sanchez (2016); Biddle (2014).

2. Siegel (2003).

3. Segrave (2013).

4. Larson (1997).

5. See Siegel (2003: especially p. 11).

6. Bergmann (1986:106).

7. See Farley (1978, 2017).

8. Benson and Thomson (1982); MacKinnon (1979).

9. On coworkers as harassers, see Gutek (1985). On subordinates as harassers, see Grauerholz (1989); McKinney (1994).

10. See Welsh (1999); Acker (1990); West and Fenstermaker (1995); Lorber (1994).

11. Rogers and Henson (1997).

12. Tsotsis (2011).

13. Perez (2014).

14. Although TaskRabbit has since ended its corporation-focused branch, companies continue to hire through it and other sharing economy services. For instance, several Kitchensurfing chefs mentioned being hired to cook for company meetings or parties, and other businesses and organizations have announced that Uber car services and Airbnb room rentals will be reimbursed on expense reports just like taxi and hotel expenses.

15. Rogers and Henson (1997:224).

16. Rogers and Henson (1997:224); also see Hochschild (1983) on emotional work.

17. Hall (1993).

18. Rogers and Henson (1997:232).

19. Goffman (1963).

20. Levin (2017).

21. Levin (2017).

22. Rogers and Henson (1997).

23. Scott and Lyman (1968:46).

24. Hondagneu-Sotelo (2001:188).

25. See Adshade (2013); Basow and Minieri (2010).

26. Fermino (2015).

27. *Street meat* is a colloquial term for a dish of "chicken or lamb, turmeric-hued rice, maybe some shreds of iceberg lettuce and a few slices of tomato, all covered in a mix of rich white sauce and spicy red sauce." The meal, which is sold out of carts all over the city, is also referred to as "chicken and rice" or "halal food" and is known for being affordable. A large Styrofoam container of street meat usually costs five to eight dollars (Krishna 2017).

28. Murray (2014).

29. Levin (2017).

6. ALL IN A DAY'S (DIRTY) WORK

1. Wilson (1996).

2. See Bushway and Reuter (1997); Kasinitz and Rosenberg (1996).

3. Venkatesh (2008).

4. Katz (1989); Merton (1938).

5. I met Michael by posting a task that entailed dropping a bag of clothes off at the local Goodwill.

6. The issue of a sharing economy firm acting as an escrow provider is not unique to TaskRabbit but is found across nearly all platforms. When working for traditional Kitchensurfing.com, chefs paid for hundreds and even thousands of dollars' worth of food out of pocket and then waited for reimbursement. Normally this occurred without a hitch, but one chef, a strong supporter of Kitchensurfing, told me that he knew of a situation involving a friend who received complaints about a meal and service. As a result, the company held on to this chef's payment and reimbursement for several additional weeks, and the chef was considering legal options.

7. Mani, Mullainathan, Shafir, and Zhao (2013).

8. Chan (2005).

9. Chan (2005).

10. Ladegaard, Ravenelle, and Schor (2017).

11. As Greenhouse (2008) notes, it's not uncommon for employers to require store managers to work more than forty hours a week. Since they are considered members of the management staff, employers are not legally obliged to pay them overtime.

12. Dougherty and Isaac (2014); Hauser (2015); Siegler (2011).

13. Bialik, Flowers, Fischer-Baum, and Mehta (2015).

14. See Office of the Attorney General of the State of New York's Research Department and Internet Bureau (2014); Lovece (2010).

15. Office of the Attorney General of the State of New York's Research Department and Internet Bureau (2014).

16. Bellafante (2016).

17. According to media accounts, landlords maintain a black list of "problem" tenants, based on records from the New York City Housing Court, and being listed can prevent someone from getting an apartment, even if the landlord-tenant dispute was settled in the tenant's favor (Satow 2014).

18. Zimbardo was a social psychologist at Stanford at the time, so his choice of the Palo Alto location was convenient in addition to remarkably prescient.

19. Kelling and Wilson (1982).

20. Kelling and Wilson (1982).

21. Kelling and Wilson (1982).

22. Kelling and Wilson (1982).

23. Schor and Attwood-Charles (2015).

24. See Hochschild (2012) for more on the outsourcing of household activities.

25. Marx (2013).

26. Dawes (1973:26).

27. Craig and McKinley (2014).

28. Craig and McKinley (2014).

29. Dewey (2015).

30. See Griebling (2012); Kalleberg (2009); Hacker (2006).

7. LIVING THE DREAM?

Portions of this chapter have been reproduced, with permission, from Alexandrea J. Ravenelle, "A Return to Gemeinschaft: Digital Impression Management and the Sharing Economy," in *Digital Sociologies*, ed. Jessie Daniels, Karen Gregory, and Tressie McMillan Cottom, 27–46 (Bristol, UK: Policy Press / Bristol University Press, 2017); and from Alexandrea J. Ravenelle, "Sharing Economy Workers: Selling, Not Sharing," *Cambridge Journal of Regions, Economy and Society* 10, no. 2 (2017): 281–95.

1. Goffman (1963).

2. Heatherton, Kleck, Hebl, and Hull (2000).

3. Landier (2005); Shepherd and Haynie (2011); Simmons, Wiklund, and Levie (2014).

4. On sex workers, see Agustin (2013); Vanwesenbeeck (2001). On the minimum wage, see Newman (1999). On blue-collar workers, see Sennett and Cobb ([1972] 1993).

5. McAfee and Brynjolfsson (2017).

6. Kitchensurfing's closure happened in two stages. First, the service began to phase out the marketplace tool (the Kitchensurfing marketplace) toward the end of 2015. Chefs were given about a month's notice in order to download messages and make backups of any records they needed. Then the Kitchensurfing Tonight service was shuttered on April 15, 2016.

7. Ravenelle (2017a).

8. Admittedly, one can sidestep the need for an attractive or conveniently located apartment if the price is low enough to draw interest regardless of the photos or location. One common strategy is for hosts to start by listing a low price when they first begin on the platform, in order to build up interest and their reviews.

9. Edelman, Luca, and Svirsky (2017).

10. Edelman, Luca, and Svirsky (2017).

11. Ghoshal and Gaddis (2015).

12. Ahmed and Hammarstedt (2008).

8. CONCLUSION

1. Entis (2014); Griswold (2016b).

2. Price (2016).

3. Price (2016).

4. As noted by Allison Arieff (2016) in *a New York Times Sunday Review* piece, "products and services are designed to 'disrupt' market sectors (a.k.a. bringing to market things no one really needs) more than to solve actual problems." Especially problematic is the focus on products for wealthier users as opposed to solving the problems experienced by what the writer C. Z. Nnaemeka described as "the unexotic underclass"—single mothers, the white rural poor, veterans, out-of-work Americans over fifty—who have the "misfortune of being insufficiently interesting."

5. Schonfeld (2016).

6. Bureau of Labor Statistics (2012).

7. Leonhardt (2009).

8. Board of Governors of the Federal Reserve System (2015).

9. Hacker et al. (2010).

10. Board of Governors of the Federal Reserve System (2014).

11. Gabler (2016).

12. Pew Research Center (2014).

13. Zumbrun (2016).

14. Board of Governors of the Federal Reserve System (2016, 2017).

15. Morduch and Schneider (2017).

16. Dynan, Elmendorf, and Sichel (2012).

17. Board of Governors of the Federal Reserve System (2017).

18. Strom and Schmitt (2016).

19. Greenhouse (2008).

20. Greenhouse (2008).

21. Strom and Schmitt (2016).

22. O'Donovan and Anand (2017).

23. *The Economist* (2015).

24. Students of research methods may recognize the Western Electric studies as also identifying the Hawthorne effect, whereby the presence of the researcher affects the behavior of the observed.

25. Greenhouse (2008).

26. Greenhouse (2008).

27. Greenhouse (2008).

28. *New York Times* (1994).

29. Uchitelle and Kleinfield (1996).

30. Greenhouse (2008); for the books mentioned, see Schor (1993), Dunlap (1996), Harrison (1997), Fraser (2002), and Uchitelle (2006).

31. Streitfeld (2004); Whalen (1995).

32. Mieszkowski (1998).

33. Mieszkowski (1998).

34. Golden (2016).

35. Greenhouse (2014).

36. Greenhouse (2014); Kantor (2014).

37. Ben-Ishai, Matthews, and Levin-Epstein (2014); Chaudry, Pedroza, and Sandstrom (2012).

38. Cass (2013).

39. Cannon and Summers (2014).

40. Autor (2015).

41. Gershon (2017: introduction); also see Boltanski and Chiapello (2005).

42. Ladegaard, Ravenelle, and Schor (2017).

43. Giddens (1998: 64–67).

44. Lev-Ram (2014).

45. Hsu (2017).

46. See National Employment Law Project (2014); Brescoll, Glass, and Sedlovskaya (2013); Stone and Hernandez (2013).

47. Kalleberg (2011).

48. Schor (2017).

49. Sundararajan (2016).

50. See Galinsky, Bond, and Sakai (2008); Williams, Blair-Loy, and Berdahl (2013).

51. Stone (2007); Moen et al. (2017).

52. Traditionally, freelancers command a higher hourly wage, which typically accounts for their slow periods and need to pay for health insurance, office space, and higher Social Security and Medicaid taxes.

53. Silva (2013).

54. After a Federal Trade Commission lawsuit alleging that Uber deceived drivers with promises of "lofty pay," the blog was taken down from the Uber site (Weise 2017).

55. Griswold (2014).

56. Isaac (2017).

57. Youshaei (2015).

58. Fottrell (2015).

59. McAfee (n.d.).

60. Rotman (2013).

61. Kolhatkar (2017).

62. Feige (1990:990).

63. Beckert and Wehinger (2012).

64. Portes (1994).

65. Portes (1994:429); see also Gershuny (1979, 1985); Pahl (1980).

66. Portes (1994:431); Venkatesh (2006).

67. Zuberi (2006:12).

68. Sapone (2015).

69. Smith (2003); Wilson (1996).

70. Katz (2017).

71. Kolhatkar (2016).

72. In 2017, the service was purchased by the ride-share app Gett. Unfortunately, while Juno began with aspirations of driver equality, after it was purchased by Gett, drivers were pressured to exchange their stock options for pennies on the dollar (Lazzaro 2017).

73. Committee on Ways and Means (2007a).

74. Roose (2014).

75. Edelman and Luca (2014); Edelman, Luca, and Svirsky (2017); Griswold (2016a; Ghoshal and Gaddis (2015); Doleac and Stein (2010); Kricheli-Katz and Regev (2016).

76. Hall and Krueger (2015).

77. A. Smith (2016a).

78. Manyika, Lund, Bughin, Robinson, Mischke, and Mahajan (2016).

79. Conley (1999).

80. Institute for Social Research (1994).

81. Asante-Muhammed, Collins, Hoxie, and Nieves (2016).

82. US Department of Labor (2017).

83. US Department of Labor, Wage and Hour Division (2017).

84. Scheiber (2018).

85. *Darrin E. McGillis v. Department of Economic Opportunity* (2017); Griswold (2017); Kokalitcheva (2016).

86. Joint Committee on Taxation (2007).

87. Weber (2015); Lang (2015).

88. Sachs (2015).

89. Harris and Krueger (2015).

90. Buhr (2017); Page (2015).

91. O'Donovan (2017).

92. Shellenbarger (2008).

93. Joint Committee on Taxation (2007).

94. Erb (2014).

95. Originally known as the Tax Cuts and Jobs Act, the lack of emphasis on jobs meant that the name had to be changed under Senate rules. The official name is the rather unwieldy Act to Provide for Reconciliation Pursuant to Titles II and V of the Concurrent Resolution on the Budget for Fiscal Year 2018.

96. Cohen (2017).

97. Alba (2015).

98. Helfand (2016:153).

99. Helfand (2016:154).

100. Waldman (2014).

101. Christensen (1997).

102. Schor (1992, 1998); Botsman and Rogers (2010).

103. Putnam (2000).

104. Ritzer (1993).

105. Lepore (2014).

106. Lepore (2014).

References

Acker, Joan. 1990. "Hierarchies, Jobs, Bodies: A Theory of Gendered Organizations." *Gender & Society* 4(2):139–58.

Acs, Zoltan J., and David B. Audretsch. 1988. "Innovation in Large and Small Firms: An Empirical Analysis." *American Economic Review* 78(4):678–90.

Adshade, Marina. 2013. *Dollars and Sex: How Economics Influences Sex and Love.* San Francisco: Chronicle Books.

AFL-CIO. 1981. "A Short History of American Labor." *American Federationist* 88(3).

Agustin, Laura. 2013. "The Sex Worker Stigma: How the Law Perpetuates Our Hatred (and Fear) of Prostitutes." *Salon*, August 17.

Ahmed, Ali M., and Mats Hammarstedt. 2008. "Discrimination in the Rental Housing Market: A Field Experiment on the Internet." *Journal of Urban Economics* 64(2):362–72.

Alba, Davey. 2015. "Instacart Shoppers Can Now Choose to Be Real Employees." *Wired*, May 25.

Albinsson, Pia A., and B. Yasanthi Perera. 2012. "Alternative Marketplaces in the 21st Century: Building Community through Sharing Events." *Journal of Consumer Behaviour* 11(4):303–15.

Alden, William. 2014. "The Business Tycoons of Airbnb." *New York Times Magazine*, November 25.

Alexandersen, Christian. 2017. "Uber Raises Rates in 8 States, including Pa., to Fund Injury Protection Insurance for Drivers." PennLive, May 9.

Andrus, Paula. 2014. "How to Launch a Business in the Sharing Economy." *Entrepreneur,* December 24.

Arieff, Allison. 2016. "Solving All the Wrong Problems." *New York Times,* July 10.

Aronowitz, Stanley, and William DiFazio. 1994. *The Jobless Future.* Minneapolis: University of Minnesota Press.

Arrington, Michael. 2011. "The Moment of Truth for Airbnb as User's Home Is Utterly Trashed." *TechCrunch,* July 27.

Asante-Muhammed, Dedrick, Chuck Collins, Josh Hoxie, and Emanuel Nieves. 2016. *The Ever-Growing Gap: Without Change, African-American and Latino Families Won't Match White Wealth for Centuries.* Washington, DC: Corporation for Economic Development and Institute for Policy Studies, August 8.

Ashby, Steven K., and C. J. Hawking. 2009. *Staley: The Fight for a New American Labor Movement.* Champaign: University of Illinois Press.

Associated Press. 2013. "US Companies Increasingly Turning to Temporary Workers to Fill Positions." *Fox News,* July 8.

Autor, David H. 2015. "Why Are There Still So Many Jobs? The History and Future of Workplace Automation." *Journal of Economic Perspectives* 29(3):3–30.

Avent, Ryan. 2014. "The Third Great Wave, Special Report: The World Economy." *The Economist,* October 4. www.economist.com/sites/default/files/20141004_world_economy.pdf.

Baker, Dean. 2014. "Don't Buy the 'Sharing Economy' Hype: Airbnb and Uber Are Facilitating Rip-Offs." *The Guardian,* May 27.

Balsamini, Dean. 2016. "The Longest Ride in Uber History." *New York Post,* December 10.

Basow, Susan A., and Alexandra Minieri. 2011. "You Owe Me: Effects of Date Cost, Who Pays, Participant Gender, and Rape Myth Beliefs on Perceptions of Rape." *Journal of Interpersonal Violence* 26(3):479–97.

Beckert, Jens, and Frank Wehinger. 2012. "In the Shadow: Illegal Markets and Economic Sociology." *Socio-Economic Review* 11(1):5–30, https://doi.org/10.1093/ser/mws020.

Belk, R. 2010. "Sharing." *Journal of Consumer Research* 36(5):715–34.

———. 2014. "Sharing versus Pseudo-Sharing in Web 2.0." *Anthropologist* 18(1):7–23.

Bellafante, Ginia. 2016. "Airbnb and the Battle of Suitcase Alley." *New York Times,* June 24.

Ben-Ishai, Liz, Hannah Matthews, and Jodie Levin-Epstein. 2014. *Scrambling for Stability: The Challenges of Job Schedule Volatility and Child Care.* Washington DC: Center for Law and Social Policy.

Benner, Katie. 2014. "A Secret of Uber's Success: Struggling Workers." *Bloomberg View*, October 2.

Bensinger, Greg. 2017a. "Uber Mistakenly Shortchanged New York Drivers." *Wall Street Journal*, May 24.

———. 2017b. "Uber Plans to Wind Down U.S. Car-Leasing Business." *Wall Street Journal*, August 8.

———. 2017c. "Uber Shutting Down U.S. Car-Leasing Business." *Wall Street Journal*, September 27.

Benson, Donna J., and Gregg E. Thomson. 1982. "Sexual Harassment on a University Campus: The Confluence of Authority Relations, Sexual Interest and Gender Stratification." *Social Problems* 29(3):236–51, doi:10.2307/800157.

Bergmann, Barbara R. 1986. *The Economic Emergence of Women*. New York: Palgrave Macmillan.

Bernstein, Leonard. 1950. "The Working People of Philadelphia from Colonial Times to the General Strike of 1835." *Pennsylvania Magazine of History and Biography* 74(3):322–39.

Bertrand, Marianne, and Sendhil Mullainathan. 2004. "Are Emily and Greg More Employable Than Lakisha and Jamal? A Field Experiment on Labor Market Discrimination." *American Economic Review* 94(4):991–1013.

Bever, Lindsey. 2016. "'She's Getting Violent': Miami Doctor Suspended after Attack on Uber Driver." *Washington Post*, January 22.

Bhuiyan, Johana. 2017. "Uber Admits That It Has Underpaid Tens of Thousands of Drivers in New York since Late 2014." *Recode*, May 23.

Bialik, Carl, Andrew Flowers, Reuben Fischer-Baum, and Dhrumil Mehta. 2015. "Uber Is Serving New York's Outer Boroughs More Than Taxis Are." *Fivethirtyeight.com*, August 10.

Bianchi, Suzanne M., Liana C. Sayer, Melissa A. Milkie, and John P. Robinson. 2012. "Housework: Who Did, Does or Will Do It, and How Much Does It Matter?" *Social Forces* 91(1):55–63.

Biddle, Sam. 2014. "Uber Driver: Here's How We Get around Background Checks." *Valleywag*, June 27.

Bliss, Charles Henry. 1902. "Labor Strikes and Their Effects on Society: A Common Sense Discussion of the Rights and Relations of Labor and Capital." Florida Heritage Collection, unpublished ms. http://palmm.digital.flvc.org/islandora/object/uwf%3A46777#page/1/mode/1up/search/bliss.

Board of Governors of the Federal Reserve System. 2014. *Report on the Economic Well-Being of U.S. Households in 2013*. Washington, DC: Federal Reserve Board, July.

———. 2015. *Report on the Economic Well-Being of U.S. Households in 2014*. Washington, DC: Federal Reserve Board, May.

———. 2016. *Report on the Economic Well-Being of U.S. Households in 2015.* Washington, DC: Federal Reserve Board, May.

———. 2017. *Report on the Economic Well-Being of U.S. Households in 2016.* Washington, DC: Federal Reserve Board, May.

Böcker, Lars, and Toon Meelen. 2017. "Sharing for People, Planet or Profit? Analysing Motivations for Intended Sharing Economy Participation." *Environmental Innovation and Societal Transitions* 23(June):28–39.

Bohr, Nick. 2016. "Uber Driver Says She Was Sexually Assaulted by Passenger." WISN, February 15.

Boltanski, L., and E. Chiapello. 2005. *The New Spirit of Capitalism.* New York: Verso.

Bort, Julie. 2014a. "Airbnb Banned from Condo Complex after Guest Caused $10,000 of Damage." *Business Insider,* October 9.

———. 2014b. "Airbnb Host: A Guest Is Squatting in My Condo and I Can't Get Him to Leave." *Business Insider,* July 21.

Botsman, Rachel, and Roo Rogers. 2010. *What's Mine Is Yours: The Rise of Collaborative Consumption.* New York: Harper Collins.

Bradford, Harry. 2014. "Most Airbnb Rentals Go Perfectly: Then There Are These Horror Stories." *Huffington Post,* July 29.

Brescoll, Victoria L., Jennifer Glass, and Alexandra Sedlovskaya. 2013. "Ask and Ye Shall Receive? The Dynamics of Employer-Provided Flexible Work Options and the Need for Public Policy." *Journal of Social Issues* 69(2):367–88.

Bricker, Jesse, Lisa J. Dettling, Alice Henriques, Joanne W. Hsu, Kevin B. Moore, John Sabelhaus, Jeffrey Thompson, and Richard A. Windle. 2014. "Changes in U.S. Family Finances from 2010 to 2013: Evidence from the Survey of Consumer Finances." *Federal Reserve Bulletin* 100(4).

Brynjolfsson, Erik, and Andrew McAfee. (2011). *Race against the Machine: How the Digital Revolution Is Accelerating Innovation, Driving Productivity, and Irreversibly Transforming Employment and the Economy.* Lexington, MA: Digital Frontier Press.

Buhr, Sarah. 2017. "A U.S. Senator Has Introduced the First Bill to Give Gig Workers Benefits." *TechCrunch,* May 25.

Bui, Quoctrung. 2017. "A Secret of Many Urban 20-Somethings: Their Parents Help with the Rent." *New York Times,* February 9.

Bureau of Labor Statistics. 2012. *Spotlight on Statistics: The Recession of 2007–2009.* Washington, DC: Bureau of Labor Statistics. www.bls.gov /spotlight/2012/recession/.

———. 2016a. "Business Employment Dynamics: Entrepreneurship and the U.S. Economy: Chart 3. Survival Rates of Establishments, by Year Started and Number of Years since Starting, 1994–2015, in Percent." U.S. Department of Labor. Last modified April 28. www.bls.gov/bdm/entrepreneurship /bdm_chart3.htm.

———. 2016b. *Employee Tenure in 2016*. Washington, DC: Bureau of Labor Statistics.

———. 2017. "Labor Force Statistics from the Current Population Survey." U.S. Department of Labor. www.bls.gov/cps/lfcharacteristics.htm.

Bushway, Shawn, and Peter Reuter. 1997. "Labor Markets and Crime Risk Factors." In *Preventing Crime: What Works, What Doesn't, What's Promising: A Report to the United States Congress*. College Park: Department of Criminology and Criminal Justice, University of Maryland. https://pdfs.semanticscholar.org/7a7e/6871dfbce8940cd88f72ad87664876d8c888.pdf.

Cannon, Sarah, and Lawrence H. Summers. 2014. "How Uber and the Sharing Economy Can Win Over Regulators." *Harvard Business Review*, October 13.

Cantillon, R. 1755. *Essai sur la nature du commerce en général*. London: Macmillan.

Cass, Connie. 2013. "In God We Trust, Maybe, but Not Each Other." AP-GfK Poll. November 30. http://ap-gfkpoll.com/featured/our-latest-poll-findings-24.

Chan, Sewell. 2005. "Taxi Partitions, Born of Danger, May Be Set for a Makeover." *New York Times*, August 9.

Chaudry, Ajay, Juan Pedroza, and Heather Sandstrom. 2012. *How Employment Constraints Affect Low-Income Working Parents' Child Care Decisions*. Brief 23. Washington, DC: Urban Institute.

Chen, Brian X. 2012. "Uber, an App That Summons a Car, Plans a Cheaper Service Using Hybrids." *New York Times*, July 1.

Chen, Michelle. 2014. "Do You Realize How Dangerous It Is to Drive a Taxi?" *The Nation*, October 24.

Christensen, Clayton M. 1997. *The Innovator's Dilemma: When New Technologies Cause Great Firms to Fail*. Boston: Harvard Business School Press.

Clifford, Catherine. 2015. "Who Exactly Are Uber's Drivers?" *Entrepreneur*, January 22.

———. 2016. "The Sharing Economy Is More Than a Buzzword. It's Changing How We Live." *Entrepreneur*. January 7. www.entrepreneur.com/article/254772.

Close, Kerry. 2015. "Uber Just Keeps on Slashing Fares." *Time*, January 29.

Cohen, Patricia. 2017. "Tax Plans May Give Your Co-worker a Better Deal Than You." *New York Times*, December 9.

Collins, Pat. 2016. "Uber Driver Attacked in Arlington after He Asks Passengers to Stop Drinking in Car." *NBC Washington*, February 22.

Committee on Ways and Means. 2007a. "Hearing on the Effects of Misclassifying Workers as Independent Contractors." Hearing before the Subcommittee on Income Security and Family Support and the Subcommittee on Select Revenue Measures of the Committee on Ways and Means, U.S. House of Representatives, 110th Cong., 1st session, serial 110-37. May 8, 2007. https://waysandmeans.house.gov/Media/transcript/10278.html.

———. 2007b. "Present Law and Background Relating to Worker Classification for Federal Tax Purposes." May 8. Scheduled for a Public Hearing before the Subcommittee on Select Revenue Measures and the Subcommittee on Income Security and Family Support of the House Committee on Ways and Means on May 8, 2007. Prepared by the Staff of the Joint Committee on Taxation. May 7, 2007. JCX-26-07. www.irs.gov/pub/irs-utl/x-26-07.pdf.

Commons, John Rogers. 1918. *History of Labour in the United States*. Vol. 1. London: Forgotten Books.

Conley, Dalton. 1999. *Being Black, Living in the Red: Race, Wealth and Social Policy in America*. Berkeley: University of California Press.

Cox, Brian L., Susan Berger, and Grace Wong. 2017. "Uber Driver Killed in Lincolnwood while Dropping Off Passenger, Cops Say." *Chicago Tribune*, May 31.

Craig, Susanne, and Jesse McKinley. 2014. "New York State Is Set to Loosen Marijuana Laws." *New York Times*, January 4.

Cronin, Brenda. 2013. "In the TaskRabbit Economy, Freelancers Are Hard to Measure." *Digits: Tech News and Analysis from the WSJ*, May 29.

Cruz, Mimi Ko. 2014. "CLRN Researcher Gains National Recognition." Connected Learning Research Network, August 19.

Curran, David. 2016. "Two Uber Drivers Shot and Killed in Separate Incidents." *SF Gate*, March 22.

Darrin E. McGillis v. Department of Economic Opportunity; and Rasier LLC, d/b/a UBER, 3D15-2758 (2017).

Dawes, Frank. 1973. *Not in Front of the Servants: A True Portrait of English Upstairs/Downstairs Life*. New York: Taplinger.

Del Rey, Jason. 2017. "Instacart Will Pay $4.6 Million to Settle a Class Action Lawsuit with Its Workers." *Recode*, March 23.

Descant, Skip. 2014. "Airbnb 'Squatter' Checks Out of Palm Springs Condo." *USA Today*, August 21.

DeSilver, Drew. 2014. "For Most Workers, Real Wages Have Barely Budged for Decades." Pew Research Institute Fact Tank, October 9. www.pewresearch .org/fact-tank/2014/10/09/for-most-workers-real-wages-have-barely-budged-for-decades/.

Dewey, Caitlin. 2015. "Everyone You Know Will Be Able to Rate You on the Terrifying 'Yelp for People'—Whether You Want Them to or Not." *Washington Post*, September 30.

Dickey, Megan Rose. 2014. "Uber Will Start Charging More for Some Rides Because It Was Losing Money." *Business Insider*, April 18.

Doleac, Jennifer L., and Luke C. D. Stein. 2010. "The Visible Hand: Race and Online Market Outcomes." *Economic Journal* 123(572):F469–92.

Dougherty, Conor, and Mike Isaac. 2014. "Uber to Portland: We're Here; Deal with It." *New York Times*, December 5.

DuBose, Renetta. 2016. "Uber Driver Attacked Taking Intoxicated Man Home." WJBF.com, February 29.

Dunlap, Albert John. 1996. *Mean Business: How I Save Bad Companies and Make Good Companies Great.* New York: Touchstone.

Dynan, Karen, Douglas Elmendorf, and Daniel Sichel. 2012. "The Evolution of Household Income Volatility." *B.E. Journal of Economic Analysis and Policy* 12(2).

Eckhardt, Gianna M., and Fleura Bardhi. 2015. "The Sharing Economy Isn't about Sharing at All." *Harvard Business Review,* January 28.

The Economist. 2011. "The Birth of the New Deal." March 17.

———. 2013. *"The Economist* Explains Itself: Is *The Economist* Left- or Right-Wing?" September 2.

———. 2015. "Digital Taylorism." September 10.

Edelman, Benjamin G., and Michael Luca. 2014. "Digital Discrimination: The Case of Airbnb.com." Harvard Business School, Working Paper No. 14-054.

Edelman, Benjamin G., Michael Luca, and Dan Svirsky. 2017. "Racial Discrimination in the Sharing Economy: Evidence from a Field Experiment." *American Economic Journal* 9(2):1–22.

Ehrenreich, Barbara. 2001. *Nickel and Dimed: On (Not) Getting by in America.* New York: Henry Holt.

Elder, P. K., and H. D. Miller, 1979. "The Fair Labor Standards Act: Changes of Four Decades." *Monthly Labor Review* 102(7): 10–16.

Ellement, John R. 2016. "Two Uber Drivers Robbed by Passengers in Jamaica Plain." *Boston Globe,* March 30.

Elliott, Bryan. 2017. "How the Developers of Hello Alfred Created a Personal Butler." *Entrepreneur,* June 21.

Entis, Laura. 2014. "We're the Uber of X!" *Entrepreneur,* August 12.

Erb, Kelly Phillips. 2014. "Credit Cards, the IRS, Form 1099-K and the $19,399 Reporting Hole." *Forbes,* August 29.

Etsy. 2013. "Redefining Entrepreneurship: Etsy Sellers' Economic Impact." Etsy.

Evans, Jon. 2013. "Meet the New Serfs, Same as the Old Serfs." *TechCrunch,* October 5.

EV Grieve. 2015. "Survey: East Village Residents Are Spending 56% of Their Incomes on Market-Rate Apartments." March 2. http://evgrieve.com/2015/03/survey-east-village-residents-are.html.

Farley, Lin. 1978. *Sexual Shakedown: The Sexual Harassment of Women on the Job.* New York: McGraw-Hill.

———. 2017. "I Coined the Term 'Sexual Harassment.' Corporations Stole It." *New York Times,* October 18.

Farrell, Diana, and Fiona Greig. 2016. *The Online Platform Economy: Has Growth Peaked?* New York: JP Morgan Chase Institute.

Feige, Edgar L. 1990. "Defining and Estimating Underground and Informal Economies: The New Institutional Economics Approach." *World Development* 18(7):989–1002.

Fermino, Jennifer. 2015. "Airbnb Taking Up 1 out of 5 Vacant Apartments in Popular New York City Zip Codes: Study." *New York Daily News,* July 15.

Fiegerman, Seth. 2014. "Kitchensurfing Raises $15 Million to Bring Private Chefs to Your Home." *Mashable,* March 31.

Fleck, Susan E. 2009. "International Comparisons of Hours Worked: An Assessment of the Statistics." *Monthly Labor Review,* May.

Foner, Philip S. [1947] 1998. *History of the Labor Movement in the United States: From Colonial Times to the Founding of the American Federation of Labor.* New York: International.

Fottrell, Quentin. 2015. "Some TaskRabbit Handymen Can Make $78,000 a Year." *Marketwatch,* March 31.

Fox, Justin. 2014. "Breaking Down the Freelance Economy." *Harvard Business Review,* September 4.

Fraser, Jill Andresky. 2002. *White-Collar Sweatshop: The Deterioration of Work and Its Rewards in Corporate America.* New York: Norton.

Freeman, Richard B., and James L. Medoff. 1984. *What Do Unions Do?* New York: Basic Books.

Frenken, Koen, Toon Meelen, Martijn Arets, and Pieter van de Glind. 2015. "Smarter Regulation for the Sharing Economy." *The Guardian,* May 20.

Friedman, Thomas L. 2013. "Welcome to the 'Sharing Economy.'" *New York Times,* July 20.

———. 2014. "Start-Up America: Our Best Hope." *New York Times,* February 15.

Gabler, Neil. 2016. "The Secret Shame of Middle-Class Americans." *The Atlantic,* May.

Galinsky, Ellen, James T. Bond, and Kelly Sakai. 2008. *2008 National Study of Employers.* New York: Families and Work Institute.

Gallagher, Leigh. 2017. *The Airbnb Story: How Three Ordinary Guys Disrupted an Industry, Made Billions . . . and Created Plenty of Controversy.* New York: Houghton Mifflin Harcourt.

Garling, Caleb. 2014. "Hunting Task Wabbits." *Medium,* December 2.

Gaumer, Elyzabeth. and Sheree West. 2015. *Selected Initial Findings of the 2014 New York City Housing and Vacancy Survey.* New York: New York City Department of Housing Preservation and Development, February 9.

Gee, Kelsey. 2017. "In a Job Market This Good, Who Needs to Work in the Gig Economy?" *Wall Street Journal,* August 8.

Geerts, Achilles, Borris A. Kornblith, and W. John Urmson. 1977. *Compensation for Bodily Harm.* Brussels: Fernand Nathan.

Geron, Tomio. 2013. "Airbnb and the Unstoppable Rise of the Share Economy." *Forbes,* January 23.

Gershon, Ilana. 2017. *Down and Out in the New Economy: How People Find (or Don't Find) Work Today.* Chicago: University of Chicago Press. Kindle edition.

Gershuny, Jonathan. 1979. "The Informal Economy." *Futures* 11(1):3–15.

———. 1985. "Economic Development and Change in the Mode of Provision of Services." In *Beyond Employment: Household, Gender and Subsistence,* ed. N. Redclif and E. Mingione. Oxford: Basil Blackwell.

Ghoshal, Raj, and S. Michael Gaddis. 2015. "Finding a Roommate on Craigslist: Racial Discrimination and Residential Segregation." May 8. Available at SSRN: https://ssrn.com/abstract=2605853.

Giddens, Anthony. 1998. *The Third Way: The Renewal of Social Democracy.* Cambridge, UK: Polity.

Glaser, Barney G., and Anselm L. Strauss. [1967] 1999. *The Discovery of Grounded Theory: Strategies for Qualitative Research.* New York: Aldine De Gruyter.

Goffman, Erving. 1963. *Stigma: Notes on the Management of Spoiled Identity.* Englewood Cliffs, NJ: Prentice-Hall.

Golden, Lonnie. 2016. *Still Falling Short on Hours and Pay: Part-Time Work Becoming New Normal.* Washington, DC: Economic Policy Institute.

Goldin, Claudia, and Cecilia Rouse. 2000. "Orchestrating Impartiality: The Impact of 'Blind' Auditions on Female Musicians." *American Economic Review* 90:715–41.

Grauerholz, Elizabeth. 1989. "Sexual Harassment of Women Professors by Students: Exploring the Dynamics of Power, Authority, and Gender in a University Setting." *Sex Roles* 21(11–12):789–801.

Green, Carla, and Sam Levin. 2017. "Homeless, Assaulted, Broke: Drivers Left Behind as Uber Promises Change at the Top." *The Guardian,* June 17.

Greenhouse, Steven. 2008. *The Big Squeeze: Tough Times for the American Worker.* New York: Knopf.

———. 2014. "A Push to Give Steadier Shifts to Part-Timers." *New York Times,* July 16.

Greenwald, Richard A. 2005. *The Triangle Fire, the Protocols of Peace, and Industrial Democracy in Progressive Era New York.* Philadelphia: Temple University Press.

Gregor, Alison. 2014. "The East Village Clings to a Colorful Past." *New York Times,* December 10.

Griebling, Brittany. 2012. "The Casualization of Intimacy: Consensual Non-Monogamy and the New Sexual Ethos." PhD. diss. Available from ProQuest, AAI3550956.

Griffith, Erin. 2015. "Why Kitchensurfing Made Its Independent Contractors into Employees." *Fortune,* September 1.

Griswold, Alison. 2014. "In Search of Uber's Unicorn." *Slate,* October 27.

———. 2016a. "The Dirty Secret of Airbnb Is That It's Really, Really White." *Quartz*, June 23.

———. 2016b. "There Is an Uber for Blood." *Quartz*, April 1.

———. 2017. "New York State Just Dealt Another Blow to Uber's Business Model." *Quartz*, June 13.

Guerrero, Maria. 2016. "Seattle Uber Driver Claims Customer Sexually Assaulted Her: Uber Responds." KIRO7.com, January 4.

Gutek, Barbara A. 1985. *Sex and the Workplace: The Impact of Sexual Behavior and Harassment on Women, Men, and Organizations*. San Francisco: Jossey-Bass.

Guyton, Gregory P. 1999. "A Brief History of Workers' Compensation." *Iowa Orthopaedic Journal* 19:106–10.

Hacker, Jacob S. 2006. *The Great Risk Shift*. New York: Oxford University Press.

Hacker, Jacob S., Gregory A. Huber, Philipp Rehm, Mark Schlesinger, and Rob Valletta. 2010. *Economic Security at Risk: Findings from the Economic Security Index*. New York City: Rockefeller Foundation, July.

Hall, Elaine J. 1993. "Smiling, Deferring, and Flirting: Doing Gender by Giving 'Good Service.'" *Work and Occupations* 20(4):452–471.

Hall, Jonathan, and Alan Krueger. 2015. "An Analysis of the Labor Market for Uber's Driver-Partners in the United States." National Bureau of Economic Research. NBER Working Paper No. 22843.

Haller, John S. 1988. "Industrial Accidents-Worker Compensation Laws and the Medical Response." *Western Journal of Medicine* 148:341–48.

Haltiwanger, John, Ron S. Jarmin, and Javier Miranda. 2013. "Who Creates Jobs? Small versus Large versus Young." *Review of Economics and Statistics* 95(2):347–61.

Hamari, Juho, Mimmi Sjöklint, and Antti Ukkonen. 2015. "The Sharing Economy: Why People Participate in Collaborative Consumption." *Journal of the Association for Information Science and Technology*. Available at SSRN: https://ssrn.com/abstract=2271971.

Hamlin, Suzanne. 1997. "Chefs and Shoes: A Bond Forged in Battle." *New York Times*, November 5.

Hanks, Douglas. 2015. "For Uber, Loyal Drivers and a New Fight for Benefits." *Miami Herald*, May 21.

Harris, Seth D., and Alan B. Krueger. 2015. "A Proposal for Modernizing Labor Laws for Twenty-First-Century Work: The 'Independent Worker.'" Hamilton Project. Discussion Paper No. 2015-10.

Harrison, Bennett. 1997. *Lean and Mean: Why Large Corporations Will Continue to Dominate the Global Economy*. New York: Guilford Press.

Haughney, Christine. 2010. "When Finding an Apartment Is Only Half the Battle." *New York Times*, November 29.

Hauser, Christine. 2015. "The State of Uber: How It Operates in the U.S." *New York Times*, July 23.

Heatherton, Todd F., Robert E. Kleck, Michelle R. Hebl, and Jay C. Hull, eds. 2000. *The Social Psychology of Stigma*. New York: Guilford Press.

Helfand, Jessica. 2016. *Design: The Invention of Desire*. New Haven, CT: Yale University Press.

Henwood, Doug. 2015. "What the Sharing Economy Takes." *The Nation*, January 27.

Higgins, Michelle. 2013. "The Get-into-School Card." *New York Times*, May 3.

Higgins, Tim, Joseph Ciolli, and Callie Bost. 2014. "Apple Inc. Market Cap Tops US$700B, Double What It Was When Tim Cook Took Over as CEO." *Bloomberg News*, November 25.

Hill, Steven. 2015a. *Raw Deal: How the "Uber Economy" and Runaway Capitalism Are Screwing American Workers*. New York: St. Martin's Griffin.

———. 2015b. "The Unsavory Side of Airbnb." *American Prospect*, October 15.

Hirsch, Barry T., and Edward J. Schumacher. 1998. "Unions, Wages, and Skills." *Journal of Human Resources* 33:201–19.

Hochschild, Arlie Russell. 1983. *The Managed Heart: Commercialization of Human Feeling*. Berkeley: University of California Press.

———. [1989] 2002. *The Second Shift*. New York: HarperCollins.

———. 2012. *The Outsourced Self: What Happens When We Pay Others to Live Our Lives for Us*. New York: Henry Holt.

Hondagneu-Sotelo, Pierrette. 2001. *Doméstica: Immigrant Workers Cleaning and Caring in the Shadows of Affluence*. Berkeley: University of California Press.

Hsu, Tiffany. 2017. "Ikea Enters 'Gig Economy' by Acquiring TaskRabbit." *New York Times*, September 28.

Hu, Winnie. 2017. "Yellow Cab, Long a Fixture of City Life, Is for Many a Thing of the Past." *New York Times*, January 15.

Huet, Ellen. 2015. "Uber Raises UberX Commission to 25 Percent in Five More Markets." *Forbes*, September 11.

Institute for Social Research. 1994. *Panel Study of Income Dynamics*. Ann Arbor: Survey Research Center, Institute for Social Research, University of Michigan.

Intuit. 2010. *Intuit 2020 Report: Twenty Trends That Will Shape the Next Decade*. Mountain View, CA: Intuit.

Isaac, Mike. 2016. "Judge Overturns Uber's Settlement with Drivers." *New York Times*, August 18.

———. 2017. "Uber's C.E.O. Plays with Fire." *New York Times*, April 23.

Isaac, Mike, and Katie Benner. 2017. "Uber Board Considers 3 Investment Offers to Buy Company's Shares." *New York Times*, August 13.

Israel, Betsy. 2002. *Bachelor Girl: The Secret History of Single Women in the Twentieth Century*. New York: William Morrow.

James, Kimberly. 2016. "Georgia Uber Driver Said Passenger Attacked Him." *Atlanta Journal-Constitution,* February 29.

JB. 2014. "Uber Slashes Prices in New York City and New Jersey." Uber Driver Diaries, July 7.

Joint Committee on Taxation. 2007. *Present Law and Background Relating to Worker Classification for Federal Tax Purposes* (JCX-26-07). Washington, DC: Internal Revenue Service, May 7.

Jost, Micah Prieb Stoltzfus. 2011. "Independent Contractors, Employees and Entrepreneurialism under the National Labor Relations Act: A Worker-by-Worker Approach." *Washington and Lee Law Review* 68(311).

Kahn, Bonnie Menes. 1987. *Cosmopolitan Culture: The Gilt-Edged Dream of a Tolerant City.* New York: Atheneum.

Kahn, Lisa B. 2010. "The Long-Term Labor Market Consequences of Graduating from College in a Bad Economy." *Labour Economics* 17(2):303–16.

Kalamar, Anthony. 2013. "Sharewashing Is the New Greenwashing." OpEdNews.com, May 13.

Kalanick, Travis. 2016. "Uber CEO Travis Kalanick's Gridlock Solution? Carpools for All." *Wall Street Journal,* June 6.

Kalleberg, Arne L. 2009. "Precarious Work, Insecure Workers: Employment Relations in Transition." *American Sociological Review* 74(1):1–22.

———. 2011. *Good Jobs, Bad Jobs: The Rise of Polarized and Precarious Employment Systems in the United States.* New York: Russell Sage Foundation.

Kane, Kat. 2015. "The Big Hidden Problem with Uber? Insincere 5-Star Ratings." *Wired,* March 19.

Kantor, Jodi. 2014. "Working Anything but 9 to 5." *New York Times,* August 13.

Kasinitz, Philip, and Jan Rosenberg. 1996. "Missing the Connection: Social Isolation and Employment on the Brooklyn Waterfront." *Social Problems* 43:180–96.

Katz, Jack. 1989. *The Seductions of Crime.* New York: Basic Books.

Katz, Lawrence F., and Alan B. Krueger. 2016. "The Rise and Nature of Alternative Work Arrangements in the United States, 1995–2015." National Bureau of Economic Research. NBER Working Paper No. 22667.

Katz, Miranda. 2017. "A Growing Number of Startups Are Ditching the Uber Model and Hiring Full-Time Workers." *Business Insider,* April 23.

Kaye, Leon. 2012. "Why Sharing Makes Sense in an Over-consuming World." *The Guardian,* January 12.

Kelling, George L., and James Q. Wilson. 1982. "Broken Windows." *The Atlantic.*

Kerr, Dara. 2015. "To Tip or Not to Tip Drivers, That Is Uber's Question." *CNET,* February 16.

Kessler, Sarah. 2014a. "Peers Says Its New Focus Is Helping Sharing Economy Workers." *Fast Company,* November 12.

———. 2014b. "Pixel and Dimed—On Not Getting By in the Gig Economy." *Fast Company*, March 18.

———. 2015a. "The Gig Economy Won't Last Because It's Being Sued to Death." *Fast Company*, February 17.

———. 2015b. "The "Sharing Economy" Is Dead, and We Killed It." *Fast Company*, September 14.

Kirchner, Elyce, David Paredes, and Scott Pham. 2014. "Is Uber Keeping Riders Safe?" *NBC Bay Area*, April 24.

Knight, Frank H. 1921. *Risk, Uncertainty, and Profit*. Boston: Houghton Mifflin.

Koebler, Jason. 2015. "Anatomy of a Seven-Hour, $583 Uber Ride." *Motherboard*. June 17. https://motherboard.vice.com/en_us/article/pga4n9/anatomy-of-a-seven-hour-583-uber-ride.

Kokalitcheva, Kia. 2016. "Uber's Employment Fight Just Got More Complicated." *Fortune*, March 4.

Kolhatkar, Sheelah. 2016. "Juno Takes on Uber." *New Yorker*, October 10.

———. 2017. "Welcoming Our New Robot Overlords." *New Yorker*, October 23.

Kolodny, Lora. 2010. "UberCab Ordered to Cease and Desist." *TechCrunch*, October 24.

Kortum, Samuel, and Josh Lerner. 2000. "Assessing the Impact of Venture Capital on Innovation." *Rand Journal of Economics* 31:674–92.

Kosoff, Maya. 2015. "2 Harvard Students Were Sick of Their Dirty Apartments, So They Built a Company That Will Do Your Chores for You." *Business Insider*, June 17.

Kravets, David. 2016. "Judge Calls Uber Algorithm 'Genius,' Green-Lights Surge-Pricing Lawsuit." *Ars Technica*, April 4.

———. 2017. "Lyft Agrees to Pay $27 Million to Settle Driver Classification Lawsuit." *Ars Technica*, March 18.

Kricheli-Katz, Tamar, and Tali Regev. 2016. "How Many Cents on the Dollar? Women and Men in Product Markets." *Science Advances* 2(2).

Krishna, Priya. 2017. "How Street Meat Conquered New York." *Grub Street*. www.grubstreet.com/2017/11/halal-cart-chicken-and-rice-oral-history.html.

Krugman, Paul. 2007. *The Conscience of a Liberal*. New York: W. W. Norton.

Kurtzleben, Danielle. 2015. "The Rise of the Servant Economy." *Vox*, February 6.

Kwon, Haegi. 2005. "Public Toilets in New York City: A Plan Flushed with Success?" Master's thesis, Department of Urban Planning, Columbia University.

Ladegaard, Isak, Alexandrea J. Ravenelle, and Juliet Schor. 2017. "'I'm Probably Going to Get One Star': Responsibilization and Worker Vulnerabilities in the Digital Age." Unpublished ms.

Lagorio-Chafkin, Christine. 2014. "How Uber Is Going to Hire 1,000 People This Year." *Inc.*, January 15.

Lamberton, Cait Poynor, and Randall L. Rose. 2012. "When Is Ours Better Than Mine? A Framework for Understanding and Altering Participation in Commercial Sharing Systems." *Journal of Marketing* 76(4):109–25.

Landier, Augustin. 2005. "Entrepreneurship and the Stigma of Failure." November. Available at SSRN: http://ssrn.com/abstract=850446

Lang, Noah. 2015. "Employee or Contractor? Online Businesses Like Uber Need a New Category." *Newsweek*, June 21.

Larson, Jane E. 1997. "Even a Worm Will Turn at Last": Rape Reform in Late Nineteenth-Century America," *Yale Journal of Law & the Humanities* 9(1). http://digitalcommons.law.yale.edu/yjlh/vol9/iss1/1.

Lashinsky, Adam. 2014. "Uber Banks on World Domination." *Fortune*, September 18.

Lawler, Ryan. 2014. "Uber Slashes UberX Fares in 16 Markets to Make It the Cheapest Car Service Available Anywhere." *TechCrunch*, January 9.

Lazzaro, Sage. 2017. "Juno Drivers File Class Action Lawsuit after Getting Stiffed in Gett Acquisition." *Observer*, June 20.

Lee, Aileen. 2013. "Welcome to the Unicorn Club: Learning from Billion-Dollar Startups." *TechCrunch*, November 2.

Leicht, Kevin T., and Scott T. Fitzgerald. 2013. *Middle Class Meltdown in America: Causes, Consequences, and Remedies.* Milton, Oxfordshire, UK: Taylor and Francis.

Leonard, Andrew. 2013a. "The Sharing Economy Gets Greedy." *Salon*, July 31.
———. 2013b. "Who Owns the Sharing Economy?" *Salon*, August 2.

Leone, Hannah. 2016. "St. Charles Man Charged with Attacking Uber Driver." *Aurora Beacon-News*, March 22.

Leonhardt, David. 2009. "Broader Measure of U.S. Unemployment Stands at 17.5%." *New York Times*, November 6.

Lepore, Jill. 2014. "The Disruption Machine." *New Yorker*, June 23.

Levin, Sam. 2017. "Sexual Harassment and the Sharing Economy: The Dark Side of Working for Strangers." *The Guardian*, August 23.

Levine, Dan. 2015. "Uber, Santander Partnership on Car Loans Is Over." *Reuters*, July 23.

Levintova, Hannah. 2016. "Uber Just Got Hit with Another Legal Fight." *Mother Jones*, October 7.

Lev-Ram, Michal. 2014. "Uber and Airbnb Are Complicating Corporate Expense Reports." *Fortune*, July 29.

Lewis, H. Gregg. 1983. "Union Relative Wage Effects: A Survey of Macro Estimates." *Journal of Labor Economics* 1(1):1–27.

Licea, Melkorka, Elizabeth Ruby, and Rebecca Harshbarger. 2015. "More Uber Cars than Yellow Taxis on the Road in NYC." *New York Post*, March 17.

Lieber, Ron. 2015. "Airbnb Horror Story Points to Need for Precautions." *New York Times*, August 14.

Lieber, Ron, and Tara Siegel Bernard. 2017. "What's in the Tax Bill, and How It Will Affect You." *New York Times,* December 16.

Lien, Tracey, and Andrea Chang. 2014. "Now Worth $40 billion, Update Uber Outraces Other Tech Models." *LA Times,* December 4.

Lightfeldt, Alan. 2015. "Bright Lights, Big Rent Burden: Understanding New York City's Rent Affordability Problem." *Streeteasy,* March 1.

Linder, Marc. 1989. *The Employment Relationship in Anglo-American Law.* New York: Greenwood Press.

Lorber, Judith. 1994. *Paradoxes of Gender.* New Haven, CT: Yale University Press.

Lorenzetti, Laura. 2014. "Airbnb's Valuation Set to Reach $13 Billion after Employee Stock Sale." *Fortune,* October 24.

Lovece, Frank. 2010. "New Law Bans Short-Term Co-op and Condo Rentals." *Habitat Magazine,* July 25.

MacKinnon, Catharine A. 1979. *Sexual Harassment of Working Women: A Case of Sex Discrimination.* New Haven, CT: Yale University Press.

Mahmood, Omar. 2016. "Uber Driver Suspended, Responds to Anti-Semitism Accusations." *Michigan Review,* March 28.

Mangalindan, J. P. 2014. "In Price Wars, Some Uber and Lyft Drivers Feel the Crunch." *Fortune,* May 28.

Mani, Anandi, Sendhil Mullainathan, Eldar Shafir, and Jiaying Zhao. 2013. "Poverty Impedes Cognitive Function." *Science* 341(6149):976–80.

Manjoo, Farhad. 2016. "Car-Pooling Helps Uber Go the Extra Mile." *New York Times,* March 30.

Manning, Robert D. 2000. *Credit Card Nation: The Consequences of America's Addiction to Credit.* New York: Basic Books.

Manyika, James, Susan Lund, Jacques Bughin, Kelsey Robinson, Jan Mischke, and Deepa Mahajan. 2016. *"Independent Work: Choice, Necessity and the Gig Economy,"* McKinsey Global Institute, October.

Marx, Patricia. 2013. "Outsource Yourself." *New Yorker,* January 14.

Mass, Alon Y., David S. Goldfarb, and Ojas Shah. 2014. "Taxi Cab Syndrome: A Review of the Extensive Genitourinary Pathology Experienced by Taxi Cab Drivers and What We Can Do to Help." *Review of Urology* 16(3):99–104.

Mathews, Joe. 2014. "The Sharing Economy Boom Is about to Bust." *Time,* June 27. http://time.com/2924778/airbnb-uber-sharing-economy/.

May, Patrick. 2015. "Apple Says It's Created 1 Million Jobs, App Store Is Going Gangbusters." *San Jose Mercury News,* January 8.

McAfee, Andrew. N.d. "The Great Decoupling of the US Economy." *Andrew McAfee* (website). http://andrewmcafee.org/2012/12/the-great-decoupling-of-the-us-economy/.

McAfee, Andrew, and Erik Brynjolfsson. 2017. *Machine, Platform, Crowd: Harnessing Our Digital Future.* New York: W. W. Norton.

McKinney, K. (1994). "Sexual Harassment and College Faculty Members." *Deviant Behavior* 15(2):171–91.

McKinney, Sarah. 2013. "A Growing Segment of Sharing Economy Users? Entrepreneurs." *Forbes*, November 9.

Merton, Robert K. 1938. "Social Structure and Anomie." *American Sociological Review* 3:672–82.

Mettler, S. 1994. "Federalism, Gender, and the Fair Labor Standards Act of 1938." *Polity* 26(4): 635–54.

Mieszkowski, Katharine. 1998. "Don't Wanna Be Your (Temp) Slave." *Fast Company*, August 31.

Mills, C. Wright. 1959. *The Sociological Imagination*. New York: Oxford University Press.

Mishel, Lawrence, Elize Gould, and Josh Bivens. 2015. *Wage Stagnation in Nine Charts*. Washington, DC: Economic Policy Institute.

Moen, Phyllis, Erin L. Kelly, Shi-Rong Lee, J. Michael Oakes, Wen Fan, Jeremy Bray, David Almeida, Leslie Hammer, David Hurtado, and Orfeu Buxton. 2017. "Can a Flexibility/Support Initiative Reduce Turnover Intentions and Exits? Results from the Work, Family, and Health Network." *Social Problems* 64(1):53–85.

Molz, Jennie Germann. 2013. "Social Networking Technologies and the Moral Economy of Alternative Tourism: The Case of Couchsurfing.org." *Annals of Tourism Research* 43:210–30.

Morduch, Jonathan, and Rachel Schneider. 2017. *The Financial Diaries: How American Families Cope in a World of Uncertainty*. Princeton, NJ: Princeton University Press.

Morgenson, Gretchen. 2008. "Given a Shovel, Americans Dig Deeper into Debt." *New York Times*, July 20.

Mose, Tamara. 2011. *Raising Brooklyn: Nannies, Childcare, and Caribbeans Creating Community*. New York: New York University Press.

Moss-Racusin, Corinne A., John F. Dovidio, Victoria L. Brescoll, Mark J. Graham, and Jo Handelsman. 2012. "Science Faculty's Subtle Gender Biases Favor Male Students." *PNAS* 109(41):16474–79.

Murray, Rheana. 2014. "Uber, Lyft Drivers and Customers Kiss and Tell." *ABC News*, July 30.

Nadeem, Shehzad. 2015. "On the Sharing Economy." *Contexts* (Winter).

Nanos, Janelle. 2013. "The End of Ownership." *Boston*, May.

National Employment Law Project. 2014. *"The Low-Wage Recovery: Industry Employment and Wages Four Years into the Recovery."* New York: National Employment Law Project.

Newcomer, Eric. 2017. "In Video, Uber CEO Argues with Driver over Falling Fares." *Bloomberg*, February 28.

Newcomer, Eric, and Olivia Zaleski. 2016. "Inside Uber's Auto-Lease Machine, Where Almost Anyone Can Get a Car." *Bloomberg,* May 31.

Newman, Katherine S. 1999. *No Shame in My Game: The Working Poor in the Inner City.* New York: Knopf.

Newton, Casey. 2013. "Tempting Fate: Can TaskRabbit Go from Side Gigs to Real Jobs?" *The Verge,* May 23.

New York Communities for Change and Real Affordability for All. 2015. *Airbnb in NYC: Housing Report.* New York: New York Communities for Change and Real Affordability for All.

New York Times. 1911. "Seek Ways to Lessen Factory Dangers." March 26.

———. 1994. "Proctor and Gamble Company Reports." January 28.

Norén, Laura. 2010. "Only Dogs Are Free to Pee: New York Cabbies' Search for Civility." In *Toilet: Public Restrooms and the Politics of Sharing.* Ed. Harvey Molotch and Laura Norén. NYU Series in Social and Cultural Analysis. New York: NYU Press. Kindle edition.

Occupational Safety and Health Administration. 2010. *OSHA FactSheet: Preventing Violence against Taxi and For-Hire Drivers.* Washington, DC: U.S. Department of Labor.

O'Donovan, Caroline. 2017. "A Senator Just Introduced the First-Ever National Gig Economy Bill." *BuzzFeed,* May 25.

O'Donovan, Caroline, and Priya Anand. 2017. "How Uber's Hard-Charging Corporate Culture Left Employees Drained." *BuzzFeed,* July 17.

Office of the Attorney General of the State of New York's Research Department and Internet Bureau. 2014. *Airbnb in the City.* New York: Office of the Attorney General of the State of New York.

Organisation for Economic Co-operation and Development (OECD). 2017. *Hours Worked: Average Annual Hours Actually Worked.* Paris: OECD Employment and Labour Market Statistics.

Oxford Economics. 2014. "An Assessment of Paid Time Off in the U.S.: Implications for Employees, Companies, and the Economy." Oxford, UK: Oxford Economics,

Page, Susan. 2015. "Sen. Mark Warner: Rethinking the Social Contract in the Age of Uber." *USA Today,* June 3.

Pahl, R. E. 1980. "Employment, Work and the Domestic Division of Labour." *International Journal of Urban and Regional Research* 4(1):1–20.

Parlapiano, Alicia. 2017. "How the 'Small-Business Tax Cut' Would Also Be a Tax Cut for the Wealthy." *New York Times,* December 20.

Perea, Christian. 2016. "What's the Real Commission That Uber Takes from Its Drivers?" *The Rideshare Guy* (blog), July 25.

Perez, Sarah. 2014. "TaskRabbit for Business Service Portal Quietly Disappears." *TechCrunch,* April 1.

Peters, Diniece, Lee Kim, Raiyyan Zaman, Greg Haas, Jialei Cheng, and Shakil Ahmed. 2015. "Pedestrian Crossing Behavior at Signalized Intersections in New York City." *Transportation Research Record: Journal of the Transportation Research Board* 2519:179–88.

Peterson, Latoya. 2015. "Uber's Convenient Racial Politics." *Fusion*, July 23.

Pew Research Center. 2014. *Views of Job Market Tick Up, No Rise in Economic Optimism*. Washington, DC: Pew Research Center.

Piketty, Thomas. 2014. *Capital in the Twenty-First Century*. Cambridge, MA: Harvard University Press.

Piketty, Thomas, and Emmanuel Saez. 2003. "Income Inequality in the United States, 1913–1998." *Quarterly Journal of Economics* 118(1):1–39.

Plaut, Melissa. 2007. *Hack: How I Stopped Worrying about What to Do with My Life and Started Driving a Yellow Cab*. New York: Random House.

Portes, Alejandro. 1994. "The Informal Economy and Its Paradoxes." In *Handbook of Economic Sociology*, ed. Neil J. Smelser and Richard Swedberg, 426–49. Princeton, NJ: Princeton University Press.

Poston, Ben, and Andrew Khouri. 2015. "Ousted Tenants Sue after Their Former Rent-Controlled L.A. Apartments Are Listed on Airbnb." *Los Angeles Times*, December 17.

Potts, Monica. 2015. "The Post-ownership Society." *Washington Monthly*, June–August.

Price, Emily. 2016. "This 'Uber for Dog Poop' App Is Definitely Fake—Sorry, Sharing Economy Enthusiasts." *Fast Company*, July 29.

PricewaterhouseCoopers. 2015. *The Sharing Economy*. Consumer Intelligence Series. PricewaterhouseCoopers. April. www.pwc.com/us/en/services /consulting/library/consumer-intelligence-series/sharing-economy.html.

Puente, Kelly. 2016. "Uber Passenger, Captured on Viral Video Drunkenly Slapping and Hitting Driver, Sues Driver for $5 Million." *Orange County Register*, January 17.

Pugh, Allison J. 2015. *The Tumbleweed Society: Working and Caring in an Age of Insecurity*. Oxford: Oxford University Press.

Pulos, Will. 2015. "Map of Average Rent by NYC Neighborhood." *Time Out New York*, August 21.

Putnam, Robert D. 2000. *Bowling Alone: The Collapse and Revival of American Community*. New York: Simon and Schuster.

Putnam, Robert D., and Lewis Feldstein. 2003. *Better Together: Restoring the American Community*. New York: Simon and Schuster.

Ravenelle, Alexandrea J. 2017a. "A Return to Gemeinschaft: Digital Impression Management and the Sharing Economy." In *Digital Sociologies,* ed. Jessie Daniels, Karen Gregory, and Tressie McMillan Cottom, 27–46. Bristol, UK: Policy Press / Bristol University Press.

————. 2017b. "Sharing Economy Workers: Selling, Not Sharing." *Cambridge Journal of Regions, Economy and Society* 10(2): 281–95.

Ritzer, George. 1993. *The McDonaldization of Society.* New York: Sage.

Rocha, Veronica. 2016. "Man Found Shot to Death in Bullet-Riddled Car with Uber Sticker in Lincoln Heights." *Los Angeles Times,* February 9.

Rogers, Jackie Krasas, and Kevin D. Henson. 1997. "Hey, Why Don't You Wear a Shorter Skirt?": Structural Vulnerability and the Organization of Sexual Harassment in Temporary Clerical Employment." *Gender & Society,* 11(2):215–37.

Rogers, Kate. 2016. "Uber Cuts Prices in More Than 100 US Cities." *CNBC,* January 11.

Roose, Kevin. 2014. "Does Silicon Valley Have a Contract-Worker Problem?" *New York,* September 18.

Rosario, Frank, C. J. Sullivan, and Joe Tacopino. 2014. "Airbnb Renter Returns to 'Overweight Orgy.'" *New York Post,* March 14.

Rosenfield, Jake, Patrick Denice, and Jennifer Laird. 2016. "Union Decline Lowers Wages of Nonunion Workers." *Economic Policy Report,* August 30.

Ross, Joel L., Lilly Irani, M. Six Silberman, Andrew Zaldivar, and Bill Tomlinson. 2010. "Who Are the Crowdworkers? Shifting Demographics in Mechanical Turk." Paper presented at the Conference on Human Factors in Computing Systems, Atlanta, GA, April 10–15.

Rotman, David. 2013. "How Technology Is Destroying Jobs." *MIT Technology Review,* June 12. www.technologyreview.com/s/515926/how-technology-is-destroying-jobs/.

Ryan, Kennedy, Kirk Hawkins, and Christina Pascucci. 2015. "Police in West Covina Investigate Discovery of Woman's Body in Possible Uber Vehicle." KTLA.com, August 26.

Rybczynski, Witold. 1993. "Alexis de Tocqueville, Urban Critic." *City Journal,* summer.

Sachs, Benjamin. 2015. "A New Category of Worker for the On-Demand Economy?" *On Labor,* June 22.

Sacks, Danielle. 2011. "The Sharing Economy." *Fast Company,* April 18.

Said, Carolyn. 2014. "TaskRabbit Makes Some Workers Hopping Mad." *San Francisco Chronicle,* July 18.

Sanchez, Karizza. 2016. "How Safe Is Uber in New York City?" *Complex,* May 20.

Sapone, Marcela. 2015. "The On-Demand Economy Doesn't Have to Imitate Uber to Win." *Quartz,* July 10.

Satow, Julie. 2014. "On the List, and Not in a Good Way." *New York Times,* October 16.

Scheiber, Noam. 2018. "Tax Law Offers a Carrot to Gig Workers, But It May Have Costs." *New York Times,* January 1.

Scheiber, Noam, and Mike Isaac. 2016. "Uber Recognizes New York Drivers' Group, Short of a Union." *New York Times,* May 10.

Schoar, Antoinette. 2010. "The Divide between Subsistence and Transformational Entrepreneurship." *Innovation Policy and the Economy* 10(1):57–81.

Schonfeld, Zach. 2016. "How a Fake Dog Poop App Fooled the Media." *Newsweek,* July 29.

Schor, Juliet B. 1992. *The Overworked American: The Unexpected Decline of Leisure.* New York: Basic Books.

———. 1998. *The Overspent American: Why We Want What We Don't Need.* New York: Basic Books.

———. 2010. *True Wealth: How and Why Millions of Americans Are Creating a Time-Rich, Ecologically Light, Small-Scale, High-Satisfaction Economy.* New York: Penguin.

———. 2013. "After the Jobs Disappear." *New York Times,* October 14.

———. 2014a. "Debating the Sharing Economy." *Great Transition Initiative,* October. www.greattransition.org/publication/debating-the-sharing-economy.

———. 2014b. "Risks and Rewards of Cultivating a Sharing Economy." *Brink,* December 23.

———. 2015. "The Sharing Economy: Reports from Stage One." Unpublished paper.

———. 2017. "Does the Sharing Economy Increase Inequality within the Eighty Percent?: Findings from a Qualitative Study of Platform Providers." *Cambridge Journal of Regions, Economy and Society* 10(2):263–79.

Schor, Juliet B., and William Attwood-Charles. 2015. "Platform Providers in the 'Sharing' Economy." *Work in Progress: Sociology on the Economy, Work and Equality,* July 28. https://workinprogress.oowsection.org/2015/07/28/platform-providers-in-the-sharing-economy/.

———. 2017. "The 'Sharing' Economy: Labor, Inequality, and Social Connection on For-Profit Platforms." *Sociology Compass* 11.

Schor, Juliet B., and Connor Fitzmaurice. 2015. "Collaborating and Connecting: The Emergence of a Sharing Economy." *Handbook on Research on Sustainable Consumption.* Cheltenham, UK: Edward Elgar.

Schor, Juliet B., Connor Fitzmaurice, Lindsey B. Carfagna, William Attwood-Charles, and Emilie Dubois Poteat. 2016. "Paradoxes of Openness and Distinction in the Sharing Economy." *Poetics* 54:66–81.

Schumpeter, Joseph A. 1942. *Capitalism, Socialism, and Democracy.* New York: Harper.

Scott, Marvin B., and Stanford M. Lyman. 1968. "Accounts." *American Sociological Review* 33(1): 46–62.

Segrave, Kerry. 2013. *The Sexual Harassment of Women in the Workplace, 1600 to 1993.* Jefferson, NC: McFarland.

Sennett, Richard, and Jonathan Cobb. [1972] 1993. *The Hidden Injuries of Class*. New York: Norton.

Shaffe, Nima. 2016. "Detroit Police Arrest Suspect in Shooting Death of Uber Driver." WXYZ.com, March 22.

Shellenbarger, Sue. 2008. "Work at Home? Your Employer May Be Watching." *Wall Street Journal*, July 30.

Shepherd, Dean A., and J. Michael Haynie. 2011. "Venture Failure, Stigma and Impression Management: A Self-Verification, Self-Determination View." *Strategic Entrepreneurship Journal* 5:178–97.

Shipler, David. 2004. *The Working Poor: Invisible in America*. New York: Knopf.

Shontell, Alyson. 2014. "All Hail the Uber Man! How Sharp-Elbowed Salesman Travis Kalanick Became Silicon Valley's Newest Star." *Business Insider*, January 11.

Siegel, Reva B. 2003. "A Short History of Sexual Harassment." In *Directions in Sexual Harassment Law*, ed. Catherine A. MacKinnon and Reva B. Siegel. New Haven, CT: Yale University Press.

Siegler, M.G. 2011. "Uber CEO: I Think I've Got 20,000 Years of Jail Time in Front of Me." *TechCrunch*, May 25.

Silva, Jennifer M. 2013. *Coming Up Short: Working-Class Adulthood in an Age of Uncertainty*. Oxford: Oxford University Press. Kindle edition.

Simmel, Georg [1902] 1964. "The Metropolis and Mental Life." In *The Sociology of Georg Simmel*, ed. and trans. by K.H. Wolff, pp. 409–24. New York: Free Press.

Simmons, Sharon A., Johan Wiklund, and Jonathan Levie. 2014. "Stigma and Business Failure: Implications for Entrepreneurs' Career Choices." *Small Business Economics* 42:485–505.

Sinclair, Upton. 1906. *The Jungle*. New York: Grosset and Dunlap.

Smith, Aaron. 2016a. *Gig Work, Online Selling and Home Sharing*. Washington, DC: Pew Research Center. November.

———. 2016b. *Shared, Collaborative and On Demand: The New Digital Economy*. Washington, DC: Pew Research Center. May.

Smith, Lindsey J. 2016. "Wall Street Loans Uber $1 Billion to Offer Subprime Auto Leases." *The Verge*, June 3.

Smith, Sandra Susan. 2003. "Exploring the Efficacy of African Americans' Job Referral Networks: A Study of the Obligations of Exchange around Job Information and Influence." *Ethnic and Racial Studies* 26(6):1029–45.

Standing, Guy. 2014. *The Precariat: The New Dangerous Class*. London: Bloomsbury Academic.

Stansell, Christine. 1987. *City of Women: Sex and Class in New York, 1789–1860*. Champaign: University of Illinois Press.

Stevenson, Howard H., and David E. Gumpert. 1985. "The Heart of Entrepreneurship." *Harvard Business Review* (March–April): 85–94.

Stone, Brad. 2012. "My Life as a TaskRabbit." *Bloomberg Business*, September 13.

Stone, Jeff. 2014. "Sharing-Economy Moves the Small Town Mindset Online." When You Put It That Way, June 7. http://whenyouputitthatway.com /sharing-economy-moves-the-small-town-mindset-online/.

Stone, John R., and Daniel C. Stevens. 2014. "Effectiveness of Taxi Partitions: Baltimore, Maryland, Case Study." *Transportation Research Record: Journal of the Transportation Research Board*, no. 1731.

Stone, Pamela. 2007. *Opting Out? Why Women Really Quit Careers and Head Home*. Berkeley: University of California Press.

Stone, Pamela, and Lisa Ackerly Hernandez. 2013. "The All-or-Nothing Workplace: Flexibility Stigma and 'Opting Out' among Professional-Managerial Women." *Journal of Social Issues* 69:235–56.

Strandell, Joe. 2015. "Can You Beat My Longest Uber Ride Ever?" *The Rideshare Guy* (blog), March 17. https://therideshareguy.com/can-you-beat-my-longest-uber-ride-ever/.

Strauss, Anselm, and Juliet Corbin. 1994. "Grounded Theory Methodology." In *Handbook of Qualitative Research*, ed. N. K. Denzin and Y. S Lincoln, 217–85. Thousand Oaks, CA: Sage.

Streitfeld, David. 2004. "No Gain, Know Pain." *Los Angeles Times*, March 2.

Strom, Shayna, and Mark Schmitt. 2016. *Protecting Workers in a Patchwork Economy*. New York: Century Foundation, April 7.

Sundararajan, Arun. 2016. *The Sharing Economy: The End of Employment and the Rise of Crowd-Based Capitalism*. Cambridge: MIT Press.

Surowiecki, James. 2013. "Airbnb's New York Problem." *New Yorker*, October 8.

Tanz, Jason. 2014. "How Airbnb and Lyft Finally Got Americans to Trust Each Other." *Wired*, April 23.

Tedesco, Austin. 2015. "Boston Police Officer Indicted for Allegedly Assaulting Uber Driver." Boston.com, April 2.

Thompson, Derek. 2011. "America's Post-ownership Future." *The Atlantic*. April 25.

Tiku, Nitasha. 2014. "Uber and Its Shady Partners Are Pushing Drivers into Subprime Loans." *Valleywag*, November 4.

Tomlins, Christopher. 1993. *Law, Labor and Ideology in the New Republic*. Cambridge: Cambridge University Press.

Tonnies, Ferdinand. 1957. *Community and Society: Gemeinschaft und Gesellschaft*. Translated and edited by Charles P. Looms. East Lansing: Michigan State University Press.

Tsotsis, Alexia. 2011. "TaskRabbit Turns Grunt Work into a Game." *Wired*, July 15.

Uber Blog. 2016. "Lower Prices; Increased Demand." January 29. www.uber .com/blog/new-york-city/lower-prices-increased-demand/.

Uchitelle, Louis. 2006. *The Disposable American: Layoffs and Their Consequences*. New York: Vintage.

Uchitelle, Louis, and N. R. Kleinfield. 1996. "On the Battlefields of Business, Millions of Casualties." *New York Times,* March 3.

US Census Bureau. 2015. *Educational Attainment in the United States: 2014.* Washington, DC: U.S. Census Bureau, January 20.

US Census Bureau, Census History Staff. 2017a. "Pop Culture: 1820," last revised July 18. www.census.gov/history/www/through_the_decades/fast_facts/1820_fast_facts.html.

———. 2017b. "Pop Culture: 1860," last revised July 18. www.census.gov/history/www/through_the_decades/fast_facts/1860_fast_facts.html.

US Department of Labor. 2017. "Fair Labor Standards Act Advisor. Am I an Employee?" Retrieved December 22. http://webapps.dol.gov/elaws/whd/flsa/scope/ee13.asp.

US Department of Labor, Wage and Hour Division. 2011. "The Fair Labor Standards Act of 1938, as Amended." May.

———. 2017. "Employment Relationship under the FLSA Presentation." Retrieved December 22. www.dol.gov/whd/flsa/employmentrelationship.ppt.

US Equal Employment Opportunity Commission. 2015. "Testimony of Fatima Goss Graves." January 14.

Vanwesenbeeck, Ine. 2001. "Another Decade of Social Scientific Work on Sex Work: A Review of Research, 1990–2000." *Annual Review of Sex Research* 12:242–89.

Veblen, Thorstein. [1899] 1994. *The Theory of the Leisure Class.* New York: A. M. Kelley.

Venkatesh, Sudhir Alladi. 2006. *Off the Books: The Underground Economy of the Urban Poor.* Cambridge, MA: Harvard University Press.

———. 2008. *Gang Leader for a Day: A Rogue Sociologist Takes to the Streets.* New York: Penguin.

Wachsmuth, David, David Chaney, Danielle Kerrigan, Andrea Shilolo, and Robin Basalaev-Binder. 2018. *The High Cost of Short-Term Rentals in New York City.* Montreal: Urban Politics and Governance, McGill University.

Waldman, Katy. 2014. "Let's Break Shit: A Short History of Silicon Valley's Favorite Phrase." *Slate,* December 5.

Walker, Edward T. 2015. "The Uber-ization of Activism." *New York Times,* August 7.

Walker, Mark. 2003. "The Ludlow Massacre: Class, Warfare, and Historical Memory in Southern Colorado." *Historical Archaeology* 37(3):66–80.

Weber, Lauren. 2015. "What If There Were a New Type of Worker? Dependent Contractor." *Wall Street Journal,* January 28.

Weber, Lauren, and Rachel Emma Silverman. 2015. "On-Demand Workers: 'We Are Not Robots.'" *Wall Street Journal,* January 27.

Weber, Max. [1905] 2002. *The Protestant Ethic and the Spirit of Capitalism and Other Writings*, edited by Peter Baehr and Gordon Wells. New York: Penguin.

Weil, David. 2014. *The Fissured Workplace*. Cambridge, MA: Harvard University Press. Kindle edition.

Weise, Elizabeth. 2017. "Uber Deceived Drivers with Promise of Lofty Pay, FTC Says." *USA Today*, January 19.

Weiss, Robert S. 1994. *Learning from Strangers: The Art and Method of Qualitative Interview Studies*. New York: Free Press.

Welsh, Sandy. 1999. "Gender and Sexual Harassment." *Annual Review of Sociology* 25:169–90.

West, Candace, and Sarah Fenstermaker. 1995. "Doing Difference." *Gender & Society* 9(1):8–37.

Whalen, John. 1995. "You're Not Paranoid: They Really Are Watching You." *Wired*, March 1.

Whitford, Emma. 2016. "Airbnb: We're Bringing 'Economic Opportunity' to NYC's Black Neighborhoods." *Gothamist*, April 21.

Williams, Joan C., Mary Blair-Loy, and Jennifer L. Berdahl. 2013. "Cultural Schemas, Social Class, and the Flexibility Stigma." *Journal of Social Issues* 69:209–34.

Williams, Mike, and D. A. Farnie. 1992. *Cotton Mills in Greater Manchester*. Lancaster, UK: Carnegie.

Wilson, William Julius. 1996. *When Work Disappears: The World of the New Urban Poor*. New York: Vintage.

Wingfield, Nick, and Mike Isaac. 2015. "Seattle Will Allow Uber and Lyft Drivers to Form Unions." *New York Times*, December 14.

Wise, Scott, and Jon Burkett. 2016. "'He Was Trying to Kill Me': Uber Driver Attacked on I-95." WTVR.com, April 25.

Worstall, Tim. 2016. "US Median Household Income Is Now Back to Pre-recession Peak." *Forbes*, August 8.

Worthman, Jenna. 2011. "With a Start-Up Company, a Ride Is Just a Tap of an App Away." *New York Times*, May 3.

Wright, Colleen. 2015. "Uber Says Proposed Freeze on Licenses in New York City Would Limit Competition." *New York Times*, July 1.

Young, Maggie. 2016. "I Was Sexually Assaulted by My Uber Passenger." *Bustle*, February 26.

Youshaei, Jon. 2015. "The Uberpreneur: How an Uber Driver Makes $252,000 a Year." *Forbes*, February 4.

Yuhas, Alan. 2015. "Airbnb Hosts Return to Find Home Trashed after 'Drug-Induced Orgy.'" *The Guardian*, April 30.

Zelizer, Viviana A. 2005. *The Purchase of Intimacy*. Princeton, NJ: Princeton University Press.

Zervas, Georgios, Davide Proserpio, and John W. Byers. 2015. "First Look at Online Reputation on Airbnb, Where Every Stay Is above Average." *Social Science Research Network*, January 28.

Zinn, Howard. 1999. *A People's History of the United States, 1492–Present*. New York: HarperCollins.

Zuberi, Dan. 2006. *Differences That Matter: Social Policy and the Working Poor in the United States and Canada*. Ithaca, NY: Cornell University Press.

Zukin, Sharon. 2009. *Naked City: The Death and Life of Authentic Urban Places*. New York: Oxford University Press.

Zumbrun, Josh. 2016. "Voter Discord Isn't over Wages." *Wall Street Journal*, August 7.

Index

Abundant Host, 46
acceptance rates, 1–2
access, 28fig. 2
accidental occupational liability policies, 110–11
Adshade, Marina, 127
advertisements: Airbnb, 44fig. 5; by Kitchen-surfing, 57, 59; TaskRabbit, 100fig. 12; by Uber, 50, 51fig. 7
African-Americans: as Airbnb hosts, 35, 39; digital divide and, 193; discrimination against, 169, 193; economic issues of, 140; as Uber users, 35; wealth gap and, 195
age issues: age of chefs, 59; age of drivers, 53; age of hosts, 49; age of sharing economy workers, 62; age of TaskRabbits, 56; child labor, 65, 70, 224n12, 225n15; Schor on, 224n1; in textile industry, 67, 225n15
Airbnb: overview, 7, 21, 22; African-American hosts, 35–36, 39; background on, 43–49; bathroom use, 88; business use of, 182, 228n14; children and hosting, 12–13; choices, 168; commercial user crackdown, 20; communication issues, 63; Couch-surfing and, 9; cultural capital and, 165, 166–67; discrimination and, 170; as dura-ble-assets-sharing sites, 27; economic impact of, 39; employee monitoring, 204;

entrepreneurship and, 6, 164–66; flexibil-ity, 168; high capital-barrier, 43, 43tab. 1, 166–68; for homeless people, 4; illegal rentals, 40, 41, 149–52; income potential, 19; Instant Book service, 170; interaction-free key transfers, 34; low pricing strat-egy, 231n8 (ch.7); marketing, 160; multi-location hosts, 40; participant recruitment and methodology, 42–43; Peers and, 72; promises of, 25; response rates, 81–82, 160; safety issues, 113–14; as sharing economy company, 26, 27–29; social interactions and, 33; striving work-ers and, 132; struggling workers and, 132; successful workers and, 19–21, 39–40, 131–32; trust and, 30; worker-client sex-ual interactions, 128–31
Airbnb hosts. See hosts
Airbnb in the City report (New York State), 40
Alden, William, 40
Alfreds, 188. *See also* Hello Alfred
algorithm-based acceptance and response rates, 5, 55; overview, 2, 5, 6; anti-trust law violations and, 71; deactivation and, 82–83; negative reviews and, 13; opaque-ness of, 84–85; TaskRabbit, 1–2
alienation, 37